Woke Is Not Enough

Woke Is Not Enough

School Reform for Leaders with Justice in Mind

T. Elijah Hawkes

ROWMAN & LITTLEFIELD
Lanham • Boulder • New York • London

Published by Rowman & Littlefield

An imprint of The Rowman & Littlefield Publishing Group, Inc.
4501 Forbes Boulevard, Suite 200, Lanham, Maryland 20706
www.rowman.com

86-90 Paul Street, London EC2A 4NE, United Kingdom

Copyright © 2022 by T. Elijah Hawkes

All rights reserved. No part of this book may be reproduced in any form or by any electronic or mechanical means, including information storage and retrieval systems, without written permission from the publisher, except by a reviewer who may quote passages in a review.

British Library Cataloguing in Publication Information Available

Library of Congress Cataloging-in-Publication Data

Names: Hawkes, T. Elijah, 1974– author.
Title: Woke is not enough : school reform for leaders with justice in mind / T. Elijah Hawkes.
Description: Lanham : Rowman & Littlefield, [2022] | Includes bibliographical references. | Summary: "Administrators, teacher leaders, and those who support school reform with justice in mind will find both practical guidance and inspiration"— Provided by publisher.
Identifiers: LCCN 2022001249 (print) | LCCN 2022001250 (ebook) | ISBN 9781475863291 (cloth) | ISBN 9781475863307 (paperback) | ISBN 9781475863314 (epub)
Subjects: LCSH: Educational change—United States. | Social justice and education—United States. | Educational leadership—United States. | School improvement programs—United States.
Classification: LCC LA217.2 .H38 2022 (print) | LCC LA217.2 (ebook) | DDC 370.973—dc23/eng/20220302
LC record available at https://lccn.loc.gov/2022001249
LC ebook record available at https://lccn.loc.gov/2022001250

When we talk about wokeness, I'm not talking about just being woke, because you can be obsessed with wokeness and suffer from insomnia. I'm talking about being fortified.

—Cornel West, "Cornel West: The Difference between Being 'Woke' & Fortified ft. Richard Wolff"

Contents

Preface	ix
Acknowledgments	xiii
Introduction: It's Your Job to Imagine the Worst	1
Chapter 1: Racial Justice	11
Chapter 2: Democratic Governance	57
Chapter 3: Restorative Justice	97
Chapter 4: Student Activism and Organizing	153
Chapter 5: Counter-Extremism	191
Conclusion: Pathways to Power	223
Notes	229
Works Cited	239
About the Author	247

Preface

The first school shootings in our country were committed by family and community members who were angry with the teacher and the school. Born of mistrust and outrage at school practitioners, educators were the first victims.

Today, we are familiar with the horrors of mass shootings in schools when student shooters have killed peers, educators, and sometimes themselves. Schools have long been sites of political tension, interpersonal strife, and sometimes even deadly violence. But it is worth noting that many of the first shootings in our nation's schools were not perpetrated by students.

In 1853, in Kentucky, the principal of Louisville High School was confronted by a man who demanded an apology for how harshly his younger brother had been disciplined the day before. After a scuffle, the principal was shot and killed. In the months that followed, there was a trial and many in the community were outraged by what seemed to be an acquittal born of political influence. A mob of thousands menaced the shooter, who took his family and moved away. This took place on the eve of the Civil War. Not long after, the man himself was shot and killed by friendly fire when he was mistaken for a Union soldier.[1]

As in this instance, many of our nation's early school shootings involved an educator killed by a student or family member aggrieved by a sense of unfair discipline. Political grievance has also fueled violence against schools, which are seen as agents and apparatus of state government.

In 1927, driven by a sense of unfairness about his property taxes, a man in Michigan planted a bomb that killed scores of children, two teachers, and the superintendent. Political grievance was not the only factor that drove him to massacre. "On the same day of the school explosion he burned down his farm, killed his wife, and then blew up his car, killing himself and five other people."[2]

Murder, suicide, mobs, political grievance, cries of unfairness, communities polarized, a nation divided—schooling past and present happens in such contexts. Schools are also, of course, places of community, friendship, and love. But education is always political and interpersonal, and questions of right and wrong are contested, often with the highest of stakes.

Today, much of what is contested concerns what's being taught. These are especially challenging times to be an educator who believes schools must teach hard history, address contemporary challenges, and be laboratories of democracy grounded in authentic dialogue and debate. Pushback and backlash from the community are real, and some educators shy away from curriculum that tackles political and personal topics, and justice-minded school reforms may be put on hold.[3]

I've been an educator for over two decades, a principal for most of that time. It wasn't until recently that I felt compelled to write a note to my sons saying goodbye, should I not return from school some evening when passions might flare in a county where guns are everywhere.[4] This was during school year 2018–2019 about the time the Black Lives Matter flag was raised at the school. This was always in the back of my mind as principal, especially when emotions such as despair or rage were tangible. In this particular time period, the vitriol that community members were speaking about students, teachers, and the school created a climate of fear for many, especially for our students of color.

I tucked the farewell card to my sons behind photos of the boys on my bookshelf, knowing it would be found should something happen to me. This from a man whose privilege and race largely protect him from assaults of any kind, systemic or episodic. Educators and students of other races are in much more danger than me, as has been true for centuries. White supremacy is no new menace. Throughout our nation's history, and before this nation even was, people of color were punished for their pursuit of learning or schooled in the most violent of ways. Later, during the eras of Reconstruction and Jim Crow, black community schools were destroyed and teachers were killed in the South; likewise in times of desegregation and urban "renewal" in northern cities, schools in black communities were shuttered or destroyed in what amounts to a cultural and spiritual attack on teaching that was calibrated to the needs of children, their families, and communities.

As in the past, so today. Across the nation, from Oregon to Arizona to Maine, educators committed to teaching aligned with the needs of students and the broader democratic society are under threat. From tirades on social media to legislation signed in state capitols, the climate is hostile to educators committed to building more just and democratic schools. It's a hard time to be a teacher and school leader. Turnover is high, from the district office to principals and classroom teachers. Between 2009 and 2016, there was a 27 percent decline in the number of people completing teacher preparation programs.[5] And this was before Donald Trump was elected president, before the COVID-19 pandemic, and before the culture wars about school curriculum and national identity began to rage afresh in school board meetings, legislatures, and classrooms.

And yet, many educators' sense of vocation and commitment to justice is stronger than ever. They know that the school must be a healthy, fair, and democratic place. They may not have all the answers, but they have clarity of conviction, which is sometimes the most certain knowledge one can have. Where that conviction takes us is often the question. And how can we take steps toward a more just school community in ways that lead to lasting change?

It is possible to be woke to injustice and yet be unsure of what to do next with the new knowledge that we hold. It is possible to see the need for reform but be unsure of how to build it. This book is for those school leaders who stand steady on principle and ready for the next steps putting principle into practice for enduring reform.

A few years ago, at the school where I was principal, a varsity boys soccer game with our closest rival had ended, the visiting team was leaving the parking lot, and a conflict was brewing. I could see it from across the parking lot. Our team was headed inside, and a boy from the other team was in his truck. "Move n—ger," he'd yelled at the black students in front of him. Our students and teammates stopped and stood in front of his truck, engine running. I ran over, my toddler in my arms. The mother of the boy in the truck got out and approached my students. She hurled the same slur. It was not safe. The truck's engine was running, my students were standing there, and the racism, rage, and fear loud and clear. I was worried to have my son in my arms, but I was afraid to put him down. I went to the truck unsure of what to do.

Some of the guidance I share in this book is tried and true and tested. But sometimes we can't see where our efforts will lead, and the only way forward is to feel the moral urgency and step into the work.

Acknowledgments

The first folks to publish something I'd written about schools were Andy Kaplan and Dan Frank at the journal *Schools: Studies in Education*. This journal invites us to share the subjective experience of school life, how our personal stories as educators intersect with the stories of students, colleagues, and the wider democratic society. Andy is an editor who inspires, gathers, and shares stories that other editors and publications would not. He gives practitioners the space to know themselves and their work more deeply. I am grateful to Andy for nearly two decades of collaboration. Only my family has read more rough draft essays than Andy.

I am indebted to my brother, Jesse, who has been a careful advisor on many past projects and to my mom, Kristin, who helped extensively with this one. My dad, Glenn, is an educator I admire deeply and an important partner to me in writing and thinking about identity, democracy, and schools. My stepfather, Bill, was once legal counsel for the state agency of education, and I'm always grateful for his cautious eye: "Lij, are you sure you want to write that?" My work is better for their gaze, and I'm the one responsible for the mistakes and lessons-not-yet-learned.

If I've learned from my mistakes as an educator, it's been because of the wisdom, honesty, and generosity of colleagues and mentors I have known. I began teaching in 1997 at Humanities Prep, a NYC public high school for transfer students. I continue to draw strength from that experience and the incredible educators that I knew at Prep. Thank you, Perry, Christina, Vince, Maria, and Doug for your friendship and inspiration.

When colleagues and I started the James Baldwin School, it was modeled on what we knew at Prep. As principal and codirector at Baldwin, I knew educators of extraordinary humanity, creativity, and resolve—some of them still working at the school today. I'm humbled to think back on the opportunity I had to work with Marie, Susan, Christine, Rehana, Seth, Rob, and so many others.

The work at Prep and Baldwin was supported by organizations that have been sustaining justice-minded school reform for decades: the Coalition of Essential Schools, Expeditionary Learning, Outward Bound, and the New York Performance Standards Consortium. When I left NYC to come back to Vermont where I grew up, I carried many lessons-learned about humane and democratic education from these networks and their leaders.

In Vermont, I worked at one school for ten years. I only recently left Randolph Union, and I already long for the meaningful collaborations I knew there, from the bus barn to the main office to the classrooms. I'm especially grateful to have worked so closely, for so many years, with Kara, Caty, Lisa, Dana, and Ken. I now work with principals-in-training as director of leadership programs at the Upper Valley Educators Institute. With my new colleagues I already feel strong solidarity.

In a loving network of family, near and far, I'm grateful to be raising two wonderful sons in partnership with their mom, Matisse. I'm also fortunate to have very dear friends in my life, old and new, like Omar and Grace.

I dedicate this book to my father, whose spirit and intellect course through it. Thank you, Dad, for the bookshelf full of your books that you gave me when I turned sixteen, and all you've given before and since.

Introduction

It's Your Job to Imagine the Worst

Most school leaders were first teachers because they have a love for kids, and love teaching and learning with them in a place called school. The teacher's best impulse and very vocation is to imagine all the beauty that children are capable of and help them become it. This disposition toward the work persists when one becomes a school leader. But we also must make room in our imaginations for less beautiful becomings. Indeed, it is our job to imagine the worst.

School leaders have a responsibility to recognize danger or potential disaster, understand how it might come to pass, and do all that we can to prevent it. This is an often-overlooked component of being a school administrator, and it is a taxing and important one.

We have fire drills, for instance, because we imagine the horror and put measures in place to avert the loss of young life. This work to imagine the worst is as necessary in the contemplating of fire and toxic spills as it is of active shooter threats and other less tangible dangers, such as the ways political polarization threatens our democracy. It is the school leader's job to consider what threatens our young people and the wider society, and then put measures in place to address those dangers.

CHILDREN AT RISK

I once followed a young man into town after he left school in distress. I didn't want to send anyone else to follow him because I was worried about how emotionally and physically volatile he was at the time. He was becoming increasingly unpredictable, in word and deed, at school and at home. He was growing out of childhood and into young adulthood, and even his mother had come to fear him at times. I'd learned this from her earlier in the week when, in my office, she said she didn't feel safe driving her son home. We called the local mental health crisis intake counselor to come down to the school to be with us and figure out what to do.

Now I walked behind him into town as the school tried to reach his family. He carried a wide smile on his face, a frozen and unmoving smile, and he wouldn't respond to me when I spoke his name. I decided to stay enough steps behind him that he couldn't quickly turn and strike me, but I had to stay close enough to him that I could intervene if needed. This seemed especially important as we approached the bridge over the river, with great rocks and cold water fifty feet below. I knew he'd experienced suicidal ideation in the past. I knew about his father, and the paranoid conspiratorial thinking that governed the father's worldview. I knew about the guns that had been in the home, and the close calls.

My job in that moment was to take what I knew of the boy and his world, imagine the danger he posed to himself and to others, and do what I could to help him to safety. Soon I would call the police, since he continued to not respond to me, and we were not able to reach any family or emergency contact. After nine years collaborating with local law enforcement, I knew them well enough to know that—unless it escalated in some violent way—they would defer to me in this situation and do what I'd advise to get the boy to safety. About a half hour later, with the boy's consent and cooperation, a police officer and I took him to the office of the same crisis counselor who'd seen him at school two days before.

Back at school, another child at school would soon be in crisis. I'll share more about him—and my relationship with him—in chapter 1. On this day, while I was in town with the other boy, this student had begun talking about shooting. He was asking peers if they'd rather kill animals or people. He had been in a heightened emotional state for a few weeks, in fact. His troubles ran deep.

There were many factors in his life conspiring to make him psychologically unstable and unwell. There was economic instability, geographic transience through his childhood years, racism and xenophobia toward him and his family, substance use or abuse by him and those around him, and much more.

What had most recently prompted this boy's elevated erratic behavior and outbursts was that he'd crossed paths with someone in the boys' bathroom who'd previously used the one where the door says "girls." This student was transitioning from female to male identity. They'd gone into the bathroom to wash their hands.

This bathroom interaction had been unsettling for me as well. I knew the student who was transitioning, and I'd been in a meeting with them, their family, and our school counselor just a week prior. We'd discussed what pronouns the student wanted school faculty and staff to use, and how the school would support them if there was a name change, and other considerations. But at that time, using the bathroom marked "boys" was just a possibility in their mind, not a certainty, and I was not prepared for the student to start using it.

I'm not saying that a school leader is the gatekeeper of a student's decision-making in this matter of identity. What unsettled me was not that the bathroom was being used by this student. It was the suddenness of the decision—and that such decisions have ripple effects, implicating others, prompting responses sometimes difficult to manage and even dangerous.

In the past, when other students had transitioned, they and their families had communicated more fully with us about the steps they were taking. We knew, for instance, what bathrooms they planned to use, and how they would approach after-school athletics where gender-specific teams and locker rooms can become factors. But in this case, there was less communication with the school.

I began to imagine the worst. What if this student decided to come to the varsity boys' basketball game later that week—and decided to use the boys' locker room where the visiting team gathers to change their clothes? What if the young men or older men—the coaches—of the opposing team objected in some way? What fans would be in the bleachers that night, strangers from the other town that we did not know? Did our athletic director have a police officer on call for the games that week? What if there was a confrontation in the parking lot after the game? I was worried that this student might take risks on campus that we were not able to help them approach safely. What if they got harassed, assaulted, or worse?

A SOCIETY AT RISK

In addition to imagining the harm that can befall an individual child, and doing all we can to prevent it, we must also think of the societal dangers that threaten the child. At the core of our vocation is not only a consideration for the intellectual and emotional health of the individual. We must also be concerned with the health of the broader society and how it impacts our children.

What can we do—as school leaders and school communities—to make our society a more just and less dangerous place? What can we do, as a school, about the homophobia and transphobia that threatens the young person in gender identity transition? What can we do about the xenophobia and racism that menaces students of color and those newly arrived to our country? What can we do about easy access to guns coupled with paranoid, conspiratorial, or apocalyptic thinking?

Leaders who care about making our society more just, fair, and inclusive have contemplated such questions. Such leaders are aware of the dangers and are working to make our schools into communities that combat them. This work is both internal and external. It is focused on the present, and it is also future oriented. This work happens through the curriculum and the culture of the school. It happens through the work the school does in partnership with other stakeholders, and approaches to contemporary problems we try to solve together. And this work is carried on in the lives our graduates go on to lead. There are victories and moments of which to be proud. Some schools help some students beat the odds, and some schools create community in ways that combat the forces that would degrade and divide us. But in many ways schools aren't helping.

SCHOOLS ARE PART OF THE PROBLEM

Environmental degradation, economic inequality, austerity regimes, deep-rooted racism, and violent authoritarian systems are ills that ravage communities across the globe, including here in the United States. These dangers are not external, and our schools are part of the problem.

Name any crisis and the odds are that a high school graduate is making it worse. How could it be otherwise? Few brick-and-mortar institutions play such a significant role in shaping both individual conscience and national consciousness. In 1940, less than half of twenty-five-year-olds had a high school diploma; today it's over 90 percent.[1] And too many students in this country graduate with flawed understandings of their nation, themselves, and other people—and they sometimes go on to do terrible things.

Derek Chauvin was a high school graduate when he killed George Floyd, bound on the ground, begging for air and mercy. And it's safe to assume David Richard Nelson had attended high school in the years before he shouted, "There is no racism!" while his partner painted over a Black Lives Matter mural the summer after Floyd's murder. "There is no oppression!" he hollered to the world on a video that went viral, a video surely shared by some in affirmation, and by others in outrage or disbelief.[2] Derek and David were once kids in school, and in their basic dispositions, these former school students are not American outliers. Their words and actions may be extreme, but an emaciated understanding of history and a crippled capacity for empathy are not uncommon in our culture.

Many people in this country were surprised to learn, on the occasion of Trump's June 2020 rally in Tulsa, about the massacre of black citizens in that city in 1921. This ethnic cleansing crime of great proportions was a shock to many because it was not taught to most, my own high school education included. We appropriately learn about mass graves dug in Auschwitz, but we don't learn about mass graves dug by white supremacists in our own country's recent past.

This is not just a problem for educators in the upper grades. At the end of the year, report cards from my sons' elementary school arrive in my mailbox. There are detailed comments, thoughtful, specific notes about my kids. These notes are found in the boxes underneath the English language arts and math standards. Underneath the science and social studies standards there is a standardized comment that all students receive describing some of the units of study. This demands radically less time.

Less is expected of teachers and schools when it comes to understanding the cultural, political, and ecological environments in which we live. This educational neglect is written into policy and radiates from Washington, DC, to state capitols, down to school districts, into the minds of kids and our communities. This neglect has roots in President Bush's "No Child Left Behind" ELA and math testing mandates, and it continued through President Obama's "Race to the Top" accountability measures. After decades now, the impact it has had on what we collectively teach, understand, and care about has been crippling. We see evidence of this collective neglect for science and social studies learning in our society's broad vulnerability to indoctrination about climate change denial and people's embrace of narratives of national history that deny core truths about who we are.

My older son is moving into an upper-elementary grade level. Over the summer, families received a thoughtful letter of welcome from the teachers who introduced their hobbies and passions and described the curriculum. There is a 96-word paragraph describing the literacy curriculum and a 114-word paragraph devoted to math.

Science and "global citizenship," or social studies—combined—get a paragraph of forty-six words, or an average of twenty-three words each, not even a third of the space given to math and literacy. The letter states, "Science and global citizenship (social studies), often the student favorites, will be a series of independent units, typically revolving around a unit project based on the district standards."

The allocation of these black ink words on white paper is a reflection of the resources that this school, like many others, allocates to learning in these domains in classrooms. Note, furthermore, the emphasis on independent work in social studies and science. In addition to there being less time and energy dedicated to these domains by the school system, there is a lack of willingness to make the learning a collective endeavor. One can predict that there will be few whole class discussions about matters of political and environmental importance, with all of the moral, ethical, local, and national implications. We must wonder about the health of a society that intentionally avoids discussing such topics. We must marvel—alarmed—at the contortions a school system goes through to deny children time on topics "favorite" to them and also deeply important to our collective welfare as a society.

THOSE WHO DO HARM

The harm being done to our society through our curriculum is often insidious and quiet. It is also extreme and bloody. We must wonder about the school experiences of those who grow up to do bloody harm. Let us wonder about the schooling of the high-school-aged boy charged with first degree intentional homicide for shooting protesters in Wisconsin during the summer of 2020. This boy, Kyle Rittenhouse, was part of a group patrolling the streets and ostensibly protecting property. Based on the reporting of local journalists, we can assume he attended a high school in a nearby town. If one looks at that town's high school course catalog in 2020, one can see that it is fifty-two pages long and in none of those pages is there any mention of "race" or "racism."[3] There is only one course description that mentions "democracy." Even if Rittenhouse didn't attend this school, consider the kind of educational neglect this kind of schooling is doing to the community of people who must send their children there. The business owners, protestors, police officers, and others whose paths crossed the night Rittenhouse killed people in the street may have attended this school or others like it. The skills, knowledge, and dispositions cultivated their schooling now inform how they act in the streets and whom they fear. And such schools are not the exception.

Miseducation like this is a misuse of tax dollars and a betrayal of our schools' responsibility to serve our democracy. It starves our children's hunger for truth and weakens their muscles of compassion. And it can pave the way to bloodshed. As Nahlia Webber, executive director of the Orleans Public Education Network, wrote in 2020, schools help "socialize Americans for White violence and Black death."[4]

Some will say this is a misguided message to place at the beginning of a book intended for school leaders working toward lasting, justice-minded reforms in their school communities. It's indeed ugly news for educators to consider our complicity in the problems of our society. But this dark cloud is ringed with silver lining: To be complicit, means one has power. Since we are part of the problem, we can be the change we seek.

This Book

The path is not always clear or simple. It is not easy to be the school leader supporting teachers to better align curriculum to the needs of the students and broader society. It is not easy to redistribute—toward justice—the people, time, and other essential school resources that have been long locked in place and always seem in short supply. Structural reform is hard because it's structural. And changing attitudes and dispositions can be harder. There are confusing contradictions, incentives that support the status quo, thorny questions, and dilemmas thick with paradox not easy to negotiate.

In chapter 1, we consider the imperative to reallocate resources in our effort to confront systemic racism, which has become more talked about and visible to white educators today than in the past. A historic wave of public outrage at black people being killed by police swept our country in 2020. Suddenly, school leaders who never before said "Black Lives Matter" have become able to speak it. Schools were closed due to the COVID pandemic, and multiracial masses were in the streets. Many called it a reckoning. However, for many newly woke school leaders, the work of confronting institutional racism faded as more mundane concerns returned along with the extraordinary logistical challenges of school operations in a pandemic. And in the years that followed, intertwined with a persistent pandemic, backlash against teaching about race in school brought new and dangerous levels of conflict.

How can school leaders keep doing anti-racist work when there is so much explicit pressure not to, or when there seem to be so many competing and urgent needs? How can we see anti-racist work as core to the work of a school in a pluralistic, democratic society? Once awakened to racial injustice and newly accountable for undoing racism in the school community, what can school leaders—especially white school leaders—do next? What can we do in the face of pressures to do nothing?

In chapter 2, democratic practice is the focus. We consider the question of whether schools can be democratic when certain people have so much power. Schools exist in hierarchies. Principals and other leaders are granted substantial positional authority. How can leaders who recognize the importance of distributed leadership and democratic practice still wield their positional power with fairness, transparency, and spare-but-occasional forcefulness?

Chapter 3 is about restorative practice, or restorative justice. Many believe that restorative practice is essential to making schools more equitable. It builds community bonds, helps repair harm, and can help dismantle disciplinary processes that push students out of schools and into the criminal justice system. If done well, restorative practice is about slowing down, reflecting, and moving "at the pace of trust." Meanwhile, school life is dominated by rigid schedules, calendars, timelines, pacing guides, and bells. How can we build restorative practice into such a system? Can it be efficient, and is it really worth the time?

Chapter 4 centers on student activism—in particular, the breaking of rules in pursuit of justice. School leaders concerned with social justice may wonder what to do when you agree with students who break the rules. All schools embody diversity—whether by economic class, race, gender, sexual identity, family background, or political views. There are always minorities and majorities. Sometimes a few student activists can disrupt the community for the causes they stand for. Sometimes they disrupt the routines and stability of the school day. What can a school leader do who supports the students' cause but must also enforce rules and norms?

In chapter 5 we consider what it means to be a school leader in a time of political extremes. The right/left polarization of our nation has worsened. As people move to the extremes, violence becomes more possible. Concerns about domestic terrorism and politically motivated violence are high. Disinformation, conspiratorial thinking, and distrust in institutions are shaking the very foundation of schooling as we know it. In this environment, it makes sense that teachers and administrators are afraid to bring politics into the classroom, and that school leaders are uncertain of how to respond to expressions of extremist ideas—especially as they are expressed more and more in the mainstream discourse of the dominant culture. There is fear of community backlash and even fear of what hurtful things students will say to each other. But trying to insulate our schools from discussions of political importance limits our capacity to develop essential habits of democratic citizenship. Silence about divisive topics only divides our nation further. Educators must be builders of democracy, not bystanders watching it crumble. What can school leaders do to help our communities confront and transcend the extremism of these troubled times, and is it worth the risk?

As readers move through each chapter, an organizing refrain will emerge: Paradox, Principle, Practicalities. Each chapter will focus on a difficult question, at the heart of which is a paradox. The paradox is perplexing; it is what makes the dilemmas and questions so difficult to navigate. But identifying and centering a core principle can help school leaders find answers that work in practice, leading us to concrete actions every school leader can take to start or sustain meaningful school reform toward justice.

IMAGINE THE WORST—BETTER

After the BLM flag was raised at the school where I was principal in 2018, my plan had been that we would lower it at the end of each year and start the following school year with fresh teaching efforts and community-building, to culminate in the flag ceremoniously raised again midyear at the ceremony commemorating Martin Luther King Jr. This, I believed, would allow every community member to wrestle—or wrestle again—with the historical facts and contemporary circumstances that demanded we stand as an institution in affirmation of the value of black lives.

But I was wrong about this plan. I was convinced I was wrong when I met with the group of students and teachers who had done the work of educating and organizing for the raising of the flag that year. A boy who identifies as mixed-race and Black, looked at me and told me what it means to him to arrive at a neighboring school's campus where the flag is also flying. "When the bus comes down the hill and turns into the driveway—that flag," he said in barely a whisper, "the Black Lives Matter flag—it's the only thing I see." He described how the flag makes him feel seen and valued and welcome. He and other students asked me how I could deny any student of color the opportunity to feel this feeling at the first day of school or any time of the school year?

One of the teachers supporting this group of students describes this as a moment when I came to see my "mistake." She has been a friend and colleague whom I've been fortunate to have speaking truth to me, challenging me, questioning me. What she calls a mistake, I am more likely to describe to myself as part of the ongoing learning process of which school leaders, faculty, staff, students are all a part. But "mistake" is appropriate. She and other students were wounded by my decision, and it was a mistake, one that I could only see because we had vessels of dialogue in the school that contained all of us. The school's commitment to democratic process and restorative practice meant that these students had even been in our faculty meeting earlier that year skillfully leading circles of dialogue about white privilege with the white adults who were their teachers and administrators.

Understanding the dangers to our wellness as individuals and as a collective requires that we see and hear each other's stories, historical and now, both group journeys and individual stories. In a healthy school, working toward justice for all, striving to meet the needs of each, school leaders need these stories in order to better imagine the worst. You can better understand what makes a safer world when you are hearing more voices and seeing the challenges—including your own flaws, doubts, and fears. This book aims to help school leaders see what concrete steps can be taken to make our school communities the places of self-reflection, empathic listening, and democratic practice that our society needs to be healthy and strong.

Chapter 1

Racial Justice

> Navigating the work of social justice in the classroom and in the community is bound up with our own personal histories that cannot be divorced from how we show up in the work and in the world.
>
> —Jamila Lyiscott[1]

> If a white man wants to lynch me, that's his problem. If he's got the power to lynch me, that's my problem. Racism is not a question of attitude; it's a question of power.
>
> —Stokely Carmichael[2]

Stokely Carmichael was a Black activist, community organizer, and courageous critic of how white supremacist power is wielded in the United States and abroad. He was also a critic of capitalism as an economic system that enriches a few and maintains brutal poverty for many. His statement that racism is a "question of power" continues:

> Racism gets its power from capitalism. Thus, if you're anti-racist, whether you know it or not, you must be anti-capitalist. The power for racism, the power for sexism, comes from capitalism, not an attitude.[3]

The readers of this book are mostly educators, working in schools in a country whose economic systems are powered by engines of capitalism. If we work in public schools, we are agents of a state that manages that economy, enabling both socialized and capitalist modes of production and wealth accumulation. Educators have powers derived from the state—just as do police, customs and border patrol agents, and soldiers. We regulate interactions of people, and we manage and distribute resources.

Carmichael is instructing us to understand that racism matters because it determines how material power is wielded. He is not concerned with a person's attitude, but with the influence a person has on how other people's lives are lived, under what controls, with what freedoms. Power is about whether a person has the resources that enable them to thrive long or make them die too soon. Power is about the body—whether it lives well or poorly—and it's about the mind that resides in that body and whether synapses fire in fear or instead describe patterns that say the world is safe.

If a person wants to be an anti-racist educator, Carmichael might imply, that educator needs to be concerned with how the society allocates resources, concerned with how we enrich some and leave many others in destitution. As educators, we need to consider what resources are at our disposal, how those resources are allocated, and whether they need to be allocated differently.

By the end of this chapter, we will be discussing the resources over which school leaders have discretion and how to redistribute them to support anti-racist school reforms. We will consider hard resources, like brick-and-mortar classrooms, as well as human resources and another resource that is typically talked of as a scarcity: time. We will also consider less tangible resources, like comfort. Comfort is a resource that, according to reformers like those of the Equity Literacy Institute, has been hoarded by some of us and requires an anti-racist redistribution. If you've been comfortable in our racist society, it's time to give some of it up.

SOULS UNDRESSED

It is not possible for an educator to effectively engage in anti-racist school reform without engaging in self-reflection. I am a white educator, and so I start with a story about being a white educator. Readers who are Black, Indigenous, and People of Color (BIPOC) may already understand much of what I'm about to say about what I've come to understand about myself.

The philosopher poet and Black intellectual activist, W. E. B. Du Bois wrote about the violence that white people will do when "imprisoned" in a fantasy of racial supremacy. In a passage from *Darkwater* that later became an essay called "The Souls of White Folks," Du Bois vividly describes his ability to see through the fantasy, to see the insides of white folks, their "entrails":

> I see these souls undressed and from the back and side. I see the working of their entrails. I know their thoughts and they know that I know. This knowledge makes them now embarrassed, now furious. . . .

And yet as they preach and strut and shout and threaten, crouching as they clutch at rags of facts and fancies to hide their nakedness, they go twisting, flying by my tired eyes and I see them ever stripped. . . .[4]

The stripped and naked facts of how white people act and think has been understood by the "tired eyes" of people of color out of necessity for centuries. "White People, I Don't Want You to Understand Me Better; I Want You to Understand Yourselves," writes Ijeoma Oluo in the title of her 2017 essay:

I know white culture, white history, white politics. I know it better than you. . . . Why do I know white culture so well? Because I'm a black woman. And while I, and just about any person of color who has spent their lives in a white supremacist society, know enough about white culture to write a book or two on whiteness and option the bestseller movie rights, y'all know almost nothing about us and even less about yourselves. Why? Because you don't have to.[5]

Her call is for white people to look inward, to see what Du Bois calls "the entrails." There are poisons that pulse inside, stuff we push out, and stuff we keep in. There are workings of mind and body that keep us feeling safe and healthy. These same workings also excrete and pollute. "As much as I'd like you to see me—" Oluo writes, "as much as I'd like systemic racism to simply be a problem of different groups not seeing each other—I need you to see yourself, really see yourself, first. This is the top priority."

White People Are White

"It took me years to figure out that white people are white people and that that's not necessarily a good thing," so opens an early chapter in *Mean*, by Myriam Gurba, a riveting book that recounts her childhood and young adult years in California.[6] It can take years, or it can come suddenly and soon, but coming to an understanding of whiteness is a part of growing up that most BIPOC people experience—and that most white people are able to avoid.

This is not to say that white people need to believe they are inherently bad, or teach this to their children. But we need to know that there is badness in how whiteness works in our society, and we need to consider how it works in and through us and outward to impact others.

One way we can do this is by telling stories about our lives. Stories are largely how people make sense of the universe, and spoken and written words can hold us accountable to the truths they reveal, or to the lies that need further undoing. If we tell stories about mistakes that we've made, the spoken word holds us doubly accountable for repairing the harm. If we tell stories that carry questions, those words hold us accountable for seeking answers or living more maturely with the uncertainty. Parents can tell such stories to their children, friends to friends, school leaders to colleagues and to students. One story that I've written and never published in full until now is about my relationship with one of the students mentioned in the introduction, the boy who asked the other kids in class if they'd prefer to shoot animals or people. In this story, I call him *"Fourteen."* (All student names in this book are pseudonyms.)

THE BOY *FOURTEEN*

Fourteen sat in a chair facing me, knee bouncing in jeans, work boots, and red trucker cap: common rural Vermont dress. But he spoke in a strange Southern drawl.

"Y'all are too sensitive," he said.

In class, he'd called a white friend "n--ger." It was a joke, he'd told his teacher, who'd brought the concern to me.

"It ain't a big deal," he said, feigning nonchalance, eyes meanwhile darting about my office. "Y'all make a big deal about this, and you make a big deal about the Confederate flag, and anything Republican."

He was new to the school. I considered his speech. I asked him how long he'd lived in the South. He spoke of years living in Texas. I spoke to his mother that evening, and she said he'd never lived in Texas.

Swastikas in the Bathroom

The year *Fourteen* joined our school, the hate speech "burn all the blacks" was scrawled on a bathroom stall. *Fourteen* wasn't a suspect, but I share this detail to provide context to his story.

We closed the bathroom, painted over the terrorist phrase. My investigation yielded no suspects. The words reappeared. Two students in the Racial Justice Alliance brought it to my attention the second time. This newly formed group was made up of several students of color, white allies, and two teacher advisors, one who identifies as white and the other as a person of color.

The Racial Justice Alliance would successfully work to raise the Black Lives Matter flag at school later that year. They would also organize the first statewide student-led conference on racism in Vermont schools. They were a courageous group working in a school, town, and state that is super-majority white. Naming and reckoning with white supremacy is new work to most people in the community. It is a fraught and important dialogue, unsettling for many, including those who deny that racism exists in their towns.

Swastikas were drawn in the bathrooms that year too. And that year a student from a visiting soccer team told one of our black students, in the parking lot after the game, to "move, n--ger!" It was a sunny Saturday afternoon. As I mentioned in the Preface, I had been watching the game with my youngest son, a toddler. I ran over with him in my arms to the visiting player's truck. A crowd was gathering, shouting. The visiting player's mom had gotten out of the truck, and she leveled the same slur. One of our students then insulted her. Her son, ready to fight, opened his door. I stood against it. The mom got back in the truck. I told them to roll up their windows and say nothing else or I'd call the police. I told our players to go inside, and I walked beside the truck to escort them out of the crowded parking lot before going to find the coaches and athletic director.

In spite of incidents like these, many people, including *Fourteen*, objected to our flying the Black Lives Matter flag that year. "All lives matter," he told me. "You're putting one race above another. That's discriminating."

Fourteen frequently accused me of being too sensitive when it came to matters of race. He called me "snowflake." He called me "liberal." He also called me "bitch." I wasn't the only target of his anger. He spoke derisively of his own family and heritage. He was a student of color, and his red trucker hat said MAGA.

A Special Age

I call him *Fourteen* because I can't share his identity, because that's his age when I met him, and because fourteen is a critical period in growing up. The age fourteen is when a young person can discover new powers, becoming more agile physically and intellectually.

At fourteen years old, a young person can suddenly wield with competence adult tools to complete adult tasks—from handling automobiles to handling AR-15s; from tractors to trigonometry; from writing software code to writing suicide notes. It is also an age when mental illness can emerge, and an age when one can feel despair. At this age, young people become increasingly aware of how the world is defined, how they might shape it, and how it is shaping them.

Christian Piciolini was fourteen years old when this young white boy joined the American Neo-Nazi movement in search of purpose and belonging. He would go on to be a leader, finding identity and meaningful work in brutality.

An age that captures imagination is fourteen. It drives narratives, fact and fiction, stories about childhood collisions with adult dangers. "I became, during my fourteenth year . . . afraid," writes James Baldwin, "afraid of the evil within me and afraid of the evil without."[7]

The world opens up and journeys begin at fourteen years old. It's about the age of Huck Finn when he sets out in Mark Twain's famous story. And fourteen years old is the age of Mattie Ross in *True Grit*, the revered Western by Charles Portis. In Cormac McCarthy's *Blood Meridian*, fourteen is the age of "the kid," a boy who has already a thirst for violence when he leaves his drunk and destitute father and joins the blood-soaked westward expansion of the United States.

How close to fourteen years old is the Black cabin boy, Pip, in Melville's *Moby Dick*, a novel about identity, madness, masculinity, violence, and whiteness? Young and distressed, Pip throws himself several times into the terrible ocean.

Ta-Nehisi Coates's son was fourteen years old at the writing of *Between the World and Me*, and it was about the age of James Baldwin's nephew when he wrote to him in *The Fire Next Time*. The men both chose this time of life to discuss with the child the damage that white supremacy perpetrates upon the Black body and mind, an effort to strengthen the child against it.

Several years before former Minneapolis police officer Derek Chauvin knelt on the neck of George Floyd and killed him, fourteen was the age of a Black boy Chauvin brutalized in similar fashion. An indictment filed in May of 2020 asserts that Chauvin put his knee on the neck of the handcuffed and unresisting child. Chauvin is also alleged to have hit him in the head with a flashlight and held him by the throat.

Fourteen Struggles

Fourteen did fine in most of his classes for a time. Teachers affirmed his intellectual engagement and dexterity. In my office, too, he was an eager conversationalist, always ready to debate school policies or the politics of the day, like the "Mexico Wall" and the "Muslim Ban." He projected confidence socially and made friendships with peers of varied backgrounds, from the boys who were farmers and hunters, to the boys on skateboards in town. He seemed to have fewer close relationships with girls, or friendships with other kids of color. He had teachers who cared for him and whom he trusted.

But while he was doing well in some ways, there were signs he was struggling. The evening of a spring concert a custodian found him passed out drunk underneath the oak tree. No Southern accent that evening, he could barely talk.

Summer came, passed, and in the fall, his school counselor and I were glad to learn that he'd begun seeing a therapist at the local mental health center. He was keeping his appointments with fidelity. A hopeful development, but our worries endured. His substance use was not abating. And he told his social studies teacher that racism is necessary to know who you are.

His condition took a turn for the worse one morning when he came across Brian—who used to be Brandy—washing their hands in the boys' restroom. After a day of brooding indignation, he made a poster mocking transsexuals and told a friend to post it on the walls. Later that day he called out in a middle-school classroom, "I sexually identify as an attack helicopter!"

In my office he told me it was "just a meme." I sat with him and looked it up online. I found a post by someone in a chatroom declaring that his true identity was Apache helicopter. In the post, he says he'd always "dreamed of soaring over the oilfields dropping hot sticky loads on disgusting foreigners":

> People say to me that a person being a helicopter is impossible and I'm fucking retarded but I don't care, I'm beautiful. I'm having a plastic surgeon install rotary blades, 30 mm cannons and AMG-114 Hellfire missiles on my body. From now on I want you guys to call me "Apache" and respect my right to kill from above and kill needlessly.[8]

How much time was my student spending in online spaces with sentiments like these? I tried to engage him in that conversation, but he told me it was none of my "fucking business." I told him that his actions and words were creating a climate of hostility and that his references to machines of war could create a climate of fear. He said something about how Obama waged war with drones and created climates of fear. I didn't disagree. He said that I was only suspending him because he was Republican.

A Man to Run From

I remember when *Fourteen* ran from me. A teacher had called me with concern that he was high. I found him in the hallway. I gave him options, but he refused to come to my office, or to the nurse, or his counselor, or the social worker.

"You can't make me," he said. "It's a free country."

I followed him. He walked faster, then ran. I can still see his small form, limbs churning, running, red hat falling on the gray floor tiles as he dashed past the auditorium and down the next hall. The boy was in fight or flight—and, I think, afraid.

I couldn't sleep that night. *I've become a man to run from*, I thought. *I have terror skin*, I thought. *I'm a white man from whom a person of color runs. The way boys like him run from border patrol agents, from police, from white men with lethal powers and twisted fears staring at the back of a boy running away. I'm part of this system.*

I thought of the powers I had as school principal. *I can make boundaries and draw borders*, I thought, *and I get to say who can go where and when.*

I can harden perimeters and restrict points of entry. I can exclude and confine. I can prohibit speech, discipline dress and lock bathrooms. I sanction comings and goings. I sign purchase orders for the books children are told to read. I approve each sign that goes on the wall. I can make Fourteen take his signs down. I can make him take his hat off. I can confiscate his phone, search his backpack, his pockets, his locker. I can suspend him. I can ban him.

Access to Guns

Months later, I felt some hope when I learned *Fourteen* was reading a book of poetry by TuPac. Better he rhyme with TuPac's indictments of poverty and racism than trumpet then-President Trump's nativist agenda. But not long after that, hope was harder to find. The therapist he'd been seeing was moving, and *Fourteen* was disrupting classrooms again. And about this same time, he was assaulted by friends of friends at a drinking party in the woods. He came to school bruised. That day, he cried. But this vulnerability was short-lived.

"I care about you," his counselor told him.

"I don't want you to care about me," he hissed.

Then came increasingly profane insults toward teachers, misogynist in theme. He started leaving school grounds without permission. I couldn't prove it, but I thought he was probably the one stashing Budweiser cans above the ceiling tiles in the bathroom.

The next month, the looping chorus of a song about kids killing kids played in a short video on his phone, looping in algebra, looping in the lunchroom. Looping in social studies, two students asked him about it and he asked if they'd prefer to kill animals or people. He said he was certain a school shooting was going to happen.

I was off campus, in town, following another student in crisis who'd left school grounds. By the time I learned of the concern about *Fourteen*, police and parents had already been notified. I got back to school just as law enforcement officers were arriving.

I found the police in the office and told them to wait. I found *Fourteen* in the hall and told him we needed to talk. I said, "The police are in the building, and if you don't follow my instructions, I will ask them for help." He cooperated. I brought him to my office. I asked the police again to wait while I talked to him.

School shootings were in the news, it seemed, constantly. The BBC called the previous year the "worst year for US school shootings," reporting 113 people killed in shootings that year.[9] And Orange County, Vermont, where I worked, has been reported to have among the highest rates of guns per capita of any county in the United States.[10] In this place, and in the current climate of fear about school shootings, it was important to take each mention of shooting very seriously.

Fourteen's parents soon arrived, and with their permission the officers questioned the boy. They asked about his access to guns. They ask some of the same questions I'd asked, like why he was certain there'd be a shooting.

"Well, you practice for it," he said, referring to our lockdown drills, routine now in so many schools. "So you must know it's gonna happen." He said *he* wasn't going to do it, but someone probably would. Then he said that the interview needed to stop, that he needed to get back to class, and he stood up to leave.

On the other side of the door, the secretaries would have heard the situation escalate.

About an hour later, as the police were getting ready to leave, he spoke to them with mocking disdain, asking in profane racial terms who they would pursue next, "Arabs, spicks, chinks, n--gers—you've got a list, right?"

Fourteen Once

If the boy in this story was contemplating a shooting, he would be a racial exception to the rule. Because when it comes to homegrown violent extremism and targeted violence that culminates in a mass shooting, the majority in of the murder in the USA is done by white men.[11]

That said, one trait that this student had in common with the men and boys who often commit mass violence is misogyny. The day I suspended him for the Apache helicopter outburst, *Fourteen* had told me, "You need to calm your pussy down." Misogyny is an ideology that is often interconnected with violent extremism.The Western States Center, in their toolkit for confronting white nationalism in schools, describes misogyny as "a key recruitment tool for white nationalist groups."[12]

Each of our adult mass murderers was fourteen once. Dylann Roof had just left his teenage years when he massacred the Black congregants in worship at a South Carolina church. A self-described psychopath, he also spoke of race war and subscribed to a flawed understanding of history that told him white people are being erased.

When Roof was just fourteen years old, his parents struggled to make ends meet. His father's once-successful business was headed toward debt and closure. His mother would soon be evicted from her home. This boy would have had good reason to believe there were forces of injustice in the world deserving of his anger.

No working-class child today can be said to be wrong if they feel some sentiment such as this. Ours is an economic and political system run by people who generate and perpetuate grave inequities. In 2018, according to *Forbes* magazine, "40% of Americans had trouble paying for food, medical care, housing, or utilities."[13] Poverty and deprivation cost our country dearly: Lives are lost every day. And young people fall prey to despair, nihilism, paranoia, self-loathing, and hate. Poverty isn't the cause of white supremacy or white supremacist violence, but economic inequality can amplify one's sense that you've got enemies, the system is broken and must be destroyed.

"Why Are There So Many?"

A teacher who worked closely with *Fourteen* had come into my office earlier that year and closed the door. "What's going on?" she said. "Why are there so many?"

She was speaking of the children wounded, abused, and troubled. She is a teacher who works with kids who have disabilities and struggles of all sorts. Most years she helps these students reach graduation with a sense of hope in their heart—and in her own. But that was starting to seem less possible.

She named a boy who lived with his parents and goats in a van. She named two girls whose fathers had seen multiple tours in Afghanistan, and were unable not to bring the trauma home. She named the child who cuts her arms and was now cutting school, and the boy whose anxiety surpassed his ability to cope, and the child from the home where guns fired in his direction, and the boy who found more security in conspiracy online than community in-person. "There are too many," she said. She named *Fourteen* and his struggles with mental health and sense of self in a place so full of dangers to students of color like him.

Broken Too Soon

In 1972, James Baldwin wrote of meeting a young adult Black man who was psychologically unwell. The young man believed he was a foreign dignitary, a prince. "This boy," Baldwin writes, "would not have been so quickly broken on the wheel of life if he had not been born black, in America."[14]

What is my part in this society that breaks the boys like the boy who ran from me? In Toni Morrison's *Beloved,* there is a schoolteacher who breaks people. I'm a schoolteacher, an educator, so what is my role in this broader system that breaks so many?

In the spring of 2021, a thirteen-year-old boy, Adam Toledo, was shot and killed by Chicago police in the alley into which they'd chased him. About a week before that, a white man assassinated six Asian American women in Georgia. And that same spring would see the sentencing of Derek Chauvin for the 2020 murder of George Floyd in Minneapolis. In the place where I live and work, I am geographically far from the locations of these stories. But it is important that I feel proximity. Across space and time, white supremacy links white lives, lies, privileges, and powers in a troubling kinship.

His Fear of My Fear

Chris Hedges is a white man with an upbringing in the church and a career as a correspondent in war-torn societies. He also teaches in US prisons. He wrote about the killings of the Asian women in Georgia, which he says were "not an anomaly by a deranged gunman." The "externalization of evil," he writes, "is not a fringe phenomenon of the Christian right":

> White supremacy, which dehumanizes the other at home and abroad, is also fueled by the fantasy that there are superior human beings who are white and lesser human beings who are not. [The murderer] did not need the Christian fascism of his church to justify to himself the killings; the racial hierarchies within American society had already dehumanized his victims.[15]

As an educator, part of my charge is to connect individual lives—including my own—to current events, contemporary politics, and historical understanding. How am I—how is my school—how is our school system—perpetuating racial hierarchies of worth? And, as a white educator, how much can I truly distance myself from the police who killed Adam Toledo, or from Derek Chauvin, or from the murderer in Georgia?

I will never forget the boy who ran from me down the hallway of the high school. I can still see his small form turning a corner. Before that, I'd never thought of myself as someone to run from, but I am—because he was.

And really, he was running because of his fear of my fear of him. White people's fears of people of color are many, including fear of losing what we've acquired or taken, and the fear of losing a sense of status dependent on the lesser status of others. This boy was right to fear white fear. What would I, or the state police, or Customs and Border Patrol, or the county sheriff, or the white boys in the woods with their boots who had already kicked him into the mud—what might such men do to him because of our fear of him?

"Education occurs in a context and has a very definite purpose," Baldwin wrote in 1980. "The context is mainly unspoken, and the purpose very often unspeakable."[16] The boy who ran from me was fourteen years old. Adam Toledo was thirteen when he was shot and stopped running. The white supremacy in our lives and institutions is fueled by fear: a fear that honoring the humanity of other people will shake the foundations of white identity and power.

A QUESTION OF POWER

Let us return to Carmichael's definition of power, from the beginning of this chapter. Whether or not a school leader's racism or anti-racism matters is not a question of attitudes held quietly or loudly professed; it's a matter of power, and how that power impacts the matters of others.

Power is, at its heart, a material matter, a concern for material things, resources that are needed to allow people to thrive. The spiritual or emotional dimension of an oppressive system is real, but it exerts itself with and upon material things, including bodies that exist in a material world.

Early childhood educator Emma Redden is a white woman who has written a book with white parents and teachers in mind called *Power Is Who Police Believe*. It offers suggestions for talking with very young children about race, racism, white supremacy, and power. Why does it matter whom the police believe? It's because of the life-or-death impacts their beliefs can have on the lives of others. Among many topics, Redden provides language to talk to young children about mass incarceration:

> The law says that slavery ended except if someone is in prison. People in prison work very hard and often make less than $1 for every hour they work. That's a very small amount of money in our country. Sometimes they do very hard or dangerous work like putting out fires.[17]

Redden is explaining incarceration in material terms, with reference to activities like working for pay, or putting out forest fires, which a young child can understand.

In one scene in which children are playing cops and robbers, with one person going to jail, Redden offers some language that the white parent can use to help the white child think clearly about what this means. The parent kneels and tells the child, "Jails are rooms that humans have to live in." The parent then says that "people with black and brown skin" are put in jails more than people with "light tan skin" even though they may break the same rules. The parent says this isn't fair and encourages the child to do something other than put people in imaginary jail in the game.

Redden is offering language the child can understand, and she grounds the understanding in concrete terms. Jail is a room. People in prison are in slavery and not paid fairly for their work. Fires are bad and it's good to put them out—but it's not fair to make people do this work and pay them so little. Redden is putting matters of race and power in material terms.

What are the material terms of school life? What power do school leaders have over these resources, and how can this power be wielded to distribute resources toward anti-racist goals?

This Spirit of Collaboration

White educators and authors like Redden have perspectives informed by their identities and experiences. In sharing their perspectives with diverse audiences—readers, students, colleagues, families—it is important to be aware of this. Redden approaches this question of authorship and audience at the beginning of her book:

> I don't assume that I am an appropriate person to make suggestions to people of color about how to educate the young people in their life about the consequences of a system created by people who look like me.... That being said, people of all races are subject to schools that neglect to teach about race, so if people of color feel like this work can offer additional tools, I am thankful to be collaborating.[18]

In this spirit of collaboration, we now consider the power school leaders have to reallocate resources in our effort to resist and dismantle systemic racism. The illness of racism has become more talked about and visible to white educators today than in recent decades. However, for many school leaders, the work of confronting institutional racism fades when the visible protest movements fade and more mundane concerns masquerade as more urgent.

How can school leaders keep doing anti-racist work when there seem to be so many competing and pressing needs? How can we see anti-racist work as core to the work of a school in a pluralistic democratic society? Once awakened to racial injustice and newly accountable for undoing racism in the school community, what can school leaders—especially white school leaders—do next?

THE PARADOX: DISCOMFORT MEANS IT'S WORKING

Many people believe that doing the right thing feels good. A paradox at the heart of finding motivation for anti-racist work, especially as a white educator—and perhaps for others as well—is that doing the right thing often isn't a "feel good" thing. There are painful self-discoveries, missteps that hurt others, and pushback and resistance from status-quo forces that can range from shunning and derision to threats and violent confrontation. Doing the right thing can create feelings of doubt, guilt, anxiety, shame, and fear.

In a white supremacist culture, when people of color feel discomfort it probably means that white supremacy is working. When white people feel discomfort, it may well mean that some aspect of the emotional or material privilege that attends white supremacy is being challenged.

People of color, in their resistance, feel the discomfort to a more dangerous degree; *discomfort* is too gentle a term. Challenging the status quo and living within it produces discomfort and worse. This country's mostly white educator corps is not used to feeling those feelings, so the paradox must be named: Discomfort means that your anti-racist efforts are working. This is not an invitation to solicit sympathy; just an invitation to understand that feelings we might normally work to avoid are a sign that we may be taking steps in the right direction.

THE PRINCIPLE: CENTER PERSONAL STORIES AND HISTORICAL FACTS

In the face of discomfort and pushback, it can be hard to maintain motivation for the work when one has the privilege not to have to. This is a generous way to frame it. One could also call it cowardice. Either way, a relevant question to ask is, how can we resist the strong incentives to avoid discomfort? How to hold ourselves accountable for fighting what we know is a cancer ruining the lives of so many, dividing and conquering people who would otherwise strive in solidarity to bring about better lives for ourselves and our children?

Personal stories and historical facts will guide and ground us. Personal stories and historical facts anchor us in truth, and the truth is the most powerful accountability tool we have. This is why "truth and reconciliation" is such a refrain in confronting atrocity and making attempts at healing: from apartheid in South Africa, to genocide in Rwanda; from efforts to remember the Holocaust and ensure never again, to the National Memorial for Peace and Justice in Montgomery, Alabama.

The National Memorial for Peace and Justice remembers the white supremacist terrorism of lynching Black people in our country. "Why build a memorial to the victims of racial terror?" the museum asks. Because "publicly confronting the truth about our history is the first step towards recovery and reconciliation."[19]

Such memorials and efforts at communal repair center both personal stories and historical facts. Personal stories tell of bodies and what is done to them. They communicate a name, a place, a family. The hair of children killed in Nazi extermination camps is collected for visitors to see. The names of lynching victims, state by state, county by county, are etched in the metal that weighs and hangs near the visitor's head.

The National Museum of African American History and Culture in Washington, DC, invites every walker through the winding journey of the museum experience to pause and enter a "Reflection Booth" and tell a story.

This is after seeing the artifacts and hearing the narratives of many stories. The experience of hearing a story invites the sister experience of telling.

Stories are how we understand our lives in place and time. We must surround ourselves in stories. In this regard, educators are among the most privileged people in our communities. By simple virtue of our profession, if our eyes are open and ears listening, we will encounter more stories of children and families than most other people will encounter in a lifetime.

Educators are also academics by vocation. The study of history is our job. Sound research and vetting of sources are tools of our trade. Few professions are better positioned to let personal stories and historical facts gather about us and help us see the truths that can guide us forward.

Stories Mistold

All stories are not treated equally. People's identities and stories can be silenced, mislabeled, mistold. Racial slurs are among the misnamings and mistellings. To not have one's story honored by the people we encounter produces a range of emotions.

> I kicked him repeatedly, in a frenzy because he still uttered insults though his lips were frothy with blood. Oh yes, I kicked him! And in my outrage I got out my knife and prepared to slit his throat.[20]

So speaks the narrator in Ralph Ellison's novel, *Invisible Man*. The narrator, a Black man, had just crossed paths with a tall blond man who'd insulted him. He demands an apology and doesn't get one. He becomes enraged but stills his knife when he realizes the man hadn't actually seen him. The slur was a misnaming. He wasn't known or seen by this stranger. The narrator feels disgust and shame at this new understanding. He then senses the absurdity of it, that this blond man was almost killed by a figment of his imagination, "a phantom," "an invisible man."

The Invisible Man then runs off loudly laughing. Most of the time, however, he is more quiet: "I remember that I am invisible and walk softly so as not to awaken the sleeping ones. Sometimes it is best not to awaken them; there are few things in the world as dangerous as sleepwalkers."[21]

Though it can be dangerous, people will ensure their stories are known. Again, schools are sites where stories can get told. Jamila Lyiscott is a scholar, activist, poet, and associate professor whose book, *Black Appetite. White Food. Issues of Race, Voice, and Justice Within and Beyond the Classroom*, explores how white privilege troubles our society and our schools. She shares of her childhood, and she tells her readers why:

This is my story. I share it because if you are an educator who has never faced their story as it intersects with the various social locations that shape how you show up in our schools and in our world, then you are destined to do this work irresponsibly.[22]

Lyiscott then asks her readers, "What are the stories that shaped your view of the world? What people and places socialized you into accepting the norms and values that script your life either knowingly or unknowingly?"

Lyiscott knows that inviting stories, and the circumstances of who shares her story with whom is not a matter without implications of power and privilege. Her time in schools has revealed that addressing institutional racism often centers "the needs and concerns of white participants, with the expectation that people of color will openly showcase their painful narratives in order to educate everyone else."[23] In her time facilitating group inquiries in schools, patterns arose, including white participants being "immobilized by the fear that any of their attempts to address racism would be viewed as racist":

> And in this fear emerged white silence alongside the expectation for people of color to carry out the emotional labor connected to this work: to tell our stories, to prove, to teach, to cry out, and to reveal the ugly belly of our pain for other people's learning.[24]

Lyiscott is highlighting a tension in her work as a facilitator of dialogue done in groups of people of different identities: Who tells what story and when? Who is permitted to be quiet? Upon whom is silence imposed? What audience meets the needs of which speaker? If I speak my truth, what will you do with it?

Above all, however, the imperative to author one's own narrative is the moral of Lyiscott's story: "My personal definition of oppression is being trapped in someone else's narrative with no power of authorship."[25] And this imperative—to author with honesty one's own narrative, in communion and intersection with the stories of others—applies to every one of us.

Likewise Crippled by Lies

Lyiscott tells us that if you haven't faced up to how your story is woven into and from the various socio-historical narratives that inform school life, then you are "destined to do this work irresponsibly."

We can't take responsibility for something we don't see, know, or understand. We can't even hold ourselves accountable to our own ideals if we have an understanding of ourselves born of lies, denial, or complacent disinterest in truth.

Few white American authors have probed questions of identity and racial oppression more fully than Lillian Smith, who grew up one generation removed from the Emancipation Proclamation in the segregated and violent Jim Crow South. Her work challenged many and earned their disdain, and earned the praise of others. Of her book, *Strange Fruit*, Alice Walker said, "The South can hardly be said to recognize itself without it."[26] And James Baldwin described Lillian Smith as "a very great, and heroic, and very lonely figure. She has paid a tremendous price for trying to do what she thinks is right."[27]

In her autobiographical and sociological study, *Killers of the Dream*, Smith brings psychoanalysis, class analysis, and feminist insight to bear on her reflections on growing up in the segregated South. Stories are teachers, and while Smith wrote for an external audience, she also wrote to and for herself, to teach herself about herself: "because I had to find out what life in a segregated culture had done to me, one person."[28]

In her writing, Smith interweaves personal stories and historical facts. She tells of the white-skinned toddler who came to live with her family as a child. The toddler had been discovered in a hovel, living on a dirt floor with a family in "Colored Town." White women of a church club conspired to have the child removed, a kidnapping cloaked in saviorship. The toddler came to live with Smith's family and slept in her room. The two children played and bonded deeply in a short span of time, as children will do. Weeks pass and then comes a phone call that reveals that the child was not a white child after all, and would have to be removed from the home.

Smith recounts her confusion, questions, and pain. Words and appearances didn't mean what they seemed. Children who loved each other could not be together. Parents who wanted their daughter to be happy were unwilling to resist the rules crushing her happiness. Of her parents, she writes, "I was shamed by their failure and frightened, for I felt they were no longer as powerful as I had thought."[29]

Most children have such moments of disillusionment, as adult ways and weaknesses clarify over time. But Smith probes deeper. She describes her compulsion to hide her fear and shame. She felt compelled to hide the adults' failings. "I felt compelled to believe they were right. It was the only way my world could be held together."[30] And as she matures, she represses her feelings—such stories—such truths—as many people do, in order to follow the rules of the world into which she was born. Such stories and truths and wounds do not disappear, though. They become wounds that never heal.

The night she comes to accept her parents' word and resigns to the story of the world as it is being inscribed upon her, she sits at the piano, and the young girl sits by her side. They now both know of the coming separation, and the girl, whose name is Janie, tries to hug her. Smith stiffens and moves away. Janie begins to cry.

As Smith grew older, this particular memory "worked its way like a splinter, bit by bit, down to the hurt places in my memory and festerd there," and as other memories congealed with it, she came to understand the hypocrisy of the world in which she was living:

> I began to know that people who talked of love and children did not mean it. That is a hard thing for a child to learn. . . . Something was wrong.
>
> Something was wrong with a world that tells you that love is good and people are important and then forces you to deny love and humiliate people. I knew, though I would not for years confess it aloud, that in trying to shut the Negro race away from us, we have shut ourselves away from so many good, creative, honest, deeply human things in life. I began to understand slowly at first but more clearly as the years passed, that the warped, distorted frame we have put around every Negro child from birth is around every white child also. . . . And I knew that what cruelly shapes and cripples the personality of one is cruelly shaping and crippling the personality of the other.[31]

Smith describes the impact this crippling has on the white Southerners of various roles and stations: mothers, children, fathers, laborers, lovers. She recounts repression, denial, lies to self, and "conscience torn from acts."[32] She describes the many resulting contortions of self and society, and grave injustices, and again contortions to excuse or silence the injustice.

Weaving personal stories with historical facts, Smith helps us understand how the contortions of white supremacy wrecked the psychic welfare and the material welfare of most whites in the South. She reminds us of the refugee status of all European newcomers to the early United States and earlier colonies. She reminds us that few whites actually owned slaves and that those who did were spiritually disabled by it:

> By the time of the Civil War in 1861 . . . only two and one-half percent owned four or more slaves. But 200,000 families out of 5,600,000 whites did own at least one slave and the ownership of one human being as slave is enough to put a Christian's conscience and mind in bondage for a lifetime.[33]

And while many were enriched, and all suffered spiritually from identifying with the fantasy of white supremacy, the racial hierarchy of people's worth convinced impoverished whites to swallow significant material deprivation for the sake of being one rung higher on the ladder of status.

> To be "superior" . . . made you forget that you were eaten up with malaria and hookworm; made you forget that you lived in a shanty and ate pot-likker and

cornbread, and worked long hours for nothing. . . . They could take your house, your job, your fun; they could steal your wages, keep you from acquiring knowledge; they could tax your vote or cheat you out of it; they could by arousing your anxieties make you impotent; but they could not strip your white skin off you.[34]

Digging your own grave, robbing your table of food, denying your children what they need to be well: This is what a lie can do.

Drained Pools

Ten years after Lilian Smith published her insights on how lies radiating from racism put the oppressor likewise in bondage, the city of Montgomery, Alabama, drained their public pool. Heather McGhee tells the story in *The Sum of Us: What Racism Costs Everyone and How We Can Prosper Together*. Weaving personal stories and historical facts, McGhee paints a vivid picture of the harm that comes to all of us when some of us deny the humanity of others.

> [T]he Oak Park pool was the grandest one for miles, the crown jewel of a Parks Department that also included a zoo, a community center and a dozen other public parks. Of course, the pool was for whites only; the entire public parks system was segregated. Dorothy Moore was a white teenage lifeguard when a federal court deemed the town's segregated recreation unconstitutional. Suddenly, Black children would be able to wade into the deep end with white children at the Oak Park pool; at the rec center, Black elders would get chairs at the card tables. The reaction of the city council was swift—effective January 1, 1959, the Parks Department would be no more.
>
> The council decided to drain the pool rather than share it with their Black neighbors. Of course the decision meant that white families lost a public resource as well. "It was miserable," Mrs. Moor told a reporter five decades later.[35]

The miserable loss of public goods concerns much more than access to pools and parks. It concerns many other public goods, and it connects to policy decisions from welfare reform to higher education access across the country. The legacy of slavery is clear, however, in terms of where one finds the most emaciated structures to sustain economic wellbeing. As of the publication of her book in 2021, McGhee notes that "nine of the ten poorest states in the nation are in the South."[36]

Truth and Freedom

The deprivation born of the lies that racism tells reveals the essential value of the truth. *The truth will set you free* is no empty cliche. Truth is freedom, and it starts with the self, which starts with the other.

"I cannot discover any truth whatsoever about myself except through the mediation of another," wrote Jean Paul Sartre in 1945.[37] Sartre was a French writer and philosopher wrestling with questions of good, evil, fascism, and freedom in a land where millions still sloshed about in the blood and ashes of the Second World War.

At a time when millions of people were dehumanized and annihilated in Europe, and a time when revolutionary struggles for freedom were taking root in Europe's colonies around the world, Sartre was well aware of the harm that comes from dehumanizing others with lies of inferiority. And he was aware of the danger lies pose to the liar.

Sartre asserts the essentially inter-subjective nature of human existence, that the truths of self and others are inseparably intertwined. "The other is essential to my existence, as well as to the knowledge I have of myself," he goes on to explain. "[M]y intimate discovery of myself is at the same time a revelation of the other as a freedom that confronts my own."[38]

If we deny the freedom of another person, we deny that other person the capacity to help us see the truth of our impact on the world, the truth of our very self. If you are not free to give me an honest appraisal of how my choices impact you, then I am not free to make decisions based on truth. I am not free to make informed choices. I am not free. This is the bondage Smith was writing of, an ocean away, in the very same era. This is the affirmation of freedom that Franz Fanon, another writer of this epoch, is demanding the world hear in his cries of "yes" and "no":

> [M]an is a *yes*. I will never stop reiterating that.
> *Yes* to life. *Yes* to love. *Yes* to generosity.
> But man is also a *no*. *No* to scorn of man. *No* to degradation of man. *No* to exploitation of man. *No* to the butchery of what is most human in man: freedom.[39]

Black Skin, White Masks is the title of Fanon's book quoted here. We hear echoes of it in the title of Jamila Lyiscott's book, referenced above, *Black Appetite. White Food.* Lyiscott's work in schools affirms a commitment to self and other together finding freedom by unwriting the lies inscribed variously into our lives by white supremacy.

In one scene, Lyiscott describes her facilitation work with a group of educators of mixed race in conversation about white privilege. "We will sit in the crosshairs," she writes, of a particularly important moment in the work. Her role, as she describes it, is to "create space for people to wrestle with difficult questions." A white woman has just brought a personal story into the space. Lyiscott, the facilitator, waits before responding. Eventually she speaks to open the space up further, noting "we have intentionally created space for discomfort as a necessary precursor of authentic dialogue. We have cultivated a space that is sacred and brave."[40] Such spaces are brave because they contain personal stories and historical facts that combine to reveal truths that are dangerous to an oppressive status quo.

THE PRACTICALITIES: REDISTRIBUTE RESOURCES

The principle of centering personal stories and historical facts compels the creation of brave spaces, and leads to mundane but crucial considerations, like who is telling the story and who is doing the listening. We're talking now about very practical matters: classroom interactions, meeting time, meeting agendas, facilitation protocols, community gatherings, curriculum content, and pedagogy, what we teach and how we teach it.

These are among the most practical elements of day-to-day school operations and involve the most important resources of the school: time and people. Yes, there are other resources that a school needs to function well. The sciences, fine arts, and other departments should have budgets for supplies that will be consumed during the course of the year. Most schools buy computers. There needs to be a roof that doesn't leak, and many more considerations.

But in the domains that most school leaders oversee, the most important resources are the people, and how the people use their time together. A school leader has a great deal of discretion over these resources—and every voice and every minute matters.

Scenario: The First Assembly of the Year

Imagine two different schools—High School X and High School Y—each with similar demographics in different corners of a large town. School is about to open. Among a thousand other important tasks, the principal at each school is working with colleagues to plan the first whole school assembly of the school year.

There are two substantial differences between these assemblies—but overall their plans for the fifty-minute gathering during the first week of school are remarkably similar. Each agenda includes the introduction of new faculty and staff, some enthusiastic announcements from the varsity soccer teams about games against rivals later that week, and a couple of pep rally–like chants led by the captains. There's also a playful contest the school counselors will lead that calls on volunteers from each grade level to come up and compete in a delightfully silly way for a new t-shirt and hat. (The sophomores will win—because they're not too cool to be goofy, and they really don't want to get beaten by their younger ninth-grade peers.) Both principals will also deliver prepared remarks, and they'll integrate a few other faculty leaders to speak about priorities and hopes for the year. Now to the differences:

The first difference is that School X had their assembly in the auditorium, with the brighter lights illuminating those on stage and the rest of the several hundred people—faculty, staff, students—sitting in rows. In contrast, School Y held the assembly in the gym, where there are bleachers on multiple sides of the massive space. There are rows, of course, but the light is bright on every face and those faces are able to look across and about the room and see other faces. Circles are common classroom and meeting practices at School Y, and the principal calls the assembly in the gym the biggest community circle.

The second difference in the assemblies concerns what the principal and faculty spoke about in their prepared remarks—and for how long. At School X the playful games went through several iterations of fun on the auditorium stage. Students love these competitions, and the counselors know that the joyful play is an essential element of childhood and must be part of school life. There remained about ten minutes at the end of the assembly for the leaders' remarks about goals for the year, which included a focus on kindness, academic excellence, and fair play.

School Y allocated their resources differently. Gathered in the "circle" in the gym, the remarks from the principal and faculty came before the games, and more time was set aside for this portion of the assembly, a full thirty minutes. (They'd planned for twenty, but it ran long and the principal let it keep going.) The focus was also on goals for the year, including the concept of inclusiveness and making the school feel safe and welcome for students and faculty of every identity. It felt to many that this was a need at the school.

The previous year there had been an increase in bullying and harassment concerns. School X had experienced the same thing. Indeed, this had been the case across the country: The nation had recently elected a white man to be president who modeled and encouraged derision and division, rooted in white supremacy, misogyny, and xenophobia.

At School Y, prior to the opening assembly in the gym, the principal had invited colleagues to volunteer to tell stories at the assembly related to their identities, claiming as a strength an identity that was being derided in mainstream culture. The idea was to have adults model for students the power of claiming their identity in a way that modeled strength. Each faculty member would share a personal story of how it makes them feel when they hear such identities being put down in the school community. And each adult would also share a hope for the school year.

One man, a beloved STEM teacher, identified as having a disability and spoke about his loss of hearing in one of his ears. An English teacher talked about her belonging to a family that includes members of the LGBTQ community, whom she loves dearly. A special educator spoke of being of Middle Eastern heritage. A history teacher spoke of his Jewish grandparents and their flight from Nazi Germany. Because he was a history teacher, he shared some historical facts, too. And he shared how it made him feel when he heard anti-Semitic comments or learned that a swastika had been found drawn on a lunch tray. In their hopes for the school year, they emphasized empathy, valuing, and learning from difference.

A lot can be understood about a school by how well students are engaged in an assembly. An assembly of any kind of crowd is a setting in which individuals can easily disengage and misbehave; side comments and distractions are muffled in the mass. But the School Y opening school assembly was very quiet, the community's task was listening, and the community felt the importance of the stories. It got loud again when the games were played. It was good to have the games come afterward. It was a release, a physical expression, a time for movement, loud voices, and playful bonding.

The principal's closing remarks stressed that these hopes for the community would be revisited and would be a goal of work in the school in every corner. Later that year, at the midyear assembly, the principal and faculty leaders would ask students to sign up to volunteer to speak to how well the school was doing in living up to this goal. Students claiming various identities would speak.

And later, at the last assembly of the year, the principal and the faculty would invite students to speak in the same terms the faculty had spoken of—and modeled—at the opening assembly: Who are you, what strengths do you claim, how do you feel when your identity is disrespected, and what hope do you have for the school community next year, when we return? A young girl of Native American heritage would speak. A boy of mixed race with a father in Central America would speak. A student of LGBTQ identity would share their story. They each would tell stories of harm and share hopes for the future. One of these students would challenge the school to raise the Black Lives Matter flag before school reopened in the fall. Not every student would cheer, but those who would cheer would be loud. The adults would listen, feeling accountable to the truths of the stories the children were telling.

The Means and the End

Personal stories and historical facts are a means and an end. Brave and inclusive spaces that contain personal stories and historical facts are what you strive for, and they are the way you get there. Once you create the vessels for personal stories and historical facts, truth will germinate in those vessels and tell you what you need to know or do next in your particular context.

Once a school has the containers for sharing personal stories and historical facts, questions about what's next will arise. Questions about how to do things differently or better will surface. The questions a school community encounters in confronting interpersonal and systemic racism could be listed for days and pages. If there are spaces for adults and young people to explore personal stories and historical facts related to racism and anti-racist goals, different questions will arise in different contexts.

And different answers will arise to common questions: What are we teaching and how are we teaching it? What do we see in our discipline data? Do we need affinity groups for students of color or for faculty? Do we need only-white spaces for dialogue? Is this a small group or large group topic? Do we have enough skilled facilitators for small group work? How does this impact you? How does this impact me?

A school needs sturdy vessels for the work of answering important questions in the local context. In some schools in rural parts of our country, the students of color are few in number, and many live with white adopted families. How questions are answered in those schools will be different from how they are answered in schools where a majority of the students are students of color. But what is true of every school is that there are ways to reallocate resources to create the spaces for the questions, interactions, and answers. People, space, time, process, and topics are among the resources and domains that school leaders control in substantial ways:

- SPACE: Where we do the work, the quality of the space, how furniture is arranged, the quality of noise, light, cleanliness, temperature.
- TIME: When we do the work in the day, and how much time is provided.
- PROCESS: How we do the work in different settings: meeting processes, classroom pedagogy, meeting facilitation, norms.
- PEOPLE: Who is in the work, their positions, their capacity, their roles and identities.
- TOPICS: The content of the work, including the personal stories and historical facts that are centered in classrooms, meetings, professional development, assemblies, and other forums.

The scenario of the contrasting assemblies reveals how space, time, process, topics, and people can be influenced by school leaders in very different ways to achieve very different outcomes. In the next several pages, we will consider other scenarios that illustrate concrete ways these resources can be used for anti-racist work.

Scenario: New Curriculum Offerings

School A and School B are both located in small towns in the Northeast. These schools each serve grades seven through twelve, a middle school and high school in one building. And, as is happening across the country, the baby boomer generation of teachers is aging into retirement, and certain course offerings are being retired with them. "Home Ec," or "Home Economics," classes, in which students learn the basics of cooking, sewing, laundry, and other systems of running a household and living independently, are no longer getting the enrollment they used to. There's a similar trend in "Wood Shop" or "Industrial Arts" classes. The high school sections of these classes have just a couple of kids in them in a given semester. At the same time, there are pressures—and opportunities—to offer STEM classes, such as computer coding and robotics. These Science, Technology, Engineering, and Mathematics classes are of interest to students, families, and employers. This social context is relevant to both schools.

Also relevant to both schools is the work of younger teachers who are challenging long-standing aspects of the curriculum. At each school, there is one humanities teacher in particular whose curriculum draws heavily from contemporary sources like Teaching for Justice, the Zinn Education Project, and Rethinking Schools. She refuses to teach straight from any textbook—though she draws heavily from Howard Zinn's *A People's History of the United States*.

In each school this teacher has recently begun advising an after-school club called the Racial Justice Alliance, modeled on the work she's seen a colleague do with the gay-straight alliance. The Racial Justice Alliance is made up of several students of color and several white students who describe themselves as allies. The club meets every other week after school and sometimes during lunch when the teacher doesn't have lunch duty in the cafeteria. The Teaching for Justice resources are often consulted by the group, and protocols for reading texts and discussing challenges are drawn from the resources of the School Reform Initiative. The principal at each school thinks this club is an important part of their extracurricular offerings and will budget, the following year, for a stipend of several hundred dollars for the teacher advisor.

In other budgetary and staffing matters, each school is trying to determine what to do in the wake of the Home Ec and Industrial Arts teacher retirements.

Given the multiyear trends toward lower and lower course enrollment, both schools ultimately decide they are not going to replace these two specific positions. Here is where the paths that the schools follow begin to diverge.

School A: New "STEM" Program

At School A, the principal, in consultation with the district office and the school-based leadership team, sees an opportunity to bring new STEM offerings to the school. The retirement of two veteran teachers on the upper end of the pay scale means there is some money to work with. The principal decides to use the funds from one of these teacher lines to help renovate the old "shop" classroom, transitioning it from workbenches, hand tools, and the warm, dry smells of sawdust to a high-tech lab with a suite of desktop computers, several tablets, a cart of laptops, and an array of robotics kits. Some of the equipment is leased, but they've got close to one hundred thousand dollars to invest, and since the funds will not be cut from the budget after the renovation, there will be money to maintain the equipment over time, renew the leases, replace materials, and purchase new equipment as the technology evolves.

With the funds from the second teacher's retirement, the principal creates a STEM teacher position. The applicant pool is open to teachers with various endorsements, and they find a wonderful candidate. School A's STEM Lab is launched with excitement across the community, including a story in the local paper with a profile of the new teacher and pictures of the clean and inviting classroom space. The principal tells the school counselors that students of all abilities and diverse interests should be encouraged to enroll in the STEM Lab classes—but the counselors needed no convincing. Many students and families had contacted them with interest as soon as public announcements were made. Enrollment in the first semester is strong, and the school is appropriately proud of their new program.

After a couple years, School A has developed STEM offerings at the lower grades to expose all students to robotics and coding, and at the uppermost level, they have an Advanced Placement Computer Science class that draws students with sophistication in mathematics to take on what is considered one of the most challenging AP classes in the country. The high school STEM Lab electives draw students who are historically underrepresented in STEM careers, including students of color and girls. The teacher who leads the Racial Justice Alliance is glad to see this. She often meets with some of these same students of color in the club.

The Racial Justice Alliance can also boast of accomplishments in the last couple years. In their first year, they invited the librarian to join their group and eventually secured her commitment to do an audit of the library's books through a racial equity lens. The librarian agreed to do this over the following summer, a valuable effort that led to substantial updates to the catalog. In the club's second year, they focused on how teachers and students were responding to comments that revealed racism and bias; they grounded their work in a toolkit produced by Learning for Justice called "Speak Up at School." By the end of the year, they'd secured an agreement from the guidance counselors to integrate these resources into the counselors' orientation for new students at the start of school. Every new student and family will get one of the booklets as a handout in the fall.

School B: A New "Applied Learning Lab"

At School B, the principal and leadership team take a different approach to reallocating the resources of the retiring teachers, decisions that eventually impact how the school's Racial Justice Alliance does its work.

This principal and leadership team also decide to use one of the funding lines to renovate a space and provide materials for new electives, and to use the other funding line to hire a teacher. But the focus is not on STEM specifically; it is on applied learning and contemporary problem-solving, more broadly.

The old Industrial Arts classroom is renovated to become a simpler space, with desks and chairs for flexible seating, a conference table, ample whiteboard space. The flexible space is called the Applied Learning Lab, and its purpose is to host classes that are focused on real-world application of skills and knowledge to solve contemporary problems in collaboration with community partners. Some of the offerings will be in the STEM domain, but teachers from across the subject areas are asked to consider teaching an Applied Learning elective.

A substantial portion of the funds from the two retirements helped renovate the space and create an annual budget for the Applied Learning Lab—for supplies, fieldwork, travel, fees, and other needs depending on the focus of the work. With the rest of the funds, a new position was created, the applied learning director, whose job is not to directly teach classes, but to support teachers in the planning and execution of the collaborative problem-solving approach that each course adopts.

The principal worked with each department chair to develop buy-in for these electives, inviting teacher passion and interest as one point of departure. Simple questions provided points of departure for developing ideas for the electives: What is the mission or purpose of your discipline? Why do you teach what you teach? What skills would you like to help students apply in doing work that needs doing in the local community? What contemporary problems need solving in our school, towns, and broader society?

Harder discussions were had in determining which other normal course offerings might rotate out of the course catalog to make room for a new Applied Learning elective. In some cases, a course that was offered every year became an offering that was offered every other year. In other cases, the core content of the new offerings aligned to the same curriculum standards as the course not to be offered.

The course offerings in the Applied Learning Lab included a diverse array of classes in the first couple years. In a class on radio journalism, the teacher and students partnered with a local college radio station to produce original youth journalism. In a class called "Climate Change and Income Inequality," students worked with local community organizers to produce events in the town to educate and raise awareness. A class in digital music production worked closely with a performance space in town to bring new youth performers to the stage. A class on local food systems worked in collaboration with a senior center to gather traditional local recipes and worked with local farmers to source local produce for cooking meals for the center.

Three other courses in the Applied Learning lab were created from extracurricular activities. The advisor of the service-learning club moved the club from the after-school hours down into the school day. As a class in the Applied Learning Lab, the club's impact expanded exponentially: There were multiple blood drives organized with the Red Cross and initiatives in collaboration with the local food shelf, veterans' home, and other organizations. In another offering, the school's Spanish teacher decided to take what used to be an after-school activity—planning the annual foreign language trip abroad—and made it a course. Instead of raising funds with parents to pay for a trip facilitated by a tour company, the students in the class now wrote grant applications to fund the trip and partnered with a human rights organization to design their travel experience abroad. Instead of tourists, the students became learners and partners; instead of hotels there were home-stays; instead of practicing Spanish in cafes and museums in Madrid, they were practicing it in living rooms and schools in Central America.

Another extracurricular offering also migrated from after-school and lunchtime meetings into the school day. The Racial Justice Alliance became a class. Instead of an hour or two of meeting time each month, the students and their teacher advisor had more than two hundred minutes every week to do their work, like any other high school class. This was a class that would run year after year. In the second year of the class, a special education teacher joined to team-teach the course and help increase access to the class for students with special education needs. With the increased time and support, the scope of the work that this group was able to achieve broadened significantly.

The principal and leadership team recognized the potential of this group to lead schooolwide discussions about racism and racial justice. They gave the Racial Justice Alliance access to faculty meetings at different points in the year, where the entire faculty could engage in personal and professional learning on topics of racial justice. Faculty and staff who had never before engaged in intentional reflection on what it means to racially identify as white, and to have white privilege, were engaged in such reflections in small groups led by student facilitators.

The Alliance was also given access to advisory classes, in which all students are enrolled, a context where every student could be engaged in conversations about racial justice. The conversations were grounded in the exchange of personal stories and historical facts, supported by resources from Learning for Justice and other organizations. When these sessions with faculty and students didn't go well, or became difficult for the student facilitators, the group's classroom became a time and place for support and reflection. The applied learning director was a support for both students and teachersin this regard.

With the three faculty supporting the students' work, and with the principal providing access to different forums, from faculty meetings to advisory classes to assemblies, the Racial Justice Alliance accomplished much in its first two years. Most importantly, they created a functional group dynamic and classroom space where support could be offered to each other. When there was stress and pain—either from without or within—there was time for reparative work within the group. With that foundation in place to support the group's own learning and collaboration, they were able to be ambitious in their plans:

- Community organizing and teach-ins to build buy-in to raise the Black Lives Matter flag at the school.
- Community forums, and school-based dialogue circles, where diverse voices were in dialogue.
- Assemblies, faculty meetings, and advisory lessons.
- Fundraisers to support a BIPOC land trust in their region.
- Community education about the murder of Emmet Till, and the activism of his mother, Mamie Till.
- A statewide conference on racism in schools, attended by hundreds of students and adults from around the state.

This course was just one of many offered as part of the Applied Learning Lab electives, but its reach was especially broad, and it was an important driver of community-wide learning and work. The principal was not an instructor in the class, nor a leader of the professional development when the group took it on, but the principal granted them access to important venues for dialogue and learning, and explained the rationale for work with public stances, emails to stakeholders, and many closed-door conversations with parents and students who struggled with the work of learning about white supremacy and systemic racism.

Important Resources, Difficult Choices

Schools A and B chose different pathways in the creation of new curricular offerings. Each pathway has value. Each principal and others who influenced the decisions had significant resources at their disposal and important decisions to make.

School A made a significant investment in STEM learning, from middle school through high school, which yielded many returns on their investment: Students of various backgrounds were enrolled in new STEM classes, from middle school through AP Computer Science. These can be empowering experiences for the students involved, opening up post-secondary pathways that otherwise might go unexplored. It is especially important that the school recruited students of color and girls into programs of study where they are often underrepresented. Some might argue that this has more practical value for those students than what the Racial Justice Alliance at School B was able to accomplish. But the pathway chosen by School B had significant impacts on the whole community.

School B made an investment in applied learning, including the specific work of challenging white supremacy through the work of the Racial Justice Alliance. The Racial Justice Alliance at School B was just one of several offerings supported by the school's resource reallocations, but its reach was extensive, because it became a major community-wide driver of learning about racism and its interpersonal and structural impacts.

Some schools may be able to have both the STEM Lab and the Applied Learning Lab—and communities should advocate for this. But many choices facing school leaders present an either/or crossroads: If we allocate resources to one endeavor, we will not have those same resources for a different endeavor. These are difficult choices about valuable resources. Consider the resources that were allocated to support the Racial Justice Alliance at School B:

- SPACE: A special classroom—the Applied Learning Lab—was created to support this class and others that were engaged in collaborative approaches to contemporary problems in partnership with community organizations.
- TIME: When the Racial Justice Alliance was an after-school club, they met for a couple hours each month, and attendance varied depending on the day of the month. When the club became a class, there were many

hours every week, and attendance was consistent, supported by all the processes a school has in place to help ensure kids attend class. In addition to the class meeting time, the group was granted access to time at faculty meetings and advisory classes.
- PROCESS: The pedagogy and protocols used in the class were often discussion-based, and suited to discussing dilemmas of emotional, ideological, and practical complexity.
- PEOPLE: Substantial human resources were dedicated to the Racial Justice Alliance at School B. First, there is the time of two teachers, as well as the Applied Learning Lab director, whose sole job is to support applications of learning and contemporary problem-solving in collaboration with community partners. To allocate the time of three professional faculty is significant.
- TOPICS: The content of the work included personal stories and historical facts that help individuals in the class and in the wider community understand the workings and impacts of institutional racism.

One of the lasting values of creating a vessel or container for the work like a racial justice alliance class—empowered with access to additional resources of staffing and time—is that it becomes an engine that drives the work, pushing the institution to be a more just community. But student-centered engines are not enough. There need to be vessels for the work at the level of faculty and staff. School leaders committed to the long project of confronting institutional racism must allocate resources to contain the work at the faculty level and sustain it over time.

Scenario: Professional Learning

Consider two different elementary schools, School C and School Z, each of which has a publicly-facing commitment to equity and academic success. And each school has at least an hour every week devoted to whole-faculty professional learning and collaboration. In a thirty-five-week school year, that's thirty-five hours of meeting time. The after-school meetings are coupled with multiple in-service days throughout the year, four of them half-days and four others full-days, creating a yearlong context for collaboration and professional learning that amounts to seventy hours or more of collaborative time outside of meetings that happen during school hours.

In schools C and Z, both principals believe that teachers need time for collaboration in teams with role-alike peers, as well as time in groups that mix people of various roles and positions. There is time throughout the year, for instance, for teachers at the upper or lower grades to meet; other times for people to meet to discuss particular curriculum domains, like math, literacy, and science.

This scenario is focused on the whole-faculty meetings throughout the year. The principal at each school outlines the meeting calendar in advance so that facilitators and any outside partners in professional development can plan accordingly. Each principal is also clear with colleagues that sometimes the priorities of the meetings shift as needs change from month to month. This was certainly the case when the COVID-19 pandemic brought school closure and then remote teaching modalities to schools in the spring of 2020. But before we discuss schooling during the pandemic, and the nationwide protest movement for Black lives that unfolded at the same time, let's look at what took place a few years prior.

First, the similarities: In school year (SY) 17–18, the professional development (PD) theme at each school was "Trauma-Informed Schooling." Following that, in SY 18–19, the school leaders at each school felt a need to respond to downward trends in scores on English language arts assessments and the focus became "Literacy for All." In SY 19–20, the schools each decided to focus on "Executive Functioning," which felt relevant in several ways: It built on learning about brain development from the trauma-informed PD, and teachers found it as relevant to literacy instruction as to student engagement in other domains.

When the pandemic disrupted school in the spring of 2020, many teachers continued to refer to what they'd learned about executive functioning as they developed online modes of schooling. However, while there were many similarities in the themes of the professional learning, the approaches were different, as was each school's capacity for anti-racist work through the pandemic and beyond.

School C: Outside Experts

School C had a substantial budget for professional development and worked closely with outside experts of good repute to facilitate workshops throughout the year on their professional learning strands. The principal worked closely with experts in the spring of the year to plan the work of the following summer and subsequent school year. Experts are in high demand, so it was important to "lock in" meeting dates on the annual calendar. This has value in terms of clarity and predictability. On the other hand, it allows less flexibility when new needs arise over the course of a school year. When Black Lives Matter protests emerged nationwide in the spring of 2020 and continued into the following school year, the leaders at School C did not feel able to make space for discussions of such in their faculty meetings.

The pandemic made certain meetings more difficult, but the outside experts remained available to meet by online video streaming. In some ways, the leadership at School C felt relief to be able to rely on the predetermined agendas and the prepared presentations of the national experts. There was ocassional mention of the racial justice protests, but there was not time for faculty discussions, personal introspection, or consideration of student needs in the local context.

School Z: Home-Grown Facilitators

At School Z there was less of a budget for outside experts. But this was not the main reason they relied more on in-house facilitation of professional learning in any given year. It was understood that local leadership and capable facilitation was crucial to maintaining spaces for courageous conversations about the difficult work of teaching.

In the summer of 2017, when the principal and leadership team at School Z began planning for the trauma-informed PD, they thought about how students were not the only population in the school that carries past and present trauma in their bodies and into the school each day. They were ready to bring in an expert to discuss trauma-informed approaches to teaching, but decided they would wait until the middle of the year for that. First they decided to build strong containers for the faculty's work, tending first to the quality of listening and learning among themselves.

During the first part of the school year, the faculty met at least once each month in small groups of six to eight people, each facilitated by a colleague. These facilitators were part of a facilitation team, which had met several times over the summer to build their own skills in facilitation and the use of protocols, including very simple "restorative circles," which they used to build trust among participants over time. They found a very useful resource in the book *Circle Forward*, which contains prompts and processes to use in schools on a wide range of topics with personal and political implications. Using these circles over the course of the fall semester, they built a foundation for learning about trauma in the student population, and the adult capacity to listen to and care for each other as difficult topics surfaced about their own practice and sometimes their own lives.

In one such circle, in response to the prompt, "How are the children?" many stories were exchanged—about the children who were students in the school, about the children some of the faculty were parenting, and about the children some of the faculty once were themselves.

After a school has established sturdy containers for conversation, personal stories can be invited and will enter, and historical facts can enter as well. The facilitators brought data about "diseases of despair" that were pushing national life expectancy downward in many communities across the country, and bringing great pain into the lives of children. They brought an article on the Adverse Childhood Effects (ACEs) Study, to help give developmental context to the impact trauma can have on a person. Race came up in these discussions.

While it hadn't been a specific focus of any prompt, at one group's meeting in October, the topic of trauma born of racism was raised. The facilitator of the group later debriefed the conversation with the other facilitators. This team of facilitators, which had formed over the previous summer, met twice a month, before and after each faculty session. The team received stipends for this extra commitment to the work. The principal suggested that they, the group of facilitators, practice talking about race, trauma, and schooling among themselves, as part of their ongoing self-directed professional development—so they could be prepared to lead or respond to the topic of race, both when it was intentionally being discussed and when it came up spontaneously. There were protocols in the *Circle Forward* book that they used to help them.

This team of facilitators maintained year after year. One or two members shifted, as some teachers' career paths changed, but new members joined who had felt the value of the small group work earlier as participants. The personal and political dimensions of the conversations they were hosting with colleagues compelled an ongoing commitment to such professional dialogue.

The principal recognized the importance of colleagues' facilitating conversations with colleagues. This didn't happen every week at the full faculty meeting time, but it happened frequently. There was still time for meetings led by district administrators and for the occasional outside expert to come and share their expertise. But meetings planned by the school leaders in collaboration with their team of facilitators were frequent enough to build strong containers for the work.

After the first year, one of the lead teachers had her teaching load reduced by one class, so that she could dedicate more time to planning and facilitating conversations about important personal and political topics as they intersected with their professional development work. This team of facilitators assisted with the literacy professional development that year, and intentionally interjected conversations about literacy and language as tools of oppression and liberation. Seeing the value of this work, the principal brought the lead facilitator onto the leadership team, so she could be in closer proximity to long-term planning and crisis response when the need arose.

At least one hour a month, year after year, teacher-facilitated professional collaboration continued to enable respectful—though sometimes difficult—conversations about challenging personal and professional topics. The groups were in place when the pandemic arrived, and they continued to meet as vessels that could hold some of the collective emotional labor of the work. And when protests for racial justice swept the nation that same spring, conversations about race and institutional racism in schools were a staple of the professional dialogue at the school.

While many other schools across the country were able to use the challenging logistics of teaching in a pandemic as an excuse to talk less about race, this school was able to see the intersections and hold the space.

In the fall of 2021, the superintendent of the district met with principals to share data on what she described as "learning loss." She mandated that professional development and meeting time be used to review local, state, and national standardized testing data and to make plans to fill the gaps that had emerged according to that data. The principal of School Z brought this information back to the school leadership team. They decided that in upper- and lower-grade team meetings they would review data, including ultra local data of student work from their classes. But they would not disband the one-hour monthly meetings of the carefully facilitated small faculty groups. In those groups they turned their attention not to "learning loss," but to what learning could be gained from a study of the pandemic and its impact on the society. The facilitators were not daunted by the debate about Critical Race Theory that was simultaneously raging across the country, placing every teacher's classroom in the crosshairs of those who would assail—with weapons of silence and denial—the work of confronting racial injustice and building racial solidarity.

In no school is every teacher in the same place, or coming with the same story, when it comes to confronting the impact of racism in schools. But at this school, come fall of 2021, they were ready with strong vessels for the ongoing task of supporting each other in the work and across their differences.

Important Resources, Difficult Choices

The structure for professional learning put in place at School Z has special value because it created the capacity for sustained work over time. It began with an investment of resources to create strong vessels for teacher collaboration and the sharing of personal stories and historical facts. These groups and the facilitators who led them became drivers of professional learning and compelled the further reallocation of resources as time went by:

- SPACE: When the time came each month for these groups to meet, the facilitators ensured that there were suitable and private spaces for each of them. Classrooms and meeting spaces around the school were used, as were breakout rooms in online meetings.

- TIME: This scenario provides an example of what we might call the "One Hour Rule." If there is important work to do at the level of whole-faculty professional learning and collaboration, at least one hour a month of a school's precious meeting time is required, at a minimum. There are always competing demands, and difficult choices have to be made. In addition to the time that was allocated for the entire faculty to engage in the work, the facilitators met for additional planning time and training. And in addition to this, a lead teacher facilitator was eventually granted time in her day—one less class—to engage more fully in the work.
- PROCESS: The protocols used in the small group meetings of faculty were discussion-based, and suited to discussing dilemmas of emotional, ideological, and practical complexity.
- PEOPLE: There was attention paid to the skills and needs of the facilitators. Those who feel a responsibility for tending to the group need attention themselves. The facilitators were paid for their work, and eventually the lead teacher facilitator was paid as part of her school-day responsibilities to lead the work. In the early phase, administration was also involved, showing up and participating and modeling commitment and engagement. Eventually administrators were able to step away from the role of facilitator as more faculty stepped up and into those roles.
- TOPICS: From trauma, to literacy, to racial justice, the content of the work included the personal stories and historical facts that create the truths that hold each of us accountable for working toward justice and meeting the diverse needs of the students and families in our schools.

One might question which came first in this scenario: the exchange of personal stories and historical facts, or the resource allocation to make space and time for the exchange of personal stories and historical facts. It was during the trauma-informed PD that people first raised the concern about taking care of their colleagues during the work—so one might argue that it was sensitivity to personal life stories that sparked the initial allocation of resources. Or one might argue that it was the allocation of resources to create small, well-facilitated faculty groups that allowed people to start raising important concerns and stories about race and racism.

As school leaders consider how to hold and carry the work of racial justice reform, the important thing is to see this as a both/and situation, the means and ends intertwined. The personal stories and historical facts will compel the allocation of resources, and, at the same time, an allocation of resources is required to support the courageous confrontations and conversations that come when we excavate and interweave our stories and histories.

FIFTEEN CONCRETE ACTIONS
EVERY LEADER CAN TAKE

We haven't yet talked about a school leading or joining more ambitious racial justice reforms outside of the school, focusing on a wider redistribution of resources aligned with the priorities of racial equity at the local, state, and national level. First there need to be vessels that hold the work with kids, engines that are fueled by the energy of students' lives, and there need to be the same at the level of the faculty. Once these are in place, a particular school, in a specific political and geographic and demographic context, will have the people with the space and time to determine priorities for the work. As noted above, the work will look different in different contexts—and the contexts from town to town, city to city, and state to state across our country are extraordinarily diverse.

Questions and answers will look different in different contexts. Is there silence about race in the curriculum? Do we place a value on discussion and empathic listening in our classrooms and meetings? Do we have protocols, structures, and habits that help people to disagree while also building shared understanding? These are just a few of countless questions that echo with different relevance in different schools.

School structures will also be interrogated. Do we have systems that track student achievement, and what are the demographic trends? Do we need to alter our hiring and retention policies and practices? What do we see in our discipline data?

In terms of broader context, do we have allies in the community who can work with us? Do we have detractors in the community who need to learn from us? What is the state and local policy context, and which elected officials support courageous work about racism in schools—and which do not? What is the stance of the teachers union?

There are different battles to be fought and different coalitions to be built in different places. Regardless of where the school leader is working, however, there are commonalities that can ground and guide the work. The paradox will be felt across all schools, and school leaders can keep in mind that discomfort means your efforts to challenge the status quo are probably working. Discomfort will feel more or less acute depending on one's identity and position. This book is being written from the perspective of a white educator, whose discomfort will be different from educators of other identities—and whose guidance may even feel mistaken to educators of other identities.

The stories of the mistakes one makes and the impact they have on others are important. Navigating the paradox requires finding anchor in truth. To act in accordance with truths about self and other is the only way to be free. I can't know myself if I don't know how my actions impact you. And if I don't know myself, then I am chained by delusion.

We will find truth in the personal stories and historical facts of the world in which we walk. This principle can guide us to focus on very practical matters, including when, where, and how we learn from and with each other. The day-to-day practicalities of leading a school come down to a few basic resources, including time, space, people, and processes. The positional power of a principal is significant and derives in large measure from influence over these resources. The scenarios shared in this chapter illuminate ways that resources can be allocated to build capacity for the work of confronting institutional racism. There are powerful actions a leader can take in any school context:

- *It's a community—tell stories*: Invite and tell stories—including your own story. You may not think of yourself as a storyteller, but you have a story to tell. If you are a white school leader, you have a story to tell about being white. Model the sharing of personal stories and integrate stories into your work with students and adults. This includes amplifying literature, drama, and the visual arts. If you are not ready to tell your own story, or not ready to invite the same from colleagues or students, a poem or short story can be a powerful entry point into conversations about complex emotional topics. If you do not feel ready to facilitate a discussion about a text, there are teachers at your school who could do it. But at some point, telling stories from your own life is important. This can happen at meetings, in classrooms, in the media, in letters to the local paper, at assemblies. You do not need to tell too much, but just model the mix of power and vulnerability that comes with the telling of a personal story.
- *It's a school—be scholarly*: Model an appreciation for research, evidence-based arguments, and historical facts—including the history that was just yesterday in the newspaper and in contemporary policy debates. There are strong anti-intellectual forces and inclinations in our nation, as dangerous today as ever in the past. Reject this and embrace your role as a public intellectual. Put the work you and others are doing in historical and contemporary policy context.
- *Run meetings the way classes need to be taught*: A school leader has control over facilitation protocols. Place value on well-facilitated discussions in small groups, and model this as much as possible whenever designing meetings. As we will explore in chapters in this book focused on restorative practice and democratic governance, adults develop skills through professional learning that they can take into their work with students—and vice versa. This attention to process will help build the

vessels needed for the personal stories and historical facts essential to the work of racial justice reform.

- *Make the extracurricular curricular*: Create student-fueled engines for the work. If you have after-school and episodic gatherings of students and others focused on anti-racist school reforms, try to bring that work out of the extracurricular realm and into the school day. As we saw in the scenarios focused on the Racial Justice Alliance at School B, doing this increases significantly the essential resources allocated to the work, from meeting time in a given week to the funding used to pay teachers to support the students in their learning. Consider doing this with other organizations that are doing work that has intersections with racial justice as well, such as a gay-straight alliance or groups focused on combating climate change. And once these groups have adequate time to do in-depth work, provide them access to additional venues for learning, such as faculty meetings and other class meetings of students.
- *Cultivate teacher facilitators*: Adults will not be ready for challenging work with students in any authentic way if they are not feeling prepared to take risks themselves. This preparation happens through the doing of it—with colleagues. Teacher meetings should be facilitated by capable facilitators. If teachers are not available or ready, you and other administrators should bring your skills to bear. But ideally, over time, a cadre of teachers who are skilled and practiced facilitators of collaborative work and dialogue will be holders and drivers of the work. Support teachers who lead teams and professional learning sessions with role titles and stipends for this work; ensure that they have training and are capable facilitators of challenging conversations; provide them time or pay them for time to prepare for the meetings they facilitate, and then build meeting time for conversations about racial justice into the monthly meeting schedule.
- *The One-Hour Rule*: Wherever you are on the continuum of this work as an institution, once you have the facilitation capacity, give this work at least one hour every month of the universal faculty meeting time. One hour is the minimum, and more can be found by using additional in-service time. Why one hour minimum? Experience and research tell us that fewer topics on the professional development calendar allows us to go deeper, and that continuity and consistency matter. According to the Center for Public Education, metastudies of professional development in schools have concluded that "professional development programs that impacted student achievement were lengthy, intensive programs." They go on to state, "Programs that were less than fourteen hours (like the one-shot workshops commonly held in schools) had no effect on student achievement. Not only did these workshop programs

fail to increase student learning, they didn't even change teaching practices."[41] If this is true of typical professional development efforts, imagine the time required to have any meaningful impact when engaging colleagues in conversations about racism and teaching practice. One hour is not enough per month, but it will allow you to keep your momentum as an institution.

- *Derive relevance from need*: Often teachers concerned with student engagement concern themselves with what the students are interested in. This can result in superficial projects and allow people to hide from difficult topics. Many students at first would rather talk about hobbies and video games than hunger, economic injustice, or environmental racism. There is a place for both, but we too often err on the side of superficial interests rather than focus on addressing the basic needs of people in our community. Rather than as "interest," frame relevance as "derived from need": the developmental needs of kids, their families, and the local needs of the school and community. When supporting teachers with curriculum design, ask how the framing of the work can be grounded in needs. Another way to frame the discourse around curriculum so that it orients toward needs is to describe teaching and learning as "problem solving." From whole class syllabi, to units of study, to particular assignments, you should encourage and support teachers in designing curriculum that is focused on solving problems in the school, the community, and the wider society. There is no way that structural racism and a host of other ills will not surface if the orientation of schoolwork is toward contemporary problem-solving.
- *Champion courageous curriculum*: If not yet familiar, explore resources that are dedicated to careful lessons that center personal stories and historical facts related to racial justice and intersectional concerns such as labor history and environmental justice. Organizations that offer such resources include Facing History and Ourselves; the Zinn Education Project; Rethinking Schools; and Learning for Justice, among others. A very useful resource for elementary educators—and teachers of every grade level—is Liz Kleinrock's book, *Start Here, Start Now: A Guide to Antibias and Antiracist Work in Your School Community*. Share links to such resources and purchase resources to share with colleagues as part of the ongoing formal and informal conversation about what we teach and how we teach it.
- *Conduct an equity audit or curriculum audit*: Centering personal stories and historical facts is how to excavate the truths that generate the will for the work. Historical facts derive from the past, which includes yesterday. Contemporary data are useful, including data about your specific school. Explore how equity audits work, and consider inviting a trusted critical

friend from outside or inside the school system to conduct an equity audit at your school. The data could reveal specific areas of inequity in your school system, in terms of how people of different racial identities are impacted by the allocation of resources and access to opportunities. Indeed, the data are likely to reveal inequities. Sometimes gathering more data and studying the problem can become a tactic, intentional or not, for delaying action. But sometimes data from a local source—your own school—can be compelling. Equity audits can take many different forms and include achievement data, enrollment data, graduation rates, and discipline data—as well as observations of teaching, learning, and other interactions. Data can also be sourced from interviews with individuals and focus groups, a.k.a stories. An additional way to audit and reflect on practices in the school can be a curriculum audit, by which you look at your curriculum through a lens and reflect on what you are teaching and how. To shine a light on whether and how racial identity and institutional racism figure into the curriculum, consider using the Social Justice Standards by Learning for Justice as a lens.

- *Teach or co-teach a class*: Lead by example. Model the kind of teaching that courageously and carefully carries the work of confronting racism in the community and broader society. Many school principals will find it difficult to teach classes, but it can be done. Perhaps not every year, but find ways to teach a class that models the kind of content and pedagogy that is required for this work. Center personal stories and historical facts. Use pedagogies that support authentic dialogue and debate. Co-teaching is often a good way for an administrator to be a teacher during the school day, for it ensures another adult is in the room if you get called away.
- *Normalize learning from mistakes and inviting feedback*: Teachers are very comfortable telling students that students can learn from mistakes. Teachers, themselves, can be less comfortable taking risks and learning from mistakes—this includes teachers who are white and the mistakes they will make related to the racial identity and racialized experiences of themselves, students, and others. No one should be careless, cavalier, or unprepared when it comes to professional learning or classroom teaching on these topics. There is too much at stake. But the school leader can remind everyone that we can support each other in learning from our mistakes. The leader can model risk-taking and solicit feedback that allows for learning—and then put what is learned from mistakes into practice the next time. If and when we make mistakes or cause harm, we can model being held accountable and learning from it.
- *Deploy adults to the topic*: In addition to classroom teachers, there are other adults in schools who can join a teacher and students in discussions of challenging topics. School counselors, social workers, deans,

para-professionals, administrators, special educators who case-manage students in the class, and others can be offered as support for discussions teachers may want to have but feel unsure of how to manage. With another adult in the room, the teacher has someone to debrief with after, someone to ask questions of, someone to model engagement in the discussion for students, or someone who can step out of the room with a student in distress. Many teachers reluctant to have a conversation about racism on their own will be willing to do it if they have the supportive presence of another adult.

- *Influence the hiring process*: Whether you have a lot of control over the hiring process or play a smaller part in a larger human resources department in a district, influence the process so that there are questions that allow follow-up questions about a candidate's professional and historical perspective on institutional racism. A broad prompt like this one can be useful: "Tell us about a time you learned a lesson about inequity in schools and how this changed your practice or perspective." A candidate's response will provide points of entry to ask follow-up questions about the person's own professional practice and their historical understanding of institutional racism.
- *Allocate staffing*: Create full-time faculty positions that are tasked with supporting courageous curriculum and contemporary problem-solving in the work done by teachers and students. Schools have all manner of people hired to support instruction, from literacy and math interventionists and coaches, to technology interventionists and others. Instead or in addition, create positions that are designed to support teachers in project-based and applied learning that is focused on contemporary challenges in the lives of kids and the community.
- *You've got the mic—use it*: The position of the school leader means that you have the ability to speak to multiple audiences throughout the year, and people will listen. Use this important power to frame the work that people are doing in a broader context of striving for racial justice and other intersecting efforts to make our communities more democratic and fair. Every time you find yourself at the microphone or keyboard—or at an assembly, a meeting, a classroom observation conference, a parent conference—you have an opportunity to remind people of the deeper values and goals of the work. You don't have to use that opportunity every time, but you should do so often enough so that people know what you stand for—and what the school stands for as long as you are leading it. In addition to common terms like "equity," use words that carry special power related to the place of schools in our society and the liberatory power of education, words like "freedom," "justice," and "democracy." Speaking your values publicly also gives birth to an intrinsic motivation

that drives all of us: to mean what we say, to be trustworthy, to deliver on a promise or a vision.

"It Has to Be Personal"

In a 1962 interview, the white journalist and oral historian Studs Terkel, and the Black author and activist James Baldwin, discuss schooling, language, and poetry—in the United States and in colonial contexts abroad. Baldwin had recently returned from a trip to West Africa. They discuss other people's perceptions of our nation, and the nation's inability to do what is right for the people of our country.

Baldwin says that people are frozen in "immaturity," and are unwilling "to think hard problems through."

Terkel asks him how to unfreeze the immaturity.

"You would have to begin by doing very dangerous things," says Baldwin. "It's such an individual matter."

Baldwin then says that we have to consider the "standards" and values according to which we want to raise our children and live our lives. "On a purely social level and on a deeper level, one has to ask oneself what one really believes . . . "

Terkel observes, "It has to be personal then."

Baldwin agrees, "It has to be personal, and everyone always wants to avoid this, but this is where everything begins."[42]

A Personal Story

I once told a personal story to a whole school assembly, about a time I put myself in between strangers on a subway train headed to Harlem late at night. A Black man was singing, and five older Black riders on the train were threatening him.

It was the middle of the night, perhaps 3 a.m., and I was half asleep, in my twenties, on my way home on the number six subway train from somewhere in Brooklyn. A Black man—probably in his thirties—whom I'd seen many times on the 4.5.6 trains—got into the nearly empty car and did what he always did. He sang.

He sang arias in Italian and German. He was classically trained, I imagined, perhaps a graduate of a school like Juilliard, and his singing sounded extraordinarily beautiful to me. He also seemed to me to struggle with mental illness. There was a mix of daring and paranoia, of confident extroversion and inner trembling, a fearful fearlessness in his bearing. He rarely spoke any words, just sang. His clothes were not always clean, and his eyeglasses seemed decades old, with thick lenses, always scratched and cloudy. He didn't carry a cup, but if people offered money, he would take it.

I listened to him in the nearly empty train that night. It was beautiful, as always. He stood in the middle of the car, neither approaching me or the other group of riders on the other end of the train. The other riders were five companions, men and women, perhaps two couples and a fifth friend. They were Black and seemed to be in their fifties. They'd boarded the train a few stops back, laughing and enjoying the night and each other. I imagined they were on their way home from a party or club, perhaps drunk (like I was that night). Whatever state they were in, it was clear they had no time for the music that was now interrupting their night.

At first they got quiet and studied him, and then they found the singer funny. After a period of laughing at him and making jokes, they got impatient. They told the singer to be quiet. He went closer to them, straight-backed, singing strong. They told him to get off the train, and with that he went closer to them still, singing with more vigor. They began to menace him. He sang with more grandeur and commitment, staring them down.

One man stood up and faced the singer. The train stopped, doors opened, and the man again told the singer to get off the train. The doors closed, and he still stood there.

The force of the music and the force of the threats rose, and then I got up, not thinking. Or perhaps I was thinking what I thought when I saw younger adults posturing in school or on the sidewalk at lunch: that I didn't want to see a physical altercation. I walked down the long train car and stood between them. There was silence. The train stopped, doors opened, and the vocalist left the train somewhere underneath lower Manhattan. I had about one hundred blocks to go before I'd be home.

The five other passengers—decades older than me—were shocked and, it seemed, afraid. They asked me if I was a cop. I told them that I wasn't a cop, that I was an educator. At that, their demeanor changed. I'd intruded, and they were angry.

Part of me wanted to get off the train, to pretend I lived somewhere else. I could get off, wait at the station, and then take the next train home. But I knew I shouldn't get off the train. I needed to be with them and listen.

I'd gotten in the middle of something that wasn't my business, they told me. And they told me that I could get hurt. The women were trying to calm one man down in particular. He was pacing and very angry, and his fist was clenched. He wanted to teach me a lesson—but he also knew that it would be dangerous for him. What if he taught me a lesson? What would happen to him then? He was outraged at my intrusion, and probably outraged at the fear I'd made him feel, or humiliated by how he'd been made to feel.

Me, a twenty-something kid, had just made a man my father's age tremble because he thought I was a white undercover cop. And then he had to subdue his very natural impulse to put me in my place—because what would happen to him, then, if the criminal justice system came for him in response to what he'd done to me?

The women scolded me, told me I didn't know what I was getting into, and should mind my own business. I said a lot of "yes, ma'ams." I don't remember much about the conversation that transpired over the remainder of that ride, but I'll never forget the way that my whiteness and my access to power and protections of the state brought such anger and probabaly fear and shame into the subway car that night.

The Truths That Compel Us

At the whole school assembly where I told this story, we also announced that the theme for the school year was citizenship. I wondered aloud if I was being a good citizen in this story, or if I was interfering in something that wasn't my business, walking impulsively into a situation unaware of how I was protected by my whiteness. I didn't answer the question in any clear terms. I answered only by saying, "We can only understand citizenship through action and reflection. And in company of others. You must see yourself in the eyes of others. And they must see themselves in you." As my remarks concluded, I walked around the gym holding a mirror. I looked at my students and colleagues and, as they looked at me, they looked at themselves.

One of the people looking into that mirror, seeing herself, and seeing the students gathered about her, was a first-year teacher. Several years later, that teacher would be co-teaching a class focused on racial justice, and the students and teachers of the class would organize, in that same high school gym, the first statewide, student-led conference about racism in schools. Hundreds of students—more students of color than the small town had ever seen—would come to the conference with educators and other allies from their communities. The conference touched many people and created networks, alliances, and connections that are still active today and agitating for justice.

There is no direct line to be traced from my assembly remarks to this teacher's work several years later with her colleagues and a group of courageous kids. Indeed, when the press came to cover the story of the conference, they came to interview me, and I was glad to be able to say that I had nothing to do with it. The Racial Justice Alliance had told me in the fall that this was their plan and I'd said okay.

But, of course, in some ways, as principal, I'd had a significant role because I'd allocated resources to enable the work: time, space, and people. And in terms of process and focus—curriculum content and pedagogy—I'd used my position as instructional leader to support teaching and learning that focused on solving contemporary problems. And when it came to race, I'd cited historical facts to place our work in broader contexts and I'd told personal stories.

Frantz Fanon asserts that it is "through the effort to recapture the self and to scrutinize the self" and by enduring the lasting tensions of their freedom, that people "will be able to create the ideal conditions of existence for a human world."

He asks why we assert the superiority of some and the inferiority of others. He asks:

> Why not the quite simple attempt to touch the other, to feel the other, to explain the other to myself? Was my freedom not given to me then in order to build the world of the *You*?[43]

School leaders can use our powers to build forums for people to explain our experiences to each other. We can use our positions to help facilitate the sharing of self-scrutinizing stories and self-implicating histories. Such stories are the truths—held in tension with the truths of others—that compel us to do the work of making our communities more just.

Chapter 2

Democratic Governance

> The exercise of power can be healthy and constructive, or it can be imbalanced and harmful. Power in hierarchies is generally exercised over others. . . . Those with power over others often don't notice when that power is operating.
>
> —Carolyn Boyes-Watson and Kay Pranis[1]

It is hard to find the word *democracy* in the many bestselling books about school leadership. The book may be hundreds of pages long, and the index of the book extensive, but you'll find no mention of democracy, for instance, in the index of Richard Dufour's *Personal Learning Communities at Work*, nor in Peter Senge's *The Fifth Discipline*, nor in *Leading Change in Your School* by Doug Reeves, nor in *The Moral Imperative of School Leadership* by Michael Fullan.

School leaders and the experts who influence leadership development across the public and private sectors talk about working as teams, learning together, and collaboratively solving problems. These are all important elements of democratic practice in schools. But rarely do we come across the word *democracy*. We instead see terms like *collaborative practice, community of practice, distributed leadership, teacher learning teams*, and *professional learning communities*. Why is this? These structures enable people to name, understand, and collaboratively solve problems about matters of local concern, which is at the heart of what it means to be "democratic"—but we do not hear the word.

IN THE NAME OF DEMOCRACY

In *Schools That Learn*, Peter Senge and his collaborating authors do, in fact, name *democracy* on a few of the book's six hundred pages. Ironically, in a section called "Schooling as an Ethical Endeavor," by Nelda Cambron-McCabe, readers can learn something about why the word *democracy* is so missing in school reform discourse.

Cambron-McCabe argues that educators must see themselves as "moral stewards," teachers and principals who understand that "enculturating young people into the principles of this social and political democracy is at the heart of the civil society we value and at the heart of school's moral responsibility to society."[2]

As moral stewards of schools in a democratic society, educators will be faced with difficult choices "in the name of democracy." This is about means and ends, the process and the outcome, and it is about more than voting and majority rule. "For example," she writes, "we cannot justify racial and gender inequity on the basis that the majority voted for it."[3]

Moral stewardship in schools is about critical reflection on the practices and structures that make the school more—or less—democratic and just. Cambron-Mcabe explains that being "morally explicit" about the democratic purpose of schools is essential, and she helps us understand why rich and important discussions of democracy have evaporated from the school reform discourse:

> In recent years . . . technical rationalists have held sway in education policy circles. They argue that pragmatic solutions work, no matter what the ideology, and that most methods of teaching are "value neutral." One has only to look at the vast number of publications addressing school improvement that are directed primarily at "how to fix schools" to see the impact of this thinking. States become preoccupied with establishing standards and measuring student outcomes through tests. Educators focus their attention on techniques and strategies to respond to policymakers' mandates, often narrowing the curriculum and increasing the emphasis on rote learning.[4]

Just six other pages of this useful book contain explicit mention of the democratic goals and processes of schooling, though in her chapter Cambron-Mccabe and coauthors clearly state the importance:

> The primary goal of public schools is to educate children for the responsibilities of citizenship in a democracy. In recent years, a plethora of private and individual interests have replaced the civic responsibilities of schools. While recognizing that schools do have some responsibility to individual private goals, we believe that broader civic responsibilities must resume their place as the central mission of the public schools.[5]

The work of reinstating democracy's place in the work and discourse of leading schools is something every school leader can do. The "technical rationalists" and those who would want us to think that schooling is "value-neutral" will certainly not do it for us.

"More Than a System of Governance"

In *Democracy Matters*, the scholar-activist Cornel West describes democracy as a "way of being":

> Democracy is always a movement of an energized public to make elites more responsible—it is at its core and most basic foundation the taking back of one's powers in the face of the misuse of elite power. In this sense, democracy is more a verb than a noun—it is more a dynamic striving and collective movement than a static order or stationary status quo. Democracy is not just a system of governance, as we tend to think of it, but a cultural way of being.[6]

In this chapter we will discuss structures of democratic school governance, as well as democracy as a "cultural way of being." Deborah Meier is an educator who has centered this understanding in her work as a person who has founded, sustained, and supported democratic-minded public schools at all grade levels.

Meier helps us understand the different contexts in which democracy matters: a civil society and public policy context; a school governance and operations context; and the context of the day-to-day life of the school. In terms of the daily life of the school, Meier is concerned with what happens in the halls and classrooms: the curriculum content, the intentionally cultivated habits of mind and work, and the general norms of interaction.

The title of Meier's 2002 book, *In Schools We Trust*, is a phrase that carries each of these meanings. Schools are an essential element of the trust inherent in a democratic society's social contract. We trust educators as caregivers and partners in child-rearing. We pool our resources with the trust that they will be used to care for each other's children. We trust that schools will educate our children to the habits, skills, and knowledge necessary to citizenship in a democratic society. And in doing this heavy work, educators will only be able to carry all they're being asked to carry if there is trust among them, born of democratic and reciprocal relationships. None of this is easy. It is messy at times, and to be awake to the imperatives of schooling in a democracy is to feel uneasy with many different pressures, from within the school and from without, including how to handle authority and how to resist it. Meier tells us:

> It is within our schools, and in the governance of them, that we need to learn how to resist institutional and peer pressures, as well as respect the institutions we live with and the peers who are our fellow citizens. It's in such institutions that we need to learn to handle authority in all its many forms—both legitimate

and illegitimate—and how to take authority on—effectively. It's within such schools that we need to learn to resist what we see as improper encroachments on our rights, and to organize and expand what we believe to be our entitlements. All the habits of mind and work that go into democratic institutional life must be practiced in our schools until they truly become habits—so deeply a part of us that in times of stress we fall back on them rather than abandon them in search of a great leader or father figure, or retreat into the private isolation of our own private interests.[7]

With all of the compelling reasons to center the concept of democracy in both the purpose and process of schooling, we should return the question of why the concept has been erased from how many people conceive of school leadership and school reform.

Because Democracy Is Difficult and Dangerous

There are those who believe that schools can be value-neutral places. There is a related, decades-long, and inordinate emphasis on basic skills in English and math. These domains contain skills easily isolated from curriculum content that has personal meaning, political importance, or relevance to local communities. There are also the cross-sector marketing priorities of the industries that publish books on leadership, industries that aim to widen their market share by appealing as much to the corporate corner office as they do to the principal's office.

Above all, the word *democracy* is a dangerous term to those people in the public and private sector who work to concentrate wealth in the hands of a few shareholders and executives at the expense of the laborers who produce the products that generate wealth and the communities that live where the resources are extracted. If a leadership seminar is to be marketed effectively to everyone—from modern-day corporate oligarchs to the heads of local preschools—the word *democracy* is not likely to be part of the framework. Even if there is an emphasis on democratic processes like teamwork and collaboration, the word *democracy* itself carries too much moral weight to be included in a supposedly value-neutral space. It carries an accountability to question entire systems of injustice and inequality that structure so many of the very institutions we are striving to lead fairly. So, we find ourselves in this dangerously sterile ground where inequality will remain unchallenged, where the seeds of democracy will sprout neither root nor stem of any strength.

Finally, we may not hear the word *democracy* much in discussions of school leadership because it's a way of being that can feel confusing and paradoxical to any leader. West wrote of democracy as a "movement of an energized public to make elites more responsible." What are the implications of this for a school leader at the top of an institution's hierarchy? The leader's position is elite compared to others, with access to power that the general populace of the school doesn't possess. How can one both occupy this position and cultivate an "energized public" that would challenge that power and position?

Meier spoke of schools as places where we all—children, teachers, leaders, families—"need to learn to handle authority in all its many forms—both legitimate and illegitimate—and how to take authority on—effectively." What does it mean to take on authority effectively? Is Meier saying that, as a school leader, a person must "take on" the powers that be for the sake of the democratic life of the school and the broader community? She is. Meier is also saying that as a school leader we "take on" and wield power in our role. The school leader has authority and needs to struggle with how to use it effectively and democratically.

Hierarchies within Hierarchies

As small, stratified societies in a larger, stratified society, schools perpetuate and exist in hierarchies. The roles and responsibilities embodied in the position of the school leader can be extensive, and thus the power of the principal and other leaders is significant in many domains.

In one particularly long job description from a school district in Minnesota, the list of responsibilities is many pages long and includes this summary of the principal's role:

> Under the direction of the Superintendent, the High School Principal provides leadership for the instructional program, as well as coordinating the implementation, review, and revision of the curriculum at the building level. Manages the operation and all functions of the grade 9–12 secondary school. Supervises school staff regarding instruction, curriculum, student programs and issues, and building operations. Schedules and attends meetings, as appropriate. Leads the site improvement process.[8]

The other pages of the job description include several more detailed lists of responsibilities, which include these items, among others:

- Supervises and evaluates certified secondary staff, ensuring that the proper elements of instruction are implemented; coordinates the teacher supervision and evaluation processes with the assistant principals.
- Evaluates assistant principals and the activities director.
- Supervises secretarial, paraprofessional, and custodial staff (in conjunction with coordinator of buildings and grounds) in the performance of their duties.

- Manages staff and program improvement processes, as well as teacher professional development plans. Evaluates all staff assigned to the building.
- Screens, interviews, and recommends the selection of staff, including teachers and paraprofessionals; assigns the teaching staff.
- Assures the existence of a faculty-participating decision-making process through the department chair structure.
- Manages all staff orientation processes.
- Manages and edits the staff handbook.
- Supervises police liaison services.
- Manages all building security and staff procedures, including evacuation and emergency plans.
- Coordinates the building and grounds maintenance program at the building level.
- Co-supervises custodial services within the building.
- Interprets policies related to faculty, staff, and students.
- Responds to and resolves complaints and grievances of students, staff, and parents.
- In the absence of the assistant principal, disciplines students.
- Develops building objectives and procedures to facilitate the delivery of programs, student discipline, scheduling, and record keeping.
- Coordinates various district programs with the regular education program.
- Supervises athletic events, evening school functions, and attends school-related community events.
- Manages field trips, out-of-state trips, and related transportation requests.
- Manages school safety and security processes, including crisis management procedures.
- Supervises the completion of, or actually completes, reports required by the district or by the State of Minnesota.
- Manages all student grade-reporting processes, honor roll, and student records.
- Collaborates with other district administrators in assessing and recommending district programs and policies.
- Coordinates the total curriculum with all departments.
- Leads high standard implementation process, including curriculum development, standards assessment, record keeping, and reporting.
- Coordinates the "tech prep" program.
- Assures and implements building site-based decision-making processes.
- Organizes and manages the North Central and other school improvement processes.
- Manages the student graduation process.
- Co-supervises and manages the building technology plan.
- Manages, analyzes, and interprets data, including assessment results, for school improvement purposes.[9]

This is a long list! And it helps illuminate the place of the principal within a hierarchy. The principal is subordinate to the superintendent, who reports to powers above at the level of the school board and state. And "below" the principal, at the level of the school, the principal has many professional subordinates, and the language used to describe the principal's work with these colleagues and students is thick with terminology of positional power, like "manages," "supervises," "evaluates," and "assigns."

Tucked into the long list of responsibilities is mention of a representative system of governance, or collaborative decision-making, which the principal must assure exists in some manner: "a faculty-participating decision-making process through the department chair structure."

Some districts have made efforts to deemphasize management duties and increase the emphasis on instructional leadership in the role of the principal; be that as it may, most of the above-listed responsibilities remain within the purview of a school principal in most places. How can someone with so much authority—and so little time for so many responsibilities—lead the often-slow work of running a school with democracy in mind?

THE PARADOX: TO SHARE POWER YOU MUST ASSERT IT

A paradox at the heart of our questions about democratic leadership in a hierarchical institution is that one must establish and assert positional power as part of the democratic process. And democracy is very much about process.

John Dewey, philosopher of education, put it this way: "A democracy is more than a form of government; it is primarily a mode of associated living, of conjoint communicated experience." This "mode" involves expanding the space so that people are working together in interconnected ways. Democracy, says Dewey, is an "extension in space of the number of individuals who participate in an interest so that each has to refer his own action to that of others." This compels one to "consider the action of others to give point and direction to [one's] own." Dewey also notes that "barriers of class, race, and national territory" can keep people from perceiving how their actions impact others.[10] This incomplete perception of reality is a problem, as noted in our first chapter, because when we willfully or unwillfully hide how our actions impact others, we are not living truthfully and cannot truly be free.

But the democratic space is never without barriers, role distinctions, or hierarchies. Dewey is clear about this as well—especially in the classroom. And there are parallels between what Dewey says of teachers and groups of students in classrooms and how school leaders and colleagues govern a school.

A teacher striving for a student-centered, egalitarian classroom must be pragmatic about the importance of leadership and the place of positional power. In Dewey's prose one can find descriptions of the well-governed classroom in terms that might remind us of traditional egalitarian societies, where individual freedoms are balanced with cooperative imperatives, where status hierarchies exist, and exist to democratically serve the welfare of all.

The individuals of the classroom, Dewey remarks, "form a community group," and the teacher leader of this group is not "external boss or dictator." Rather, this person's role is to "arrange conditions that are conducive to community activity" and "communal projects." In pursuit of the common good, different people will have different roles, based on their expertise, interests, and availability. Individual freedom is important—but there "can be no greater mistake," writes Dewey, "than to treat such freedom as an end in itself." It is the common project that preserves and perpetuates the group: "The primary source of social control resides in the very nature of the work done as a social enterprise in which all individuals have an opportunity to contribute and to which all feel a responsibility." This is the "normal and proper" way to hold the community together and how also to honor the individual "without the violation of freedom."[11]

What Dewey says of the well-run classroom is equally relevant to the well-governed school. In the democratic school, the role of school leaders is not to dictate because-I-said-so, but to frame an authentic and worthy common task, such that the imperatives of completing the task together dictate who does what and why. Leaders should frame the work in this way, and then use their power to allocate resources to support individuals and groups in completing the common task, solving the problems that they share. Throughout, it is important that everyone knows who has what powers in the larger system and collaboratively influence how those powers are mobilized to serve common goals.

THE PRINCIPLE: CLARITY OF PURPOSE, TRANSPARENCY OF PROCESS

Clarity of purpose and transparency of process are key elements of democratic governance—in schools and in state and national systems. Unfortunately, we don't always have models of such in the behavior of our elected leaders, and this lack of transparency should and will raise concerns about corruption and cowardice. It compromises trust in the system.

For instance, consider the lack of transparency and unreliable data from the federal government on gun violence. According to the Center for American Progress, there is a "dearth of detailed and timely data about gun violence in the United States."[12] This lack of transparency is a problem across government bodies. The Centers for Disease Control (CDC), Bureau of Alcohol, Tobacco, Firearms and Explosives (ATF), and the Federal Bureau of Investigations (FBI) are all part of the problem:

> CDC data on nonfatal gun victimizations are so incomplete that many researchers advise against relying on them. In an annual report, ATF makes only the most cursory data available about the origin of guns that are recovered in connection with violent crime; moreover, it has not released a comprehensive analytical report about gun trafficking in two decades. Data released by the FBI related to hate crimes and fatal use of force by police officers are similarly deemed too unreliable to be useful.[13]

This lack of transparency compromises the political will to act on measures that could reduce gun violence, which a majority of Americans favor.[14]

If the federal government were behaving democratically, accountable to the needs and will of the American people, there would be more timely and transparent dissemination of data on gun violence in our country. But when people with power work in anti-democratic ways, lax oversight and a lack of transparency are tools of their trade.

The end results of power wielded without transparency are violence and deprivation. The basic needs of people go unmet, and violence comes to many. The power wielded by the US Armed Forces is a case in point. Granted, the armed forces are armed, and their purpose is to use violence when necessary to protect a nation's people and their interests. But the lack of accountability for how this power is used enables violence of terrible proportions, including the deaths of innocents and the unethical treatment of enemy combatants.

Our nation, through our military, is guilty of war crimes and torture which are enabled, in part, by a lack of transparency about how our government uses our resources. In many cases, we employ private military contractors, accountable to company shareholders, rather than soldiers accountable to the US citizenry through chain of command. We inadequately audit the Defense Department—and when audits are conducted, they are failed.[15]

Recent wars tell the story of our unchecked military power and the public-private partnership that is our military industrial complex. As reported by the journalist, pastor, and activist Chris Hedges, "at least 801,000 people have been killed by direct war violence in Iraq, Afghanistan, Syria, Yemen, and Pakistan and 37 million have been displaced in and from Afghanistan, Iraq, Pakistan, Yemen, Somalia, the Philippines, Libya, and Syria." This "human tragedy," says Hedges, "is reduced to a neglected footnote" because of the lack of accountability. He predicts:

[N]o one will be held accountable for the debacle or for the other debacles in Iraq, Syria, Libya, Somalia, Yemen or anywhere else. Not the generals. Not the politicians. Not the CIA and intelligence agencies. Not the diplomats. Not the obsequious courtiers in the press who serve as cheerleaders for war. Not the compliant academics and area specialists. Not the defense industry.[16]

That power unchecked leads to violence is not a matter irrelevant to the work of an educator. The power of the school system can be wielded democratically, with accountability to the people of our communities, or not. The power of the principal can be used transparently, with methods of distributed leadership that engage faculty, staff, and students in the collective work of making the community well—or not. The curriculum of the school can correlate to the needs of the individuals and the broader community—or not. The graduates of the school can leave the place knowing the value of democratic relationships—or not. The barriers that divide us can be broken down—or reinforced.

The end result of an education system unaccountable to the people it serves is violence. As noted earlier in this book, Nahlia Webber, executive director of the Orleans Public Education Network, asserts explicitly that schools help "socialize Americans for White violence and Black death."[17] Webber is concerned with the kind of curriculum that can train white students to discount the humanity of Black students, a discounting that enables structural violence as well as the kind of violence we see in murders committed by agents of the state:

> Black children are suspended, detained, "demerited" and isolated in schools for trivial things every day. And there's a killer cop sitting in every school where White children learn. They hear the litany of bad statistics and stereotypes about "scary" Black people in their classes and on the news. They gleefully soak in their White-washed history that downplays the holocaust of Indigenous, Native peoples and Africans in the Americas. They happily believe their all-White spaces exist as a matter of personal effort and willingly use violence against Black bodies to keep those spaces white.[18]

The teachers who write, interpret, and teach the kinds of lessons Webber describes go to work every day in a school led by somebody. It is important that the leader lead with democracy in mind. This requires that we explicitly name our intent to use our power toward democratic ends, and it requires transparency about how our power is being wielded. Without clarity of purpose and transparency of process, we will find that our democratic systems are weak, lacking the broad and varied engagement needed to make those systems strong, and lacking the measures to hold leaders accountable for how their power is employed.

PRACTICALITIES: SPEAK ITS NAME, MAKE ITS SHAPE, LIVE IT VARIOUSLY

School leaders committed to democracy in theory may find it difficult to use their positional power to cultivate democracy in practice—for many reasons. The system is hierarchical by design. The job responsibilities are innumerable and the related tasks often urgent. It is hard to slow down and include others. And there's little explicit guidance about democratic leadership, since the discourse of leadership has been blanched of the concept. This happens, as we have noted, because democracy is dangerous. The democratic spirit challenges the status quo in an era of privatization, wealth hoarding, and the control of vast resources by a shrinking number of people. In the face of such challenges, how can we deepen our commitment to democracy in theory and practice in schools?

Paradoxically, democratic systems require not the retreat from positional power, but that leaders use it intentionally to shape school life. School leaders can live well with this paradox by keeping in mind the principle that democracy thrives on clarity of purpose and transparency of process. This principle leads us to consider practical matters, from the very words we use to speak about the work, to how we literally shape human interactions in the school community, to the various ways that democracy is lived by various stakeholders, based on their different roles and needs.

Speak Its Name

Thomas Jefferson was an early leader of this republic. He was a conqueror and enslaver who wrote very public words that gave the world the language to name his sins even as he lived them. "We hold these truths to be self-evident, that all men are created equal" is a phrase that has, for hundreds of years, broadcast the hypocrisy of an American slaveholder into every corner of this country and world. Jefferson wrote in the Declaration of Independence that "all men are created equal, that they are endowed by their creator with certain unalienable rights, that among these are life, liberty and the pursuit of happiness." These words resonate for their clarity, for their truth. They set a standard and have helped hold to account the leaders of the nation born in the wake of the words.

To voice moral principles in no uncertain terms gives the human community—which lives in language and passes its ways down through generations in stories—the tools needed to affirm what's good and to call out failings. Freedom fighters through the ages have held up the Declaration of Independence as a mirror that reveals both what is right and how far we have to go to get there. Black traditions of activism and literature have done this illuminating work for centuries.

In Ralph Ellison's *Invisible Man*, the novel's protagonist sits as a child at the side of his dying grandfather, a man who was born into slavery. The grandfather's deathbed instructions haunt and confuse the grandson for his whole life. In the last pages of the novel, he revisits the scene and its haunting questions. The grandfather had told him to "yes 'em to death and destruction." What did this mean? He wonders:

> Could he have meant—hell, he *must* have meant the principle, that we were to affirm the principle on which the country was built and not the men, or at least not the men who did the violence. Did he mean say "yes" because he knew that the principle was greater than the men, greater than the numbers and the vicious power and all the methods used to corrupt its name?[19]

Grandfather is telling the boy to affirm the truth and democratic promise of the words from the Declaration of Independence in spite of the fact that the men who authored the words betrayed the principle.

It is the spoken principle, the words in ink, the vocal assertion to listeners near and far that allows the idea to be known to self and others. We must speak it if we are to be compelled to make it so. Consider the two phrases below. Which of them is the most compelling?

"Teachers at this school belong to intentional learning communities of practice."

Or:

"Teachers at this school belong to a democratic community."

The first phrase uses the language of contemporary school reform. The second phrase just uses the word *democracy*. Which is the more compelling for its simplicity and idealism? The answer is obvious. Excavating the idealism from the jargon is a very practical step that school leaders committed to democracy can take.

It may surprise some school communities to hear you speak it, because we have come so far from valuing the concept in word and deed. Even the most progressive school reform organizations, whose core work is to seed and support democratic practice in schools, seem to hesitate to put the word in print. The School Reform Initiative (SRI), for instance, is much respected for their protocols that get people talking, collaborating, and learning in authentic and respectful ways. Their work supports democratic practice in schools. But even when they critique the language of school reform, they speak of fostering "intentional learning communities" without speaking democracy by name:

There is considerable conversation about "learning communities" in schools and the literature about schools. Some communities are "professional;" some are "purposeful;" others are "communities of practice." There is a lot of talk and lots of different (and often confusing) language. Moreover, Richard DuFour who coined the term "professional learning community" has remarked that the "term has been used so ubiquitously that it is in danger of losing all meaning." ... In SRI's view, in order to make a difference, learning communities need to be rigorous, collaborative, focused on learning, and built upon shared norms and values. In other words, they need to be intentional.[20]

All of what the authors say is true—but we must put our work in a broader context, that of the democratic project that is our nation's promise. This language signals our great aspirations, helps us see our terrible shortcomings, and spurs us in our essential strivings for a better school and better world.

Case Study: A School Striving to be Democratic

To further illustrate the practicalities involved in striving to be a democratic school community, we turn to a 2017 case study: the James Baldwin School, a New York City public school with an explicit commitment to democracy in its mission and core values.

The James Baldwin School (JBS) was an outgrowth of Humanities Preparatory Academy, another small, community-minded New York City public school.[21] Like its parent school, JBS intended to be an institution that would empower youth and teachers both. Since opening in 2005, the school has more than tripled in size, and the faculty has known several principals. There have been growing pains and some hard transitions. But at the time of the case study, after twelve years, the distributed leadership structures had lasted, as had restorative justice forums, student-led town meetings, and faculty meetings guided by consensus-seeking processes.

By many other measures, the school was dong well. The *Atlantic* magazine mentioned the school for its work in restorative practice,[22] and an article in *The Nation* described the school as one of the "successful public schools" serving "communities of color" in New York City.[23]

The widely consulted NYC school-review website, Insideschools.org, described JBS as "a small transfer school in a huge building that attracts students who were not successful at some of the city's most selective high schools and others who are looking for personal attention in a small environment." Data on the site in 2017 indicated that most students were Black or Hispanic, and over 70 percent of students were eligible for free or reduced lunch. The review noted, "Dedicated teachers and a college counselor work closely with [these students] to make sure they graduate and go to college, even if it takes some students more than four years."[24]

In terms of more standardized measures of success, such as the 2017 NYC School Quality Report—an annual evaluation of schools based on student achievement data and other inputs—JBS was rated as "good" to "excellent" in every metric.[25]

How is democracy part of the equation?

Mission and Core Values

JBS was a replication project, transplanting core elements of the parent and mentor school, Humanities Prep.[26] A team of Humanities Prep teachers and leaders worked for a year to plan the school, collaborating with external partners and a group of tenth-grade students, who would transfer in to become the founding student elders of the new school. The core elements of the new school included:

- A codirectorship, made up of a principal codirector and a teacher codirector
- Consensus-based faculty governance
- An advisory program
- Student-run town meetings
- Restorative practice
- Performance assessment and thematic curriculum
- A mission statement and seven core values

Researchers who study democratic schools will tell us that mission and values are essential ingredients of these institutions. Münire Erden and H. Elem Korkmaz, after an exhaustive survey process that engaged practitioners and allies of democratic schools around the world, found that "the most important category in founding a democratic school is its 'values and philosophy.'"[27] And these values are not to be guessed or inferred; they are made explicit. As Michael W. Apple and James A. Beane note in *Democratic Schools: Lessons in Powerful Education*, "Democratic schools, like democracy itself, do not happen by chance. They result from explicit attempts by educators to put in place arrangements and opportunities that will bring democracy to life."[28]

The JBS mission statement was written by Perry Weiner, founder of the parent school. It is less concise than a typical mission statement. It reads more like a manifesto. Democratic purpose and practice are clearly named:

> It is our mission to provide a philosophical and practical education for all students, an education that features creativity and inquiry, encourages habitual

reading and productivity, as well as self-reflection and original thought. We agree with Socrates that the "unexamined life is not worth living," and it is our desire to prepare students to live thoughtful and meaningful lives. We are committed to inspiring the love of learning in our students.

This mission can best be accomplished in a school that is a democratic community. As a democratic community, we strive to exemplify the values of democracy: mutual respect, cooperation, empathy, the love of humankind, justice for all, and service to the world.

The James Baldwin School is college preparatory. Our curriculum and pedagogy prepare students for the rigors of college work and motivate them to desire and plan for a higher education. In preparing students for college we believe that we move students toward higher levels of intellectual engagement while they are in high school.

It is our mission, as well, at the James Baldwin School, to provide a haven for students who have previously experienced school as unresponsive to their needs as individuals. We wish for all students to find their voice and to speak knowledgeably and thoughtfully on issues that concern their school, their world. We aid students in this endeavor by personalizing our learning situations, by democratizing and humanizing the school environment, and by creating a "talking culture," an atmosphere of informal intellectual discourse among students and faculty.

In order to achieve this, we intend:

- to restore a true understanding of the First Amendment: that freedom of expression is the highest democratic right and must be therefore taken seriously, and that democracy can only continue if opinions are based on evidence and meaningful thought;
- to encourage students to become passionate thinkers, seekers of truth and beauty, advocates for justice;
- to create an environment in which individuality is respected and cherished, an environment in which human beings are valued for the content of their character and the quality of their thought;
- to address the problem of student cynicism through promoting intellectual behaviors which lead to students' discovery of their own humanity and the value of human life, human feeling, human culture, human history, and the human endeavor;
- to promote an ongoing dialogue about the educational process, and to create an atmosphere of mutual intellectual and artistic endeavor in which students and teachers learn from each other;
- to cultivate the natural idealism of youth through promoting and honoring community work, and to acknowledge and engage the vital interdependency of the practical and the philosophical by creating meaningful external learning situations in the community at large;
- to advocate for peace and nonviolence through an understanding of history, modeling respect and mutual esteem, and actively exploring and

promoting alternatives to hurtful conflict in the realms of both interpersonal and political life;
- to provide moral alternatives and to help students become morally sensitive people, and to establish the connections between the academic disciplines and moral action, the connections between learning and community, thereby creating a just community in our school;
- to employ the best progressive principles of education, to promote emotional as well as intellectual development, and to cultivate the various learning styles and intelligences present in all students. To this effect, we advocate that depth of inquiry, not coverage of material, guide classroom instruction.

Always subject to interpretation and reflection, the mission statement was never subject to revision—though occasionally someone might bring up the idea. Why not revise it? Because it is important for every community to have sacred texts, those constellations of words and stories that are given special reverence. The mission, with its emphasis on democratic schooling for a democratic society, was one of those texts. The school's core values comprised another kind of sacred text at JBS:

- Respect for Humanity
- Respect for the Intellect
- Respect for the Truth
- Respect for Diversity
- Commitment to Peace
- Commitment to Democracy
- Commitment to Justice

Lofty, broad, and flexible, core values such as these demand constant revisiting to have practical meaning and importance. At one time, the faculty handbook included a more detailed description of each value, as a point of departure for ongoing reflection, and to aid teachers in connecting these values to learning intentions in the classroom. The description of Commitment to Democracy included various indicators. One of them was "Citizenship in School," which emphasized contributing to the creation and revision of classroom rules and participating in schoolwide forums for discussion and governance. Every community—with people joining and departing—is always in process of becoming itself, and so forging a common understanding of community values is an ongoing process. For this reason, discussing the core values became an important element of many activities at the school, from the orientation process, to curriculum and activities in Advisory class, to behavioral contracts, to restorative justice interventions, to annual student-generated awards and faculty-conferred graduation honors. The core values grounded each of these processes, compelling ongoing reflection by students and faculty about the meaning of a Commitment to Democracy and the other ideals.

Governance

Full-faculty consensus-building process was an important way that the school worked to operationalize the commitment to democracy voiced in the mission and core values. At JBS, as at other schools,[29] active participation in democratic decision-making processes is made an explicit expectation of all faculty.

"Creating Curriculum *and* a School" was the title of the section of the faculty handbook that provided a teacher job description focused on three essential aspects of working at JBS: teaching in the classroom, being an advisor, and being a teacher-leader who participates in school governance. One of the expectations of a teacher and advisor at JBS was a "commitment to, and practice of, our core values; infusing them into our curriculum, culture and lives." The expectations of teachers as school leaders included "attending and participating in consensus-based staff meetings for school governance."

Consensus-seeking is a means to surface multiple perspectives and to collectively realize a good response to a given problem or challenge. Faith is placed in the wisdom of the collective, and power is granted to each individual to shape the outcome of a discussion, indeed to block a decision from moving forward if there are significant concerns that a person can't live with.

In addition to articulating the expectation that each teacher be an agent in the consensus process, it also became important, as the handbook was revised over the years, to include explicit mention of the role of the meeting chairperson, discussion facilitators, and those people who had positional power in the school, including the principal.

As the school grew in size, efforts to value every faculty voice became more challenging. It became clear that any meeting for collaborative problem solving—or governance—should intentionally and transparently make use of the capacity of the chairperson or principal.

If consensus hadn't been reached in the time allotted, and if further deliberation wasn't an effective path, the chairperson or principal had a twofold responsibility: to determine next steps based on the ideas and information that had been shared, and to record any major concerns that participants had voiced, so that those concerns could be revisited when the time came to evaluate the effectiveness of the decision. By acknowledging the explicit roles of meeting leaders in consensus-based work, one thereby makes explicit the ways that a principal or any committee chair is accountable for seeking and listening to multiple and dissenting perspectives.

Even egalitarian communities have—and need to learn how to use—differentiated roles, positional powers, and status hierarchies based on wisdom and experience. As long as the essential forms and norms of democratic process are in place, and as long as a leader's authority can be transparently mobilized to serve the common good, the occasional reliance on positional power can be important to meeting the goals of the group.

Some will disagree with this perspective. Erden and Korkmaz summarize the beliefs of the many democratic school leaders they surveyed in their research: "A general evaluation of all of the findings of this study leads to the following rough definition of democratic school: It is a democratic community where everybody—be they adult or child—has equal rights and power."[30] It is a mistake, however, to define a democratic school in this way.

Democracy in schools isn't about the purely equal distribution of power or voice. Just as in the classroom, it is a mistake for teachers to strive for purely student-directed learning, so at the level of governance it is a mistake for a faculty to idealize modes of interaction in which each voice—no matter, age, experience, or position—is said to carry equal weight or authority. It's not that individual voices and personal freedoms don't matter. Rather, it's a mistake to be guided by such a pure vision because, quite simply, hierarchies exist, both formal and informal, and to not acknowledge them only makes it more possible that the power at the top of the hierarchy be misused.

When good-intentioned leaders and collaborators obscure the fact that a hierarchy exists, this allows those with the positional power to be less accountable, and—most importantly—it prevents the collective from using that power to meet its goals. When, however, we are transparent and intentional about the positional power located in certain roles, it allows us to know what the power is, who has it, and how it can be used in service of common objectives. This transparency can be as simple as being explicit about the authority of a timekeeper in a group work protocol, or as complex as finding clarity about the positional power of the principal in governance structures for distributed leadership.

Leading in Collaboration

Even in a consensus-seeking process, hiring is one area of decision-making where the principal should be directly involved and typically have the final say, grounded in the carefully considered input of stakeholders. It is important that principals have this role because, once a teacher is hired, it is typically the principal who has the individual and often lonely responsibility of rating a teacher's work satisfactory or not, professional or unprofessional. A person's professional fate hangs in the balance, as does the experience of the students they serve.

The special powers a principal has are not ones to be happily hoarded and wielded in isolation. Indeed, the weighty responsibilities singularly located in the position of the principal are one reason why protracted, democratic, collaborative processes are important. It is also why leaders at the top of the hierarchy should practice collaboration. This could be principal and coprincipal, principal and associate principal, or some other configuration of peer relationships at the highest levels. At JBS this took the shape of a team called the codirectorship, a partnership between a teacher codirector and a principal codirector.

The codirectors modeled collaborative deliberation at all levels of school functioning, from the weekly agendas of meetings, to student suspensions, to hiring committees, to strategic planning. In essence, the purpose of the codirectorship was to ensure that teacher voice was always at the table. At first, the school didn't have role descriptions of the teacher codirector or the principal codirector. Such role descriptions were drafted in the second year, as the school began to anticipate the succession process, because the position was envisioned as having a three-year term.

Deborah Meier and Paul Schwarz discuss succession and the departure of founding leaders in their reflections on how democratic practice at schools is often "eroded" over time and "mostly finally dropped."[31] With such stories in mind, the process of succession of the teacher codirector was made very intentional and clear.

The three-year term for the teacher codirector was intended to allow multiple teacher-leaders to step into the role over time. In year two, the school formed a governance committee to clarify the role, solicit interest from teachers, and guide the transition process. The plan was that candidates would declare interest in a letter to their colleagues. The entire faculty would then be invited to reflect, in writing, on which of the candidates they felt could best fulfill responsibilities of the teacher codirector. This was not a vote but an affirmation of strengths and critical-friend feedback on areas for growth. The selection committee, chaired by the principal codirector, was to include the current teacher codirector and four other faculty. The final selection was to be made based on colleagues' responses to candidates' letters, the committee's evaluation of ability to fulfill the role, and a discussion with each candidate of how s/he perceives the role taking shape in new ways in the future. The committee was to strive for consensus.

But neither in year two nor in year three did anyone declare formal interest in the role. This was partially because the founding codirector was doing well in the position, and partially because the role was an intimidating one. During the school's fourth year, a teacher who had joined JBS largely because of the commitment to democracy and social justice decided he would be willing.

"My reason for considering this so seriously," he wrote in his letter, "is my faith that our school will be stronger with distributed knowledge and leadership." He went on to discuss the democratic values of the school in connection to students: "I am confident that there are qualities I bring to the table that would be strengths as a co-director. Primarily, I am dedicated to the mission of the school. I believe deeply in our school's approach to creating an educational community that supports students in forming identities and building skills to become engaged members of a democratic society." He also voiced his dedication to democratic values in the context of governance:

> I am committed to the idea that our school is strongest when all voices are involved in shaping it. I believe I can continue to build on our efforts to effectively make collective decisions and expand our democratic processes to include more stakeholders, especially students and families. Last year, the teacher co-director position was described to me as a constant and vigilant representative of classroom teachers in decision-making. This is a role I feel passionate about and would be honored to play in our school.

He closed his letter with humility and a request for support from his colleagues should he be given the job—which he was. This teacher also remained in the role beyond a three-year term, straddling a period of leadership changes when there were four different principals over four successive years during a challenging period in the school's evolution. It was a period during which the codirectorship might have dissolved and many veteran faculty might have left the school. This didn't happen, however, and the codirectorship and a broader commitment to democratic governance were two major reasons the school could endure these transitions.

Of the twenty-two faculty at the school during its sixth year, fifteen were still there after year twelve. And while a few teachers had moved on, only one teacher had left JBS to work at another New York City school. This is significant. In a system as large as New York City, with one million students, there are many opportunities for good teachers to leave one school and work at another. It matters that so many mid-career professionals chose to stay at JBS during the challenging transition years.

A veteran science teacher, who had been with the school since year four, was asked if he thought that democratic governance was something that kept the school strong during the transition years. He said, "One of the reasons I came here was because the school had a set of core values, including a Commitment to Democracy." He reflected on his own involvement in school governance and remarked that there were three proposals he was currently working on, ideas for school improvements that he'd brought or was going to bring to the full faculty for feedback and refinement. He noted the value of faculty-facilitated meetings and teacher-led professional development. "I'm still here," he said, "in part because of how the school is governed."

Improving Clarity and Transparency

During one period of leadership transition, the teacher-leaders did much to improve the clarity and functionality of procedures for faculty consensus-building and decision-making. One of the benefits of leadership transitions—though they are hard—is that they provide a school the opportunity to clarify roles and operations essential to the welfare of school.

In the school's challenging seventh year, a small committee met to work on illuminating the subtleties and clarifying the core simplicities at the heart of consensus-based deliberations. The result of their work was a handbook called "JBS Decision-Making Process." The purpose of the handbook was to clarify when and how consensus-based deliberations were used in the governance of the school.

The authors noted at the outset that "there is not sufficient faculty meeting time to make all decisions through the Whole Group Consensus Process and many decisions do not have the scale to warrant the use of faculty meeting time required to achieve whole group consensus." The handbook then provides examples of different types of decisions:

- Whole Group Consensus Decisions: Decisions made with the consent of the full faculty. (Not a majority vote.) Criteria: Long-term philosophical or structural shifts to the school.
- Delegated Decisions: Decisions made by committees or individuals in specific roles in consultation, then presented to the codirectors for approval. Criteria: Pertaining to a discrete issue with a scope limited to a particular group.
- Codirector Decisions: Decisions made by the principal and teacher codirector in consultation. Criteria: Decisions that are short-term, do not impact whole school, are in need of immediate action, or it is determined that there is not sufficient time available for a Whole Group Consensus decision.

In addition, there are descriptions of "Union Chapter Decisions," which concern topics that could impact "contractual obligations," and decisions that fall only within the purview of the principal, which include supervisory or personnel matters.

As noted above, pragmatism and clarity about positional power in a democratic community are essential to the sound functioning of the group. This document is clear about when the principal's power matters, and it makes clear that even in cases where the principal or codirectors make the decision, it is still expected that those decisions "will be made in consultation with the faculty, specific stakeholders or other school leaders depending on the type of decision being made." The authors of the guide also describe the responsibility of the principal in cases when whole-group consensus processes get stuck: "In cases where the Whole Group Consensus process becomes stalemated and timely action is required, it is the responsibility of the principal codirector to determine the next step, based on a measured weighing of the various perspectives shared to assure a timely decision is made."

The faculty who helped shape this document know from experience that "Commitment to Democracy" can ring clear and true to the ear, but be far from clear and transparent in practice. They take pains to give specific guidance on how democracy works at this school. And just as teachers do in the classroom, steps in the process are scaffolded, including graphic organizers or templates to help teachers draft proposals. The handbook also includes a "Consensus Tracker," a tool to use in meetings to follow a discussion as it unfolds, noting what strikes you as a "pro" and "con," allowing you to change your mind and note it as the deliberation evolves. The handbook describes other tools that meeting facilitators can use to gauge how a proposal is taking shape over time. And sometimes it takes a lot of time. Some proposals enter the process and take a year or more to be refined. Other proposals find more expedient paths. It should be noted, however, that for all the emphasis on democracy in the JBS governance handbook, there is little reference to voting, except when it comes to processes governed by union rules. This is intentional.

In a democratic school, minority voices should not be counted in such a manner that they can be discounted. In a group of twenty people, a vote of eleven to nine can efficiently yield the adoption of a measure that a minority of nearly half the community opposes. In contrast, the slow-democracy processes outlined in the JBS handbook reveal how those minority voices are accounted for at various stages, their opinions allowed to shape and reshape a proposal until it becomes something that more people can more fully endorse and own. And in the end, it is about owning it: seeing the challenges faced as both mine and yours, together shaping a vision of how to address our common needs, and then articulating each individual's role in getting the common work done.

Dewey's description of "social control" in the classroom holds true here at the level of governance: JBS teacher-leaders and administrators are committed to running this school as a "social enterprise in which all individuals have an opportunity to contribute and to which all feel a responsibility."[32] But it is a social enterprise fraught with the challenges of any social enterprise.

Even when using the well-wrought processes that the JBS leaders put in place, doubts can arise, people feel left out, some voices are loud, some quiet, it takes too long, it moves too fast, there are contradictions. And yet the school's commitment to gathering face-to-face, in circles large and small, and helping faculty work through these challenges together is clear.

Democracy's Basic Shape: The Circle

Power and endurance derive largely from core muscles that get their strength from good habits and simple practices. In some ways, the subtleties of democratic process can be complex and hard to illuminate, but in other ways, they're easy to define—in terms of a few good habits and simple practices.

There is an essence to democracy, a simple shape: the circle. This is another key characteristic of how democracy endures at JBS—and in most places. The circle is the elemental shape of the democratic spirit.

In the circle we find a group of people—large or small—facing each other, listening to each other, deliberating a common concern, making meaning through collaboration and empathic exchange. At JBS the circle is the common form of interaction and deliberation. This is one way the school lives its democratic mission with integrity.

Integration, or integrity, requires that there be many small instances of living one's values, repeatedly, integrated throughout a day, a school year, a lifetime. What we want to see integrated throughout a school with a commitment to democracy is a small group of people facing a common question, working together to shape a response. An observer should find various and frequent instances of this kind of interaction in the school. Let us consider the various ways that circles structured the daily, weekly, and annual modes of interaction at JBS:

- The admissions process: This is for most students their first impression of the school. JBS is a transfer school, with students joining throughout the year. The admissions interview serves as the first step in an orientation process. Students are asked to write a reflection on one of the school's seven core values and make connections to their own lives. Typically, two applicants are then brought together with two faculty members and there's a discussion. The first substantive interaction a student has at JBS is in a circle.
- Advisory: This is a structure we will discuss more in-depth in this book when we get to the chapter on restorative practice. At JBS, Advisory was typically a small group of ten to fifteen students that meets every day for forty minutes. As part of the Expeditionary Learning network, Crew is the special name given to Advisory: In this journey, on this vessel, "we

are all crew, not passengers." The normal shape of Crew or Advisory interactions is a circle.
- Town Meeting: Typically, this assembling of students takes a different shape each week: sometimes whole-school, sometimes smaller groupings of Advisories. The meetings are often prepared in advance by an Advisory and facilitated by students. The topics range widely. The purpose is student-leadership development and the cultivation of the habits of civil discourse. The basic norms of town meeting mirror those in Advisory and in the classrooms, such as the "One Mic" rule, don't talk while someone else is talking. If a larger circle isn't possible, efforts are made for students to talk to each other face-to-face.
- Classrooms: From group work at tables to whole class discussions, one rarely finds chairs in rows.
- Restorative Justice: Whether it's a Fairness Committee hearing,[33] a peer mediation, or a post-suspension reentry process, high-stakes behavioral interventions happen face-to-face, in circles, and solutions are determined collaboratively.
- Student-Led Conferences: With three or four chairs around a table, or a few desks pulled close, at these conferences, students meet with their advisor and members of their family to discuss personal and academic goals and progress.
- Oral Defense: As part of the New York Performance Assessment Consortium,[34] JBS is a school at which the highest-level academic work culminates in the oral defense of papers and projects in the core academic disciplines. This happens before a panel of faculty and external evaluators from the wider community. Like the first admissions conversation, a JBS scholar's journey ends in a small group of people, facing each other, wrestling with common questions.

The student experience outlined above is likewise a teacher experience. This is significant. If we want the adults of our schools to be skilled in the norms and processes of democratic interaction, the bulk of our interactions with students must also be structured in democratic ways. This is both a matter of integrity, and a practical matter of practice and time on-task. It takes time to develop expertise, and teachers spend a lot less time meeting with adults than they do working with students. So, if the adults are going to practice processes that value each voice, learn how to facilitate the co-construction of knowledge, and understand how individuals can feel empowerment when a group gets work done collaboratively—it is important that they hone this skillset in the classroom as well as in meetings of adults.

At JBS there's traditionally a lot of adult meeting time. In addition to practicing democratic habits with students, adults at JBS go to meetings at which students are generally not present. Some meetings are dedicated to working in subject-specific departments, others are focused on the work of being an advisor, others are whole-faculty or committee meetings focused on schoolwide concerns. The meeting agendas focus on a mix of topics, including what Carl Glickman would call "core impact decisions" having to do with the instructional program, student achievement, professional development, the allocation of resources: "These decisions align the school with its educational values."[35]

In *Renewing America's Schools*, Glickman offers comprehensive guidance on many aspects of what it means to govern schools that are committed to the core purpose of schooling in a democratic society. "What democratic governance does," he writes, "is strive for decisions that focus on matters of school-wide education, are fair and equal and distribute power, and are morally consistent with the school's goal of democratic engagement of students."[36]

Glickman is careful to note that in addition to choosing the right content for the focus of our deliberations, process matters too, and all rules or protocols by which decisions are made must be clear in advance to participants. Indeed, just as we need carefully crafted learning intentions and clear guidance for students in our classes, we need to be clear about how a democratically run school is governed and where a faculty member should expect to experience those circles of distributed leadership and collaborative process.

Varied Democratic Experiences

In all this discussion of democratic experience, we have yet to mention having students at the decision-making table with adults. Actually, this is not true. The list of ways that students experience circle interactions and dialogue at the school includes some important instances of young people being at the table, making decisions or taking the lead. The forums for restorative justice, for instance, are authentic decision-making meetings, at which students exercise their knowledge and insights to shape the life of the school in meaningful ways.

The school once designed a post-suspension reentry process after a terrible end-of-school-year fight, at which students had a primary role in deciding if other students would be allowed to be present at the graduation ceremony. The stakes can be very high in such matters. Time must be made in the schedule for these meetings, which shows the priority placed on students' having time to participate in such decisions. Likewise, students are empowered when time is made in the weekly schedule for student-led town meetings, the content and facilitation of which is much in the hands of students.

Is it possible for a core value of democracy to live with integrity in a school even if students are not equal partners to adults in the governance of the school? The answer is yes.

This is not to say that schools shouldn't have young people representatively involved in school governance with adults. This should be a priority. There is much to be gained from having young people at the table with adults in decision-making: The eyes of youth are skilled at seeing hypocrisy and inconsistency; the insights of youth offer corrective perspectives and new solutions that adults can't see; the presence of youth can remind adults of the deeper purpose of their work; and intergenerational gatherings are typically settings where people of all ages better behave themselves.

For these and other reasons, young people should be represented at some governance meetings. But representative structures that allow a few students into a meeting can't be a replacement for the more essential work of cultivating the agency and engagement of all students, and this can only happen through the work that happens in those spheres of school life where all students participate: the classroom.

Restorative justice forums and town meetings are important, but it is to the classroom that we must look if we are to know whether democratic schooling is truly aligned to the needs and capacities of young people. There are few schools that will truly empower any large number of students through representative positions or governance structures, or even through direct democracy, like casting ballots in a vote. The way to empower students is by driving voice, choice, and responsibilities for important tasks down into the day-to-day classroom, and simultaneously out into broader community through curriculum that tackles important contemporary topics.

It is interesting to consider whether the norms and processes of democratic interaction at the level of faculty governance have parallels in the classroom. In other words, does valuing teacher voice in teacher meetings and school governance have corollary in the valuing of student voice in the classroom? An English teacher, one of the founding members of the JBS faculty, offered these reflections:

> The setting of classroom norms is negotiated in many of our classes. As a member of the community, the facilitator [teacher] comes in with experienced norms that make the classroom environment run smoothly. This becomes a starting point for students to also contribute norms that they feel might create a better learning environment in class . . . This is certainly aligned with what happens at our staff meetings where we review the norms, and an invitation is extended to add to these.

In addition, this teacher praised the work of a colleague who involves students in developing lesson plans and determining the content of learning. She sees students working on "professional lesson plans" to guide the learning in this class, and she notes that "this is incredibly empowering for them." She also draws parallels between student self-assessment and teacher goal-setting, between teachers sharing their own reflections on professional practice and student-led conferences where students share their reflections on their goals and growth. She notes:

> Whenever teachers provide the opportunity for students to assess their semester's contribution to a course, self-assess their proficiency levels, submit a proposal for an alternative project or are given an opportunity to choose from a selection of alternative projects—these are democratic opportunities.

It would not be surprising if a visitor to JBS, who spent time in both faculty meetings and in classrooms, were to find many parallels between these two settings.

Walt Whitman once wrote, in a poem called "An Old Man's Thought of School," that America could look to boyhood, girlhood, the teacher, and the school for signs of what the future brings, light or shadow, good or evil. He is right, of course. And just as a nation can look to its schools to gauge its wellness and the integrity of its values, so can a school look to its classrooms.

Chances are, if you find the adults using careful discussion protocols to seek solutions at the level of school governance meetings, you'll find similar discussion protocols for the collective construction of meaning at the level of the classroom. If there are norms for talking about heavy topics in a faculty meeting, chances are you'll find similar norms in the classrooms. And the classroom with students is where it matters most, for the classroom is where most school people live most of the time. It's where you have the time to get good at the skills and habits democracy requires. Being able to listen with empathy, to ask questions of different kinds, to clarify roles in a collaboration, to take an impassioned stance, to make a principled compromise, to empower truth to speak to power, to wield positional authority in service of the collective—each of these attributes is as important to good teaching as it is to democratic governance.

Curriculum Content

Being committed to democracy in a school is about form and process, habits and skills. But content matters, too, just as much. Let us remain at the level of the classroom. What does a school's commitment to democracy look like in the classroom—not just in terms of *how*, but in terms of *what*?

In addition to protocols for building trust and enabling student voice, in addition to skillful differentiation and inquiry-based instruction, what is the *content* that a democratic school posits as worthy? We can answer this question by looking at some samples of what has been taught at JBS. Living democratic values with integrity is not only about how we work together; it's also about what we're working on.

In a democratic school, the content of the work that students and teachers do together will reflect the pressing needs of the school community and broader democratic society. Consider some of the courses that students have been able to choose from at JBS. Here are two social studies classes, for instance, that place contemporary concerns in historical perspective:

> Borders: How open should our borders be? Today immigration policy is at the center of a boiling debate in this country. This academic expedition will explore the political, social, and economic significance of borders between countries. Students will combine their learning from historical immigration policies with their research on other immigration controversies in the United States, past or present . . .
>
> Revolutionary Women: This course is an exploration of women and girls as powerful individuals and change makers throughout the world, past and present. Women often are left out of mainstream history or are confined to damaging stereotypes. Students will dig deeper for stories of radical and revolutionary women who have been making history all along . . .[37]

Such courses embrace matters of familial and personal importance to students, which are also matters of importance to any citizen in our country today. It is fitting, in a school named after James Baldwin, that students will engage in studies such as these. Baldwin is a writer whose words emanate from a place that is deeply personal and honest. He hides neither his love nor his anger, neither his questions nor his convictions. And it is armed with this—his love, rage, questions, and convictions—that he both assaults the hypocrisy of America and affirms its promise of freedom and democratic community.

Like their school's namesake, teachers at JBS often posit the truths of students' personal experience as their points of departure; and with the strength derived from the honest interrogation of that experience, and the self-knowledge that this reflection engenders, they connect the learning to wider circles of meaning, which include our nation, the ongoing American experiment in democracy, with all its blessings, flaws, and potential. English class offerings have included:

I Write Therefore I Am: Memoir, Identity, and Transformation: Why do people write their own life stories (memoirs)? Why do people draw and paint themselves? How does writing your own narrative help define who you are (your identity)? . . . Can memoirs and self-portraiture be empowering, or even liberating? In this academic expedition, we explore how expressing identity in memoirs and visual art can transform anyone willing to enter that journey.

Native Son in the Promised Land: Is racism still alive all over our country, from our big cities to our small towns? If so, how does it operate systematically to place some in power and others (based on their race, gender, sexuality) on the outskirts with less power, value, and worth? How can it affect a person's psyche to be powerless and on the margins; to be considered a problem, an outcast, a menace?

Math and science teachers can also place a commitment to democracy and the common good at the heart of their curriculum; here are two such courses:

Got Water?: This is an expedition that will use water as its first lens of study. Students will collect and analyze statistics based on the results from their water taste test. Students will find evidence to support the Flint water crisis. Students will use statistical techniques to analyze the lack of drinkable water as a global health concern in order to develop the abilities and confidence needed to analyze any subject . . .

Climate Change: Our New Normal: Experts claim that climate change is upon us, is happening right now, but how do we experience climate on a day-to-day basis? And how will the "new normal" affect us in the future? We will look back into our climate past to get some perspective on the projected changes. We will also explore earth systems interactions in urban areas to ensure our survival here in New York City, a vulnerable coastal region.

"If the central goal of schools were to prepare students to engage productively in a democracy," Carl Glickman writes, then students and teachers would be focused on the concerns of their "immediate and future life" and their "immediate and extended communities."[38] When the curriculum of a school embodies this imperative, it is a further reflection of how the school strives to live democracy with integrity.

Democratic Schools: A Contemporary Imperative

Working with young people in schools is child-rearing work, and it's among the most difficult and important work a community has to do. It gets even harder when you add to it the responsibility of rearing citizens in a nation that aspires to be a democratic society. And it gets harder still when you aspire to organize your school itself as a democratic community: The tensions between positional power and equity of voice are not easy to live with and never neatly resolved; the need for space and time for dialogue can feel impossible to come by in a system of rigid calendars and constraining schedules; the developmental differences between maturing children and adults make it challenging to determine who should make the rules and decisions—a tension that can be as difficult to negotiate in a school as it is in a maturing family.

The educators at the school in this case study, and schools with similar commitments to democracy, struggle constantly with these tensions. But such schools can endure for many years and through some difficult transitions in part because of the transparency and intentionality with which they struggle with these challenges.

This is a practical matter of leadership choices and faculty engagement. Democratic practice shapes the lives of the adults in the school as much as the youth—and it pays dividends in terms of stability and collegiality, year after year. On average, teacher turnover and principal turnover are higher than is healthy for most schools. How principals connect and interact with their faculty matters. Many teachers new to the profession leave it, and the main factor is how the principal works with the faculty. Researchers have found:

> [T]he most important factor influencing commitment was the beginning teacher's perception of how well the school principal worked with the teaching staff as a whole. This was a stronger factor than the adequacy of resources, the extent of a teacher's administrative duties, the manageability of his or her workload, or the frequency of professional-development opportunities.[39]

How well a leader works with the teaching staff is a matter of how democratic those collaborations are. This case study has highlighted the importance of pragmatism and clarity about positional power. One indicator of this is the effort taken to articulate exactly when and how full-faculty consensus should be the means of making decisions, and when it is not. This case study also illuminates other practical priorities for operationalizing democracy in practice.

First, the founding texts of the school name democracy explicitly as the purpose and process of the work of the place. These texts and such commitments are routinely revisited as new people join the community and are audible in the discourse and visible in the curriculum.

A second practicality of being a democratic school is making democracy's shape: the circle. One can find this elemental shape of democratic interaction across the community, from disciplinary interventions to classroom interactions, faculty meetings, family conferences, and presentations of student work.

A third practicality of approach is found in differentiated democratic experiences for youth and adults. The school does not treat everyone the same, but puts the same energetic focus on helping students and faculty feel agency in the places where they spend the most time and have the most developmental readiness and role-related responsibility. Students spend most of their school lives in the classroom, which is where the majority of effort is made to help them speak their voice and shape their environment, including in the world outside the school through a curriculum engaged in considering our society's pressing problems.

These approaches to operationalizing democratic practice are relevant to schools of any size. Leaders of schools big and small can translate these practical considerations into concrete actions to bring democracy to life in their school communities.

FIFTEEN CONCRETE ACTIONS EVERY LEADER CAN TAKE

We live in a society shaped by powerbrokers who view with suspicion if not disdain many of the essential elements of our democracy, including free and equitable public schools, a free press, and free and fair elections. Local newspapers are bought and downsized by hedge funds. Journalists are threatened and sometimes assaulted. Public school resources are channeled to private contractors. Free elections are compromised—less by foreign meddling than by homegrown Jim Crow–style intimidation and deterrence.

Educators long committed to democratic schools might say they saw this coming. Debbie Meier warned in 2003: "The real crisis we face is not a threat to America's economic or military dominance but the ebbing strength of our democratic and egalitarian culture."[40] Let us hear this warning afresh. The need for school leaders committed to democratic life in word and deed is as urgent as it ever has been. Concrete actions every school leader can take include:

- *Excavate and name it*: Democratic practice is already at work in your school. At the level of the faculty, it may go by other names like "collaboration," "professional learning," or "communities of practice." Excavate the concepts and terms *democracy* and *democratic* from these practices and name them as such. This work of naming could be collaborative in itself. Faculty teams and leadership teams could be asked to help find and name the practices in the school that are democratic.

Engage colleagues in a discussion of why this is important; define what is democratic; find the places where democracy lives, even in small ways; ask whether and how these practices can be improved and expanded in your school.
- *Share it*: Write about where and how democratic practice lives in your school and publish that writing. Internally share your reflections and convictions with the faculty at an important meeting or in an important letter or memo. Put it in your faculty and student handbooks. There are bound to be parts of those handbooks written by your district's legal team, which can't be altered, but there are other parts that can be updated or written by the school leader. Find an opportunity to share your thoughts more publicly, in a letter to the editor of a newspaper, for instance, or in parent communications. You could put your comments in a contemporary political context or not. If you feel confident speaking out about anti-democratic forces, you could do that and give broader context to why democratic practice in your school is important. If you don't want to comment on contemporary events, you can share reflections on work done by faculty and students of which you are proud. There will be many people in your community inspired to hear your reflections on these matters. An additional benefit is that speaking publicly helps us hold ourselves accountable to living up to our commitments. It helps others hold us accountable, too.
- *Praise the pedagogy*: Curriculum content is important, but let us focus here on pedagogy, how teachers teach, not what they teach. There are plenty of teachers who teach "civics lessons" in a way that invites little participation from students and is essentially undemocratic in its mode. So, content aside, who at your school teaches in ways that are democratic? There are teachers who sit students in circles and value every voice. There are teachers who use protocols for discussion that ensure students listen empathically to each other. There are teachers who support students in public speaking and debate. There are teachers who engage students and community members in projects that take time and require collaborative problem-solving. Praise these teachers' work in tactful ways. Especially find ways to share this kind of practice with the new teachers you hire.
- *Ask hiring questions with democracy in mind*: Pick a quote about the democratic purpose of schools and ask a question about it in your hiring interview. Make it one of the first questions, so that you let it make a first impression. There are quotes to choose from in this chapter. Debbie Meier's reflections on how schools must cultivate democratic habits of mind in adults and students could help you or your interview committee frame interesting questions that reveal a candidate's commitment to

schools as democratic communities. Such questions, furthermore, communicate your own commitments to those you might be hiring.
- *Form hiring committees with students and other stakeholders*: The most important decision a school leader makes in any given year is whether to offer a particular human being the job of being teacher of the children in your school. If your school or district is accustomed to one or two people interviewing candidates and making offers, work to change this practice. An interview committee is an ideal opportunity for a leader to model and develop skills in democratic engagement and the facilitation of a consensus-seeking process. Diversity of role and identity is important to the committee. Including students on the committee is valuable for many reasons, one of which is that they are exposed to adults having respectful conversations about high-stakes matters. Social media, what they consume in popular media, or overhear their families watching on mainstream news will expose them to very few examples of adults engaged in mature conversation seeking consensus on important decisions.
- *Seek consensus*: Seeking consensus doesn't mean that you'll get there. But the journey is an important one. It shows a commitment to many elements of democratic process, including that the people of the place have the power and responsibility to solve their own problems collaboratively. Consensus seeking, when facilitated carefully, also gives voice to minority perspectives in ways that voting doesn't always do. A place to start for definitions and protocols is the School Reform Initiative (SRI). SRI also does work in schools to facilitate and train facilitators. Skillful facilitation and the use of protocols is important because it helps clarify steps in the process and what happens if consensus isn't reached. This is where it's important to have transparency about the role of the facilitator or leader in the group who has positional power. A certain amount of time may be allotted for a consensus-seeking process, but consensus may not be achieved by the end of that time, so it should be clear that the person with positional power has the role of determining if more time will allotted to the process, or if a decision will be reached by other means.
- *Plan in terms of years not months*: Democracy is slower than autocracy. Democracy is slow because it requires that the people impacted by a decision be involved in making it. As you consider your school's professional learning priorities for a given year, or the school reform projects that are given primacy, consider your work in terms of years, not months. Many teachers and other faculty will express "initiative fatigue" if there is something seemingly new that demands their attention every six months. The fatigue may well be real, and it's not just a matter of being "tired of new initiatives." It's literally a matter of energy wasted,

or energy invested without adequate time for return on the investment. In contrast, it can be a sign of respect for teachers' time—as well as a signal of stability, integrity, and conviction—when the school leader guides the faculty to focus on one or two important priorities for several years in a row. Many teachers will appreciate hearing—at the return to school at the end of the summer—something along these lines: "This year we will retain our focus on X. We will be building on your work last year by . . . "

- *The Five-Year Rule*: School people often think of school life in annual terms, and most of our ceremonies and rituals to mark the passage of time recycle year after year. But cycles of substantial professional learning and structural school reform take more like four or five years. School leaders should keep this "five-year rule" in mind when planning both the phases of one's career and planning the work of sustained school improvement. If, for instance, you are endeavoring to develop an advisory program at your school, or to reform curriculum with racial equity in mind, it is important to have both short-term goals and a longer, five-year, vision of the work. Keeping this in mind can help you pace the work in order to have the democratic involvement of many stakeholders.
- *The One-Hour Rule*: As noted in chapter 1, for every major responsibility that a teacher holds, there should be at least one hour of meeting time per month dedicated to that work in collaboration with peers in similar roles. There can certainly be more than one hour a month, but one hour is a minimum requirement to keep the work moving forward. If a teacher is on a grade team, a content-specific team, and is also expected to participate in a PLC focused on another area of learning—each of those focus areas needs at least one hour each month. And the leaders or facilitators of the work will need even more time to plan and debrief the meetings.
- *Support PLCs, by whatever name*: Much of the literature about Professional Learning Communities leaves out the word *democracy*, but they can be a democratic structure. The School Reform Initiative prefers the term *Intentional Learning Community* and describes them as "places where educators work together to learn the skills of reflecting, collaborating, deprivatizing practice, and exposing and exploring fundamental assumptions"; they are places "where groups build shared norms and values and hold each other accountable for being faithful to them."[40] The PLC structure will not have value, however, if adequate time is not allocated to the work in the calendar of meetings, or if people can opt out because it's voluntary. If you strive for a democratic community, people must have choices but should not be permitted to opt out of democratic and collaborative practice. PLCs can also be compromised by disengagement because it feels irrelevant to the participants. Just as

curriculum relevance should be derived from needs of individuals and communities, the work of the faculty must be grounded in the needs of the faculty and wider community. Another factor that will compromise a PLC is poor facilitation. Invest in a trained cadre of facilitators, including you and other school leaders, who must be seen leading and invested in the work.

- *Champion courageous curriculum*: As mentioned in chapter 1, a school leader should become familiar with resources that teachers can use to develop curriculum content with justice in mind. The resources noted earlier are relevant when it comes to the democratic purpose of schools as well: *Facing History and Ourselves*; the *Zinn Education Project*; *Rethinking Schools*; and *Teaching for Justice*. Additional resources relevant to schooling dedicated to democratic ends and means include the *News Literacy Project* and *Educating for American Democracy*. School leaders can validate the utility and importance of such organizations by routinely sharing links and purchasing resources to share as part of the ongoing formal and informal conversation about what we teach and how we teach it.
- *Work closely with student government and students in leadership positions*: Serving in traditional student government positions can be an important leadership opportunity for a few students. They are typically not a structure for universal student engagement, but they can have value for bringing the unique perspectives of young people into adult conversations, especially if the youth voices at the table are not those students who are being best served by the status quo. Often, positions like class president and organizations like student councils do not intersect with school leaders in collaborative ways, nor do they often focus their time on school policy, structures, or curriculum. If they do, it is important that school leaders work closely with these groups and be transparent with them about what access they have to influencing such matters. Students should not work hard for the sake of a reform initiative if, in the end, their project didn't have a chance of getting the support of the adults would be largely responsible for implementing it over the long term. The leader must be clear with the student government about such matters to avoid reinforcing cynicism or distrust in the democratic process and in government more broadly. The leader must also be clear that universal structures in the curriculum are even more important than student government when it comes to all students having access to work that empowers them to solve problems on matters of importance to them. A school with curriculum standards that embody universal expectations for public speaking, project-based learning, political and historical understanding, and collaborative contemporary problem-solving is doing

much more to cultivate democratic practice than the school that has five to ten students active in student government, no matter how visible and vocal those students may be.
- *Audit your standards*: Most schools have curriculum anchored in state or national standards. Many schools also have standards for "transferrable skills" or "habits of mind" and "habits of work." Some schools have adopted standards at that intentionally drive the curriculum toward civic responsibility and democratic engagement, such as the Learning for Justice "Social Justice Standards." Audit your standards. Look for ways that your standards embody expectations for democratic habits and the kind of knowledge citizens need to be empathic and powerful civic-minded participants in their communities. Your audit might reveal that some small changes could make a large degree of difference when translated into actual actions of teaching and learning. For instance, a standard in English Language Arts that says "students will write effectively for a range of audiences" could be imbued with the spirit of democracy with the addition of a few key words: "students will write effectively for a range of *authentic* audiences *in the school and wider community*." All of a sudden, instead of the standard prompting teachers to ask students to write just to them, teachers will need to ask students to do work that has them engaging with wider "authentic" audiences, such as the school leader, the school board, other students, their local paper, or their state representatives. Auditing your standards and looking for opportunities such as these could be a quiet leadership retreat activity, or a more collaborative process involving teachers and others over a longer period of time.
- *Lead through distributed leadership, representative governance, and collaborative problem-solving*: Many of the actions listed above will contribute to what Cornell West would call a culture of democracy, a way of being. We have been less focused on school systems of governance. But governance, as revealed in the James Baldwin School case study, is important to the democratic life of the school. The adults of the school should be engaged, through distributed leadership and representative structures, in routine opportunities for collaborative problem-solving in areas where they have agency and investment. The size of the school will determine how complex or simple these governance systems should be to allow adequate time and space for the work. But we can name two of the essential components that have general applicability across schools: group size and length of meeting. A meeting for deliberation on important matters should probably be forty to sixty minutes long, and ten people in the room may be too many. There needs to be time for every person to check in and connect, and then adequate time

for everyone to weigh in on the deliberations, hopefully more than once, in more than a soundbite. Our ideas can shift as we listen to the ideas of others. In other words, groups must be small enough to have time to deliberate in the time allocated.
- *Make the circle*: In the meetings that you facilitate, bring people together in circles. Even large meetings of scores of people, which will need to break out into smaller groups, can start or end in a circle where everyone sees every other person's face. One area where a school leader can use circles, and what restorative justice practitioners call "circle process," is in disciplinary or behavioral interventions. Modeling and training is important. Though many people will learn by doing, sometimes outside expertise will be useful, and if circle process is unfamiliar, there are some good off-the-shelf resources to help you learn as you go. The book *Circle Forward,* which will be referenced more in the following chapter, is a resource that every school leader should have on their shelf. Start with this text if you'd like to have at your fingertips some simple scripts and prompts for a variety of topics. Leading this work yourself, and modeling how to learn from it, will necessarily integrate other people into the work and train them in democratic modes of interaction. For instance, a post-suspension reentry circle is likely to involve students, parents, and faculty or staff. Your collaboration with faculty in this process will mentor them into the ways of the work.

METACOGNITIVE DEMOCRACY

What can we learn from schools that consider themselves explicitly committed to democracy? In his leadership ethnography of ten public schools with stated commitments to democracy, Doug Knecht, dean of children's programs at Bank Street College of Education, found seven important patterns. These urban schools spanned grades K–12, served students of a wide range of academic needs and demographic identities, and were of various sizes. After visiting these schools and asking their leaders to discuss the connection between democracy and their approach to schooling, seven patterns or themes emerged. Knecht phrases these themes like the learning intentions that many educators write for students. He starts with the subject, "we," by which he means the educators who are committed to schooling "with and for" democracy:

- Content and Learning Experiences: We intentionally develop informed citizens who are grounded in democratic values with an understanding of

how our democracy works by an exploration of issues we have faced and currently face as a nation of constitutionally empowered people.
- Diversity and Humanity: We intentionally develop empathic and inclusive citizens who perceive strength in diversity by appreciating others in light of differences and who feel their individual value is validated by the ways of the larger community.
- Critique and Reflection: We intentionally develop inquiry-minded citizens who evaluate and discuss complex issues using evidence to construct arguments and who reflect on their own choices, involvement, and emotions in relation to the issues.
- Participatory Governance and Justice: We intentionally develop confident and vocal citizens who are practiced in shared decision-making and restorative justice processes.
- Action Taking and Change Making: We intentionally develop involved citizens who are experienced in analyzing, planning, and implementing authentic efforts to improve their community and make social change for increased equity.
- Adult Modeling and (Re)Making: We intentionally create parallel democratic experiences for students and adults so that the kids can hear about and see models of the kinds of learning and processes of making and remaking the community that we want them to develop and to remind adults of how challenging it is to foster and live these democratic ways.[42]

How these elements of democratic schooling exist in a kindergarten classroom is different than in the upper grades, but the commitment is one that all leaders share. There is no assumption that democracy is a topic for just a couple of high school social studies classes and not for the rest. Democracy is both the purpose and method of these schools. It's what they do and what they strive to do better.

The ironic and compelling twist at the end of Knecht's account is that the seventh pattern across these schools is that the explicit democratic purpose of their practices frequently goes unsaid:

Each school leader acknowledged and described throughout the interview how his or her school community and culture, classroom practices and curricula, and adult and student governance structures address issues and skills of democratic participation to one degree or another—and, importantly, each school has participatory systems, which often include families, for iterating and improving all these pieces of the school. Yet, in general, the school leaders also acknowledged that, in the day-to-day work, there is a lack of an explicit connection made between, on the one hand, the cultural, structural, and instructional efforts to build committed, tolerant, and engaged citizens (of all ages) and, on the other hand, the concept and language of practicing democracy. In short, democracy is rarely named when it is happening—when the habits, mind-sets, and skills for being a participant in a democratic environment are being practiced.[43]

In his conclusion, Knecht poses a question to the school leaders of these schools, and to all of us: "How well do students and adults know that they are learning, within their school settings, to be stronger participants in our larger democratic society?" And "to what degree is making this connection explicit in school communities important?" The answer is that it's very important. Naming it strengthens "the relationship between our public school system's role in citizenship readiness and the health of our democracy."[44]

The importance of metacognition in student learning has been widely proven and accepted. It helps us learn when we think and talk about what we are thinking, doing and feeling. This strengthens our sense of purpose and our understanding of how well we are achieving our goal—or how far we have to go.

Just as teachers do with students, school leaders are uniquely well positioned to help us all be more metacognitive about democratic practice in schools, making it more explicit in our work, both the how and the why. Leaders can model metacognition about the democratic purpose and practice of schooling by talking about it as our intention and reflecting on the process. Our metacognition about matters of democracy involves connecting the concept explicitly to what is happening in classrooms. And at the leadership level, it involves asserting our commitment, wondering about the just use of our power, asking for help, inviting accountability, and standing in solidarity with others who share our commitment.

Chapter 3

Restorative Justice

You are a school leader who is aware of contradictions. You believe in the creative and liberating power of education, and yet you work in a system that has perfected regimentation and confinement.

You know the health and rejuvenation of your society demands disruptive and youthful critique, and yet your school can stand only so much youthful disruption.

You strive to empower young people to challenge the status quo, and yet getting through any given day demands that rules as-they-are be followed.

And the contradictions are deeper and more troubling still. You believe your school can be a place where youth learn the names of oppressors—indeed, how to unseat them—and yet you know the schoolhouse is but a few steps from the master's house, and your tools are also his tools, and you are an agent of his state. You are a student of history. You know this nation was built on a foundation that included genocide and slavery. You know that to assemble, sit, move, order, measure, rank, sort, reward, admit, dismiss, and discipline students is done in this context, with the weight of that history.

PUNISHMENT CONCERNS YOU

In particular, the school's discipline system concerns you. It concerns you in both senses of the word. As a school leader you have a say in this system. It is your professional concern. The moral dimensions also concern and worry you. You see how discipline systems can punish young people, how punishment makes them feel, and how school consequences can mirror the racial and socioeconomic biases of the criminal justice system. You see how schools rank and sort according to how people across the land are unjustly ranked and sorted. You see who gets suspended and who doesn't, and who gets suspended again, and who doesn't come back. You're familiar with the historical facts, the data, and you've heard personal stories. You know the school-to-prison pipeline is real.

You are working to address these concerns. You know that restorative practice is used to disrupt oppressive disciplinary systems in schools, but you've also heard they can fall flat. You know that they take time to develop and lots of time to implement. Time is a precious resource. Who has the time? Teachers are always teaching, and then they need their preparation time. Your school counselors are swamped. And when it comes to major behavioral infractions, and the related investigations that administrators must conduct, just getting through one harassment investigation can take days.

You also know there could be substantial pushback if the discipline code is changed. Pushback will come from parents, teachers, even students who are accustomed to the status quo. Yes, you have discretion as a leader, but there are mandatory minimums that the community is accustomed to when it comes to suspensions, loss of privileges, detentions, and any number of other consequences.

In addition to being resource-intensive, restorative practice is also individualized, resulting in different outcomes for different people. This will feel unfair to some. Accusations and feelings of unfairness are sentiments you do not want to inspire. A leader who is perceived as being unfair will make people angry and resentful, or withdrawn and dismissive. You do not want to erode the sense of community you've worked so hard to cultivate. And yet you know that there are ways to make your school community even healthier, more bonded, and fair. How can restorative practice be a thread woven to make the fabric of the community stronger?

THE PARADOX: TRADITIONAL DISCIPLINE AND RESTORATIVE PRACTICE CAN GO TOGETHER

For the school leader beginning or deepening a school's work in restorative practice, a paradox inherent in the work can be just as grounding as it is puzzling at first. The paradox is that traditional consequences, like suspensions, can go hand in hand with restorative practice.

A suspension, which removes a person from the community—when combined with a process of repair and return—can be a very powerful intervention if the school feels like a place of belonging. James Baldwin has written, "You can't betray a country you don't have."[1] In other words, cycles of harm and healing only have meaning when the school feels like it belongs to the student, and the student feels that they belong to the school.

Ostracism

Comparing "traditional" school disciplinary practices to restorative justice reforms is interesting in that it can actually unsettle our notions of what is traditional versus what is progressive or new.

Exile and ostracism, for instance, are age-old human responses to harm, and they can be used effectively if the community finds ways to value every individual in the process of removal and return. Adults use ostracism frequently in school, and often in parenting. A child is told to take a time-out. A child is sent to her room. Students are told to move their seat, or wait in the hall, or go to the office. Students are sent to detention and suspended.

These techniques can deepen harm and produce shame, and suspension is often used to push out students who might challenge us, thus furthering systemic neglect and mistreatment. But it doesn't have to work that way. If done right, the traditional consequence of ostracism can be a step in a restorative process, and a meaningful and fair response to the violation of community values.

I once worked closely with a teacher colleague who was new to the profession and struggling to maintain a respectful climate in the classroom. He told me that sometimes certain kids needed to "just get out." His students were arriving at the principal's office too frequently. I met with the teacher to discuss what I first wrote him in a note:

> Suspending students from class can be an effective strategy, just like suspensions from school, to force certain conversations and reflection, to develop behavior contracts, and to broaden the child's "circle of accountability" to include more people, such as the codirectors, advisor, or parents. However, the classroom environment and community, like our school community, is among our most sacred entities. Excluding people from it (to have them re-enter) should be a strategy of last resort.

We discussed how removal from class, while a last resort, is not an end, but the beginning. It initiates a process that includes a reentry meeting with the student and perhaps other faculty to clarify expectations and establish future consequences, listening to the child all the while to better understand the root causes of the behavior, which could include our choices as adults. As with removal from class, so with suspension from school: It is an ostracism that can start a process of reflection and return.

Dwayne and Roland

Consider a student at this same school, Dwayne. His removal was a consequence for physically assaulting another student, Roland. Suspension was a standard consequence when there was violence in the community. But there was concern that it might not be effective in this case, because Dwayne was just a few days new to the school.

Dwayne had been there so short a time that the school hadn't built with him the requisite sense of belonging. Removal should inspire some feeling of regret and desire to return, and these feelings are only likely if some sense of home has been established first.

When Dwayne arrived at the school, he brought colossal mistrust of teachers and various aggressive and lewd habits of interaction with peers. He was having trouble establishing relationships with everyone. He didn't feel at home. So, after the violent incident, during his suspension, the task facing the adults was not simply to provide him with schoolwork, maintain contact, and prepare a mediation between him and Roland, the boy he'd hurt. The school had to do all of this, but there was more basic work to do. The suspension had to be shaped into an opportunity to nurture bonds of trust that had barely begun to form—all the while removing his physical presence from the classrooms and hallways for a time.

The suspension was several days long, and the school needed all that time to prepare the reentry. Though suspended, Dwayne was asked to come to school for meetings. School leaders, a counselor, and a social worker spent several hours with him and his parents, and several hours of time with him alone. There was time spent with the other boy, Roland, as well.

Dwayne, who was new to the school, acknowledged feeling threatened by things Roland was saying to and about him. He admitted feeling disliked and hurt, especially because Roland was sharing stuff that he'd heard from kids who'd known Dwayne at his former school. Those kids had said he was a person who "wasn't worth liking." This was painful for him to hear. He felt unfairly followed by a negative reputation and helpless to shed it.

After a few days, Dwayne was still angry and defensive, but after his time away from the general school population, combined with individual meetings, some progress had been made. One part of the work with him was an inventory of positive qualities. He was asked to see strengths in himself and to look for them in Roland. It took some time, but he was eventually able to verbalize positive qualities in Roland, that "he's generous to his friends" and would "go the distance for them." Notes were kept on these meetings and given to the faculty members who would be facilitating the conflict mediation between the boys.

The traditional suspension combined with the extensive time preparing Dwayne's return paid off. The school administration and faculty listened to him, asked questions, got to know him a lot better. By removing him from the school through a suspension, he was shown that there were high expectations for peaceful problem-solving in the community and that violence was not tolerated. By engaging him in a process of repair, the school showed that there were high expectations of him and belief that he had a place in that same community. He also learned that the school was willing to forgive—and that he was able to as well. In the years that followed, he and Roland never had another conflict.

Monica

In very different circumstances at a different time of year, Monica was a student the school had come to know well. Her story of ostracism and return is very different from Dwayne's, but it illustrates the important blurring of lines between traditional discipline and restorative approaches to harm and repair.

It was spring, getting hot, and emotions were running high. Monica and her friends formed one group, and Sara and her friends the other. Over the course of several months, there had been constant ups and downs. There would be insults, and then mediation and repair, only to be followed by fresh affronts. There were text messages of disrespect, physical posturing, or a shoulder bump in the hall. There was name calling, and a slur written on the bathroom wall. There were threats, too, and expectations of violence. Classrooms were disrupted, and hallways could erupt in shouting. At this small school, everyone felt it.

Each girl—Monica and Sara—had her motives and needs. At the heart of it for Monica were two compelling circumstances. One was that on the periphery of Sara's group was a girl who'd once dated Monica's boyfriend. This made the girl a rival in Monica's mind. The other circumstance was that the previous year, in another context, Monica had been beaten very unexpectedly, publicly, and painfully by an emotionally disturbed older girl. This older girl was no longer at the school, but the conflict with Sara and her friends, and the talk of violence, plucked at thick cords of meaning inside Monica. She was angry and afraid and determined not to let herself again be attacked and made a public victim.

Over the previous years, the faculty had developed very strong bonds with Monica, and many of the other girls and their families. The school was intent to guide them toward a peaceful solution. But the school's efforts—individual counseling, mediations, family meetings, warnings that participation in the graduation ceremony was at stake, even an off-site half-day retreat for the factions hosted by a counselor and social worker—all seemed to have little lasting impact.

There was some consolation, however, that there had not been a physical fight. The faculty felt this was a victory—until it happened.

Monica and two friends jumped Sara and two of the other girls on the sidewalk outside the school. Allies piled on, some trying to deescalate, others making it worse. A phone was lost in the scuffle on the sidewalk. Local police happened to be on the block at the time, so they got involved and the situation was, for the moment, taken out of the hands of the school's authority. In the midst of tears, punching, and screaming, suddenly some of the girls were in the heavy hands of the cops, who quickly decided the missing phone was a matter of larceny. Then there were handcuffs, humiliation, and police custody all night for four of the girls.

On the broad scale of pain that any day can trouble the children of our nation, this was not the most extreme: No one was killed or hospitalized, and the charges against the girls were eventually dropped. But it was a terrible experience for the girls. And the adults of the school felt like failures.

It was June and everyone was exhausted. But for the adults and for the girls, it was just the beginning of several stories of removal, return, and repair.

A Public Reckoning

Some families decided to keep their daughters out of school for the remainder of the year, beyond any suspensions that the school imposed. There were just two weeks left before the last day, and the families of three seniors decided that they'd simply do their coursework from home. The school leadership allowed this, but no one was comfortable—even most students and families—with the idea that there wouldn't be some restitution and closure. Nor were any school leaders or faculty—despite some strong differences of perspective on these events—willing that seniors on either side of the conflict would participate in the graduation ceremony if there wasn't some repair.

It was decided that in order for any of them to march at graduation, they had to engage in a public accounting before school faculty and younger students, to confront the past and consider the legacy of their actions in the eyes of their younger peers.

Just as suspension is kin to age-old stories of ostracism, so, too, the school's forum for repair was cousin to something ages-old. It had elements like Gacaca, a practice for communal restitution in Rwanda. Similar structures exist among the First Nations of North America and in other cultures in other times. It happened in a circle, was intergenerational, and was a public accounting.

The school had an advisory program, a class that met most days of the week and was a way of providing small-group and individual support for academics, social-emotional needs, and community-building. In a circle designed to hold reflection on the impact of the conflict, there were thirteen younger students, one from each advisory, and as many of the advisors as could attend. This group of people met first, without the seniors who had been involved in the conflict in the room. It took place in the after-school hours.

The younger students were first asked to reflect on why their advisors had chosen them for the meeting. Some needed coaxing but eventually each spoke of some positive quality that their advisor had seen in them. These proclamations of their own strengths both served to validate why they'd been selected and helped the students set high expectations for the meeting and for themselves. The student who says they were chosen "because I'm a good listener" sets a high expectation for good listening in the meeting. Other than the school leader who was facilitating, the other adults in the room did no talking at this point.

The younger students were then asked to imagine what it would feel like to be one of the seniors at that moment. Some responded judgmentally with what they thought the seniors *should* be feeling, such as "she should be ashamed of herself." But this wasn't the prompt. They were again asked to simply imagine what the girls were *actually* feeling. They came up with a list of possible emotions: The girls might feel nervous, embarrassed, angry at themselves, or regretful. Several younger students noted that it would take bravery to come into the circle that afternoon.

Each senior, one at a time, came in accompanied by her advisor, who sat beside her. It was important that each girl feel support at her side. The senior was told that her younger peers thought it took courage to come before the group. The senior was asked to reflect on the lessons she'd learned, and if anything made her proud or made her feel regret. After she spoke, the younger students were asked to paraphrase what they'd heard and to do this with "I" statements, such as, "Monica, what I heard you saying was . . . "

After hearing the younger students' paraphrasing, the senior was asked if there was anything else she wished to add or comment. The group heard her thoughts, and then the group turned to a conversation about how to make the school community even stronger next year.

This happened four times, with four girls, a two-hour process in total. Each senior admitted something she would have done differently. Some of the most meaningful comments came from Monica and Sara, who made simple, unsolicited statements of being sorry for choices they'd made, and for how they had unsettled the community. They'd not been told that an apology was an expectation, which made it powerful. Each time it happened, the conversation was paused so that the younger students could be asked if anyone was willing to accept the apology. Various students spoke to say yes.

The apologies and the future-focused conclusion of the meeting provided some closure and hope. The thoughts from the students on how to strengthen the community were good ones, and the adults took notes: peer resources for conflict resolution, more guidance groups, and after-school classes to allow students to know each other in extracurricular settings and to help decrease the likelihood of cliques. The group decided that each senior who participated would be allowed to take her place at the graduation ceremony.

No Return Without Restitution

There was one senior, Angela, who hadn't been willing to engage in the reparative meeting with the younger students. In the end, she couldn't have marched in commencement anyway, because she was two credits short of graduating. But she was still a member of the senior class, had been at the school for years, and she fervently wished to attend the ceremony. It was difficult, and she and her family pleaded and were angry, but the school leadership refused to let her come to graduation, a ceremony to which everyone else in the school was invited. She had disrupted the community with violence, and she'd refused to participate in the process to repair the harm.

A year passed. Angela and her family reached out again. Angela had completed her coursework over the summer and received her diploma as an August graduate, which came with some congratulations but without a full ceremony. Now she wanted to wear a cap and gown at the traditional June ceremony the following spring. But the school's expectations for repair and accountability hadn't changed. She would need to participate in a process of restitution. This time, she was willing. Students and staff were again gathered, and a few days were taken to prepare. A year had passed, but it was clear that this story of exile and return still had the potential for healing.

When the circle was convened, Angela acknowledged playing a big part in the feud, fueling the tension between the groups. She went on to share her experience of getting arrested on the sidewalk that day and how it had affected her. On the topic of why she wanted to be at the ceremony, she said it was because, even though she was now enrolled in college, she didn't "have closure" on her high school years. After other questions and reflections, including an apology to the eldest student in the room, whom Angela knew better than the others, Angela was asked to leave so the group could deliberate. Should her request to attend graduation be granted? The students shared their feelings first. In the end, everyone agreed that she should participate in the graduation ceremony because, in the words of one student, "she and society and our school will be better for it."

PRINCIPLE: HARM IS REPAIRED IN A COMMUNITY OF BELONGING

Each of the restorative justice interventions described above was created by people close to the problem they were seeking to solve. There was no outside expert or consultant guiding the work. Restorative practice was familiar to people in the school, however, in formal and informal ways. The adults at the school understood the paradoxical relationship between traditional school discipline and restorative justice, namely that these two seemingly different approaches can support each other well in certain situations. This paradox can be navigated if certain principles are kept in mind and taken to heart, including the idea that repair is created by people whose needs are understood in a community where they feel belonging.

Alejandro

Alejandro looked down, then looked up. We were seated in a circle. The desks had been pushed aside, and we sat in chairs. There were a few voices in the hallway, students going where they needed to go, but in our circle, it was quiet.

"I think it would be a Commitment to Peace," he said, naming one of the school's core values.

The teacher-facilitator asked Alejandro to explain further. "He violated my peace, the peace inside me." I listened. He was talking about me, his school principal. The two other students and the other staff member also listened.

"I was really upset," he said, and then wandered his eyes upward—but he wasn't rolling his eyes, just thinking. Actually, rolling his eyes was a signature expression, which Alejandro would exhibit in moments of frustration, teasing, or insolence. But he wasn't doing that now. He was letting his eyes wander above us, looking into his memory of the incident. "What he said, it really upset me. I was so upset I just left. I was thinking about it all weekend."

More questions followed, from the facilitator, from the other teacher and the other students. It was the phase of the meeting when the group determines if a school core value has been violated, and, if so, which one. The process had already clarified the circumstance of the incident itself, and how each person experienced it.

Four school days earlier, Alejandro had been brought into the office by one of his teachers. This was not an unfamiliar occurrence—it had been happening for years. It was still early in the school year, and there were some discouraging signs of those same past behaviors that had so effectively sabotaged his progress in previous years: cutting classes, giving up on his work, severing bonds with adults who could help him, speaking provocatively and disrespectfully—all reasons for him being removed from classes. And here he was again: almost eighteen years old, brought to the office by his teacher after refusing to put away his phone, and after he'd already been reprimanded for casting slurs across the room.

Alejandro and the teacher stood before me, and after the teacher finished explaining, I sat back in my chair and gave a sigh. Alejandro might have anticipated this. He crossed his arms and waited for the questions and concerns. But I didn't want to follow the same path we'd been on for so long. He was eighteen years old, and it felt too late and too high-stakes for this student and the adults of the school to fall again into the same habits: his cutting, disruptions, removals from class, and soon a suspension from school, meetings with advisor and guardian, a behavioral contract that lists the immature behaviors he mustn't exhibit, and so on and so forth, stating the obvious, again and again.

I was aware, firsthand, of the general state of his engagement this year, because I had him in an English class I was co-teaching with a special educator. I impulsively decided to interrupt our cycle. I leaned forward and told him, "Maybe you should just leave."

He was silent. What might have been a smirk faded from his face. "What are you talking about?" he said.

I explained, quickly, sternly, quietly: "It's not working out. Here we are again, just like last year, and just like the year before that. You're cutting classes—again. And cursing, and using electronics in class—again. And you're frustrated with your teachers—again—and with your advisor, who knows you so well and cares for you so much. 'She's annoying,' you told me. Well, if we annoy you so much, then why don't you just leave? Maybe you need to consider some other options: other schools, other pathways to graduation, maybe a GED program and then on to college. We'll help you find it, but whatever it is, no more of this. Enough. You don't have time for it, Alejandro." He stared at me, shook his head, and looked away. Then he cursed at me and left.

I called and left a message for his guardian. It was hard to say where this was headed, but if old habits needed to be interrupted, it seemed that they were. Alejandro seemed sincerely shocked, though it remained to be seen what decisions would follow.

On the following school day, a Monday, the school's social worker reported that Alejandro was so upset by the suggestion that he leave that he was calling for a convening of the Fairness Committee.

A Grassroots Structure for Restorative Practice

The Fairness Committee, as described by Vassar College professor of education Maria Hantzopoulos, is "a non-traditional model of school 'discipline' that seeks to create, through dialogue and by consensus, appropriate responses for community norm violations rather than simply mete out prescribed punishments."[2]

This process plays out in different ways at different schools, evolving as educators from one place take it to another. It's a grassroots effort to reinforce belonging, foster mutual understanding, and generate local solutions to local problems. It can be a means for one community member to hold another accountable for harm, and it can also be a means for conflict resolution.

At our school, no adult had been taken to Fairness before, but it was very good that Alejandro wanted to make use of this process. He either needed to recommit to being at the school or he needed to consider an alternative path. We would support him either way. By using the Fairness Committee, he seemed to be saying he was in the right place, and this was affirming, because many people at the school—above all, Alejandro—had invested a lot of energy and hope in sustaining his engagement through hard times.

Alejandro had overcome many obstacles, and he continued to struggle to surmount others in order to stay in school. He was living with a very strong advocate and guardian, but his past group home guardians and social workers did not always serve him well, and he'd had a troubled upbringing as a child. His parents were dead, buried in a country far away.

Alejandro's journey—to our country, to our school, to fluency in English, to mental health—had been an arduous one. That journey was yet incomplete, with many dangers, including inconsistent care in the foster care system. Add to all of this that Alejandro openly identified as gay and that to be dark-skinned, adolescent, and gay is to belong to one of the most vulnerable demographics in our nation.

I knew all of this. But I hadn't realized, until the committee meeting, how much value he placed on a traditional high school diploma. He told the group that I had violated his inner peace, that suddenly his principal had become another voice in a chorus of denigrating voices predicting that he would never finish school, that he was a failure. He said he was determined to get a high school diploma even though many had told him that he couldn't, and he was going to prove them wrong.

I raised my hand, and the facilitator called on me. I acknowledged what Alejandro was saying, paraphrased my understanding, appreciated his honesty. I suggested to him and the group that perhaps I had violated a different core value, respect for humanity. "Showing empathy," I said, "is one of the ways we say we can live this core value at our school. And since I reacted so harshly, in that moment, and didn't speak in a way that invited Alejandro into the conversation, I didn't give him—you, Alejandro—a chance to say how much a high school diploma means to you. I didn't give myself a chance to empathize with you. I was trying to say what I thought you needed to hear, which wasn't exactly the kind of empathy that comes from listening to you share your perspective."

After reaching consensus on which core value had been violated, the remainder of the dialogue was devoted to determining consequences for the violation: actions that Alejandro and I would undertake to help restore our relationship. One consequence we agreed to was simply the Fairness meeting itself—which was restorative. Another consequence was that I would apologize to Alejandro for unknowingly echoing the denigrating voices in his life. He accepted this apology.

This meeting was an important forum for Alejandro to assert his commitment to the school before an audience of his peers, his teacher, and his principal. And everyone participating was able to validate a collective commitment to the core values and to democratic structures for addressing and resolving conflict.

In addition to the focus on the actions that had disrupted Alejandro's sense of peace, the student and teacher committee members were able to solicit from Alejandro an acknowledgment of his own problematic behaviors. And it should be noted that this was not the only forum where those behaviors would be discussed. In another meeting with Alejandro, his classroom teacher, and advisor, he would be reminded that another instance of classroom disruption would, as it had in the past, result in suspension from school and a reentry process.

A Menu of Interventions

Though adults were not typically brought by students to the Fairness Committee, it was important that the student community know it is possible, for this further invests them in the power that the structure holds—a power intended, above all, for them to wield.

This is one of many behavioral interventions employed at the school, including suspension, family conferences, mediation, counseling, behavioral contracts, and, in extreme situations—like a fight that couldn't be deescalated—calling upon security agents or police. On this menu is a mix of traditional and restorative consequences, all of which can work to reinforce community members' sense of safety, belonging, and mutual understanding.

It's important that schools have a menu of interventions to choose from, according to the type of infraction or disruption. However, the main behavioral intervention that determines whether or not restorative practice is alive and well in any community is not on any list of structures or interventions. It's the way people interact with each other from day to day: the ways of being in hallways and classrooms, the habits of speaking and listening at meetings. It's in those simple rituals like opening a gathering of staff or students with an opportunity to appreciate or apologize. It's in those cultural norms that can be difficult to codify except in the most basic of rules most strictly enforced, like, please listen and don't talk while someone else is talking.

One of the most essential behavioral interventions that healthy schools make in the lives of their students, and the adults, has to do with cultivating the simple habits that value an individual's humanity in a society that often devalues it. And schools can do this—valuing the individual—not at the expense of the collective, but as a means to sustain the collective.

Continuing the Dialogue

When Alejandro mobilized the Fairness Committee as a means to hold his principal accountable to the school's core values, and to affirm his commitment to his own education, it was a successful effort in healing, restorative practice, and student voice. A school needs many similar instances throughout a school year and in diverse forms to sustain a healthy school community. But a school must also consider a boy like Alejandro's work and grades, to ensure that the school is doing all it can to engage him and meet his academic needs.

Alejandro eventually reengaged in school enough to be successful in the second unit of the course I was teaching, a unit on writing short stories. Earlier in the class, during the first unit on writing poetry he'd done no work at all. He'd refused to write a word, refused even to brainstorm ideas. Part of the issue was that he couldn't be convinced that poetry didn't have to be personally revealing—though he'd seen plenty of examples of such.

He refused to engage in something that he thought had to be about his inner life or his past. At one point he covered his face in his hands and just said, "I can't, I can't, I can't," and left the room.

But later in the semester he was able to take advantage of the short story unit to write about a struggling family, about pain in a fictional household. In this short story, his narrator remarks toward the end, "Once I witnessed a beating on Mom which also made me cry, but I couldn't show it because then I would feel like I lost my battle against all of the feelings I held back from all of these years."

"Battle" is what it feels like for teachers, too, sometimes, to do this work of fighting with, and for, student voice and belonging. There are walls that hold feelings back, and educators bump up against the defenses they've built to protect themselves from their own pain, and from the injustice and hardship of the world that brings it.

But little by little, if we and they persist, students can access their feelings, honor who they are, and demand the world do the same. With help, Alejandro seemed to be scaffolding this process for himself in the class.

The class used open-form "free writes" to initiate the composition process, after reading several model pieces in the genre. After short story writing, as the class began the next unit on personal essays, Alejandro participated in the free write, where, in the very last line, as if an aside, he mentioned the deaths of his parents. He'd spoken of such to his advisor and the school social worker, but this was the first time he'd ever written about it.

By the end of the unit, the students would be asked to revise their essays at least twice. As many teachers know, revising work that is personally meaningful is one of the best ways to improve students' academic skills, for they are motivated to do the work on a personal, emotional level. For Alejandro and me, the revision process was also the continuation of a dialogue we'd begun earlier that year in the forum for restorative justice.

PRACTICALITIES: UNIVERSAL SUPPORTS FOR DIALOGUE AND COMMUNITY-BUILDING

In terms of cultivating shared understanding and sense of belonging, it is important that the day-to-day work of every teacher's classroom be a place where we are cultivating habits of interaction and skills that can be called upon in the intensive interventions that happen more episodically throughout the year.

Indeed, when it comes to seeding and growing restorative practice in a school community, the intensive interventions are important and engage a small number of people in important work, but they actually require less collective energy and commitment than the schoolwide, or "universal," structures that sustain a culture of restorative practice and values.

Daily, universal practices in classrooms and occasional intensive interventions are both important to maintaining a restorative school culture. The school leader has an essential role in sustaining restorative practice in each domain, the universal and the intensive.

The remainder of this chapter focuses on the practicalities of what school leaders can do to deepen restorative practice in their school. It is not necessary that this chapter articulate a specific framework for restorative practice. There are various frameworks, orthodoxies, approaches, definitions, and protocols suited to countless varied circumstances in diverse school settings. There are books just a few online clicks away, some of them probably already on the bookshelves of readers of this book, which frame the theoretical underpinnings of restorative justice or restorative practice.

Some of the books worth exploring include: *Circle Forward: Building a Restorative School Community*, by Carolyn Boyes-Watson and Kay Pranis; *The Little Book of Restorative Justice*, by Howard Zehr; and *Circle in the Square: Building Community and Repairing Harm in Schools*, by Nancy Riestenberg. For more on the structure called the Fairness Committee, readers can consult a series of essays by Hantzopoulos and others in the journal *Schools: Studies in Education*.

In these works, and in my own experience, an essential element of restorative practice, which informs the practical measures that will be recommended in this chapter, is the understanding that in every community people possess the knowledge and skills needed to repair harm that occurs in their community.

By people, we include those who do harm, those who are harmed, and community members young and old. If they are ready and willing, almost any person in the community who has been touched by an incident can be involved in the work of acknowledging harm and engaging in repair.

By community, we mean a place where people have a sense of belonging and mutual understanding, and where they are continually striving for such. The geographic and political scale of "community" can be more narrowly or widely defined: a classroom, a school, a nation. Harm happens and repair is needed across societies of all dimensions. Here we are concerned with the work of cultivating belonging and mutual understanding in the classrooms where all students spend time, as well as in the intensive interventions where fewer people work to address more intensive harm and mend substantial breaches of community values.

The anecdotes above describe intensive interventions in the upper grades. There was also mention of the role of advisors and a structure called Advisory. And there was some limited discussion of classroom interactions and curriculum. We need to discuss all three of these domains in more detail, and as they pertain to different grade levels:

- Universal Supports in Classrooms
- Universal Supports through Advisory
- Intensive Restorative Justice Interventions

It is in the universal domain where the skills of empathic listening and respectful dialogue about high-stakes topics are developed. And it is in the universal domain that schools develop the sense of belonging in students that is needed for them to care about repairing harm through the hard work of restorative justice interventions. Students who don't feel a sense of belonging are both more likely to harm others and more likely to lack incentive to repair. To explore these topics, we will next consider three scenarios at different grade levels.

Universal Supports: A Third Grade Scenario

Sitting in a circle is not uncommon in elementary schools. Imagine two third grade classrooms where each day the teacher begins with a morning circle. These classrooms are across the hall from each other in the same school.

There's a lot that the classrooms have in common, but there are some subtle and important differences. One thing they have in common is that by nine o'clock each morning, the class needs to move into the literacy work for that day. The morning settling-in and circling-up needs to be wrapped up by that time.

One teacher facilitates a morning circle that lasts twenty minutes. He reviews the schedule for the day with the class, introduces a vocabulary word that they will encounter later in the day, and—the kids' favorite part of the circle—he reads a page of knock-knock jokes from a joke book that contains hundreds. The morning circle routinely ends in giggles. For the next half hour, the students have choice time. They can quietly play, read a book, or help the teacher with several morning chores and routines, like feeding the fish and setting out the math baskets that contain manipulatives for the math lesson later in the morning. Aside from the occasional disagreement about sharing a toy, book, or beanbag—which the teacher skillfully deescalates should it arise—the children are happy.

Across the hall, the morning circle lasts at least twice as long. It begins in similar fashion. The teacher reviews the daily schedule and shares the vocabulary word for the day. This is an element of their lesson planning, among others, that the teachers and district curriculum coordinator have agreed to have in common.

After these routines, the teacher transitions to a morning ritual: appreciations and apologies. The students are invited to share something positive they noticed or heard another student do or say the day before, and they can also offer apologies if they have something to apologize for. On the wall is a poster that reminds them of what makes an effective appreciation or apology, including that it be about specific words or actions. Another criterion is that such gestures are not a performance to make people laugh or to entertain. The teacher will typically share her own appreciation or apology as part of the ritual, modeling specificity and sincerity. She keeps track, at her desk, of the apologies or appreciations she has offered, to ensure that each student in the group is offered one from her over the course of the first weeks of the school year. She lets the students know that she is doing this and says that it's not a competition and that it's not hard to find things to appreciate in people.

There are some other guidelines that the teacher has developed for this ritual over time. She's been refining it for several years, adjusting it based on who is in a particular class. She gives them some options, for instance, when it comes to accepting an apology. If a student is not yet ready to accept an apology in the circle, she acknowledges this, and will follow up with the student, or students, after the morning circle to check in.

The appreciations and apologies ritual doesn't typically take very long, maybe five minutes, so she has ample time to get their talking piece for the week and facilitate a circle where each student is invited—not required—to share a reflection in response to a prompt.

This kind of circle process is something the teacher learned about in a book written by another elementary school teacher, Liz Kleinrock. In her book, *Start Here, Start Now: A Guide to Antibias and Antiracist Work*, Kleinrock describes the "Circle." This is some of what she writes:

> One of my favorite ways to dialogue is to invite students to participate in a Circle, which is rooted in Indigenous and First Nations cultures and practices. This process ensures that community members are heard, and that those who wish to speak are able to do so without interruption. In a Circle, an item of significance is chosen as a talking piece, and when the talking piece is in someone's hands, it is their turn to speak.[3]

In this classroom, the talking piece is an object that one student chooses each week from a shelf where students have put objects that are special to them. It is passed from one person to the other, and unless it is in your hands, you don't speak. When it is in your hands, you are invited to offer your own reflections into the circle, rather than respond to or debate something someone else has said.

Sometimes the teacher asks the circle of students to respond to a quote of the day, a short song, or a picture. She'll ask a simple question like, "What does it make you think, or wonder, or feel?" After the circle process, she transitions the group to a few minutes of choice time before the literacy lesson. If students have shared anything in the circle of significant emotional content, she will ask them about it during choice time, or later in the day, or she'll discuss it with the school counselor or principal.

These two teachers have started their days in different ways, but by the appointed time each morning, each classroom has transitioned to the district-wide literacy lesson. Academic rigor and intellectual development are a priority in both classrooms. But in the second classroom, rigorous interpersonal intelligence is also being prioritized.

That winter, there's a student in the sixth grade who publicly transitions from male to female identity. Students talk about it in the younger grades, through whispers in the halls, comments on the bus, observations at recess. Unfortunately, there was also an incident of homophobic graffiti on the school's front doors and then also in the bathrooms. The younger students talked about that, too, wondering what the words meant and who did it.

If we only judge from how they start their day, it is clear which third grade classroom has the habits of listening and careful talk needed to have an authentic conversation about what is going on in the school. With an investment of twenty minutes a day in a circle process, where there is adult guidance and safe parameters, one of these two classrooms has one hundred minutes every week for careful talk and listening. The universal practice embedded in the daily classroom helps develop the skills needed for intensive interventions and when conversations about harm and repair are needed in the community. There is no directive to discuss what happened in the younger grades, but the teacher in this classroom asks the guidance counselor to join her for the morning circle, and they acknowledge what happened in the bathroom, and ask if the students have questions. They answer what questions they can answer in public.

Afterward, the teacher and counselor discuss what to do with what they heard from the students, including making a calls to parents who would want to know what their children were asking about. They also went together to the principal to ask what schoolwide communication might be going home regarding the homophobic incident and how it had impacted some of the younger students.

Universal Supports: A Fifth Grade Scenario

Imagine two fifth grade classrooms. As in the scenario above, there is teacher discretion that leads to differences, but there is much they have in common in terms of units of study and pacing. In both classrooms, after lunch and recess, there is time for silent reading. The librarian does a great job of helping the teachers match the classroom books to the reading levels and interests of the students. Monday through Thursday, after silent reading, the Spanish and music teachers rotate through the classrooms. But on Friday the fifth grade classroom teacher is in charge after silent reading, and the focus is on current events. This current events activity lasts for about thirty minutes, sometimes a bit more, sometimes less.

Several students present a current event each week, which is charted on a calendar that allows each student to make a presentation multiple times over the course of the school year. Each teacher uses the silent reading time that comes prior to these presentations to help the student or students prepare. The students are well supported. This is the case in each classroom. Beyond these similarities, there are differences:

In one classroom, two students and the teacher make a presentation each week. The student presentations take about five minutes, if there are questions from other students. If there are no questions from students, the teacher will help fill out the five minutes by asking questions that the presenter is likely to feel comfortable answering. The teacher then does her own more elaborate presentation for about fifteen minutes on a current events topic she knows will be engaging for all students, typically involving a video. The teacher thoughtfully picks a topic that is typically connected to something she knows students are studying in Spanish or music class. Toward the end of the year, she typically picks current events in anticipation of the theme for the annual fifth and sixth grade science fair. There are always plenty of student questions for her that she answers gladly. If she doesn't know the answer, she isn't afraid to say so and do a bit more research and share the answers on Monday.

In the other classroom, just one student presents a topic each week. The student presentation and discussion take about fifteen or twenty minutes, not the whole half hour, because there is some time needed for transitions at the beginning and end of the presentation and discussion. The transition involves moving furniture. Students do not remain in their desks for the current event presentation, they take their chairs and arrange them in a circle. The teacher does this because student-to-student discussion follows the student's presentation of the current event. The teacher has had the previous four days during silent reading to find time to help the student prepare. Part of these preparations involves the two of them agreeing on two or three discussion questions, which will be shared with the class after the student's presentation.

The teacher typically plays a role in finalizing these questions, for she wants questions that both connect to the specific event the child has chosen, but are general enough that any student can have a point of entry into a response. For instance, one week a boy chose to make a presentation on a hurricane, a major weather event two states away, where his grandparents lived. The questions that the teacher proposed they ask the class after the presentation were: Have you ever been worried about the weather? What have you noticed the government or emergency responders doing when there is a weather emergency? What can families and communities do to stay safe when the weather is worrisome?

There are five or six norms, or "agreements," that the class uses when having these discussions. The teacher reminds the class of the norms at the start of the discussion, models using them, and affirms the use of the norms along the way. She uses the same norms for discussion of whole-class texts when the students read a piece of literature or science writing, even though they don't always sit in a circle. Four of the norms are:

- Use "I" statements. Speak from your own understanding and personal experience.

- Disagree respectfully. If you disagree with something, that's okay, but disagree with the idea, not the person.
- Be curious. Seek deeper understanding of what other people say. Ask questions of peers and the teacher.
- Step up—step back. Share your thoughts, and if you have spoken, consider waiting to speak until others have a chance.

The teacher is especially affirming when students ask each other questions, for her goal is have student-to-student conversation. She is also affirming when students share something personal that is appropriate but which might be a risk in terms of vulnerability. She cautions and redirects students if they seem to be sharing something that might be sensitive about other people, such as the personal life of a friend or parent.

Sometimes the teacher finds it useful to call a parent to let them know what their child shared in the class, or she speaks with the guidance counselor or principal to get their take. The principal has told her that she's okay with her conducting these kinds of discussions as long as she's asking general and not leading questions about the lives of the kids and the world they live in. The teacher feels like the principal supports her. Indeed, though the principal doesn't ask all teachers to do this sort of thing, she admires this teacher's commitment to the classroom norms and discussion process. On more than one occasion, she has spent time on the phone with a parent of one of her students affirming the value of asking open-ended questions, even about political topics, and having student discussions. This happened, for instance, when there were protests about police brutality in a city not far away, which some students wanted to discuss.

As mentioned, other than how they run the current events portion of the week, the two teachers in this scenario have parallel units of study and daily agendas. And even though they run the current events portion of the day differently, in both classrooms the students enjoy the current events time on Fridays very much.

However, when harm arises in the community later that year, some students are more ready than others to discuss it respectfully.

It happened in the spring, when there was a contentious run-off election for a high-level elected office in the state. Political action committees flooded the region with political campaign rhetoric on television and social media that exacerbated divisions among many adults, and it trickled down to their children. One candidate's stance on immigration was made a central issue.

The school is located in a racially diverse suburb where there are families of white, Black, and Asian American identity. Friendships exist across these differences. But on the playground one day, a group of two white and two Black girls were using stereotypical anti-Asian speech when talking to three

Asian American boys. The girls put their fingers to their faces and pulled the skin about their eyes to make them narrow. They laughed. The first time, the boys walked away and didn't tell anyone. The next time it happened, they told their parents, who called the school counselor.

Of these seven students, three were in one fifth grade classroom and four in the other. The counselor informed the principal, who investigated, meeting with each student, and concluding that indeed the incident occurred as reported. She took care of the important formalities related to an incident of harassment, communicating with all parties involved and sharing her findings, then she met with the guidance counselor and the two teachers to get their input on what else is needed to keep students safe and ensure the incident doesn't happen again.

They discussed a menu of options, including small group mediations between individual students, larger group interventions with the students who made the offensive gestures and comments, learning activities to help them understand anti–Asian American discrimination and violence in historical context.

They also discussed the possibility of whole-class learning and discussions. The teacher who routinely engages her whole class in student-to-student discussions of current events, and who has norms for discussion in place, was open to this idea. The teacher who doesn't teach student-to-student discussion habits didn't want to take it on, but she said she'd very much like to observe and see how it went in the other class, should they opt for this intervention.

The school counselor wasn't sure where it would lead, but she felt it was good that some of the students involved were in the classroom where careful listening to each other was something that was explicitly taught. She anticipated they'd be meeting in some constellation of small or large groups soon and that she'd have to help facilitate. After school she went into the classroom and copied down the discussion norms onto her own piece of chart paper to hang by the table in her office.

Universal Supports: A Seventh Grade Scenario

Imagine a middle school building, two stories, with the sixth and seventh grades downstairs. Upstairs the 8th grade social studies and science teacher collaborate on several units each year. One of them is focused on the decline of ancient civilizations and what human and environmental factors are at play. The students are asked to research and understand various points of view and then bring evidence for their own arguments to a discussion format that the teachers call Socratic Seminar because of the emphasis on questions, particularly students asking questions of other students.

Students do research in both social studies and science class that they record in an "entry ticket" that they must finish to be "admitted" to the seminar. This allows each teacher to assess content understanding, and it ensures that students have talking points at the ready for the seminar discussion.

The seventh grade social studies teacher was in a department meeting with his eighth grade colleague over the summer when there was discussion of the effectiveness of the eighth grade Socratic Seminars as a method for collaboration as well as means to address social studies standards. The seventh grade teacher brought the idea to her team, and it led them to a new plan for their final unit of the year.

The seventh grade team was used to working with interdisciplinary curriculum themes and overarching questions. The curriculum wasn't integrated fully, but the themes and essential question brought some continuity across the classes for students, and it always helped spark some interesting discussion among the teachers.

For the final unit of the year, as students prepared to leave school for summer, they were focused on the themes of home and community. In recent years, there had been an increase in homelessness in their county, including some seasonal population changes based on migrant agricultural laborers moving through the region. The teachers took on the topic of home and community to help their students have a broader vocabulary and understanding of the forces that work to bring housing insecurity to certain families. They also found ways in this unit to affirm the diverse cultural traditions in the families of the students in their community. Their essential question was "Is home where you are or how you feel?"

In science class, where the teacher is required to end the year with an earth science unit, she connected to the theme by focusing on three related topics: climate changes that can create population dislocation; geographic and meteorological factors that contribute to some lands being fertile for certain crops and not others; and how pollution impacts people in different ways, depending on where they live. In English class, the teacher engaged students in personal writing about "feeling or being at home." Students read poetry on the theme by authors of a variety of cultural identities. In social studies, the teacher wanted to show how public policy impacts where people call home, and she focused on two case studies of public policy and housing, one drawn from the era of the Homestead Act, one that teaches about racially segregated neighborhoods in the mid-twentieth century. The math teacher, who typically found it harder to integrate work explicitly on the theme, engaged students in making graphs that showed population flux over several decades in the region where they lived.

Typically, at the end of the unit, student work from each class was compiled to make a poster that hung in the hall. Students assembled the poster in English class, bringing their graphs from math class and artifacts from the other classes. These posters would hang in the hall until the last week of school, when students would take them home with their other belongings.

The culminating product changed substantially when the seventh grade team decided to emulate the eighth grade team's way of channeling content from various classrooms into a culminating Socratic Seminar. Instead of putting content of various classes on a poster, students channeled their research and notes into the culminating discussion. And rather than time spent assembling the poster, the English teacher helped them assemble their "ticket to participate," the graphic organizer for their thoughts, their arguments and supporting evidence. The English teacher also helped students practice the discussion format, with its emphasis on student-to-student interaction.

The teachers were excited for their new approach. Unfortunately, as this multi-week unit was nearing conclusion, there was an incident in the middle school boys' locker room. Several toilets were clogged with paper towels and apples from the lunchroom. The flush sensors were tampered with such that they flushed many times, spewing countless gallons of water into the locker room. The PE class had gone outside to play on the ball fields for their lesson, and when they returned to the gym and locker rooms, water was seeping toward the expensive gymnasium floor. The personal belongings of students who had left backpacks on the floor were soaked.

Custodial staff had to be reassigned from various locations in the district to come clean up the water immediately, before the gym floor got damaged. PE classes were unable to access the boys' locker room and part of the gymnasium for the rest of that day and two following days as fans and dehumidifiers blew. Eighth graders were upset with seventh graders, for it was known to have happened during a seventh grade class period.

Seventh graders were upset with seventh graders, too. Some students knew who did it and why—it had been a dare—but the principal's interviews with students didn't yield any confessions or concrete corroborating evidence.

Some students took it lightly, and some, especially those who'd had belongings damaged, took it seriously. After listening to student comments here and there, reading the principal's email about the incident, and hearing about how upset the custodians were, the seventh grade English teacher met with her colleagues and asked that they delay the culminating seminar for a few days and make use of her classroom to hold a conversation about the incident. She'd done work to support their discussion skills and thought they could do it.

It wasn't hard to see connections to their themes of home and community, and the teacher wanted the students to discuss how the incident impacted people in the community and what could be done to address the harm that occurred. Her colleagues agreed. The science teacher, who worked closely with the custodial staff when lab experiments involving water and other materials were being used, suggested that they invite someone from the custodial staff to come to the discussion.

This discussion about the harm that had happened only took one period. It didn't follow the same format that the Socratic Seminar would, but the discussion norms were similar, and the questions focused on what makes a school or home a good place to be. The English teacher hadn't done anything like this before, so some of the prompts she used changed from one class group to the next, as she tried them out. With two of her questions, she did "go-arounds," where each student was asked to speak to a question. One of these questions was "How did the locker room incident impact you or people you know?"

After these rounds the teacher facilitated an open discussion by calling on students and encouraging others to engage. She also encouraged them to ask questions of each other to seek deeper understanding of how the incident affected the school community.

The classes had discussions of different personality and tone. In one group, students worked hard to make light of it, and other students worked hard to convince them of the seriousness. In one class, it was all seriousness from the start, because of the presence of one boy who was so upset he refused to participate. His cell phone, which he'd gotten for his birthday, had been ruined by the water that soaked his backpack.

A member of the custodial staff was able to join one group, and this brought a new dimension to the conversation. The students weren't used to thinking about the impacts, in general, of their actions on those who were in the building after they'd gone, taking out the garbage and cleaning the space.

This teacher had no training in restorative practice, but she was taking a restorative approach, focusing on harm and how to repair it. Each group was asked a final question, "Based on what we are hearing about how different individuals were affected, what should we do?" The teacher wrote down the ideas and said she would share them with the principal, the PE teachers, the custodians, and the other teachers on the seventh grade team.

Some suggestions were as simple as "the kids who did it should apologize." Other suggestions included mention of punishment, like, "the boys who did it should confess they did it and take their punishment." Other suggestions included a communal approach to repair, like "we should do a fundraiser to help pay for the phone that was damaged." Some students loudly championed this idea, for it gave them a way to help a friend in need. Other students resisted, saying that it wasn't their responsibility, but that the kids who did the damage should pay for it.

Some students wondered, what if the families of the kids who did it didn't have money to pay for the phone? The teacher wasn't sure what to do when the conversation turned to topics like this, such as who might have done it, or their families, or their motivations. But in general she guided the conversation away from those topics by saying, "Our goal is to talk about the impact of this incident and how to make things better from here, but if you have specific thoughts about who did it and why, you can talk to me after class." She knew that the kids who did the harm were in her classes. She didn't want them to feel shame, but to feel accountability to the group—and, hopefully, accountable to their own sense of right and wrong.

In one group, one student said, "There's nothing that can be done to fix this situation now. But hopefully after hearing all this, they won't do something like this again." When the teacher shared her notes with her colleagues, the principal, and others, she also expressed this sentiment. She also had her hopes that the students who did it might come forward to take responsibility. And she wanted to talk more with her colleagues about the idea of a fundraiser for the phone that was ruined. She knew they couldn't do that kind of thing every time a student's belongings got damaged in school, but she wondered if this was a special case. She wasn't sure and needed to talk about it more.

She also wasn't sure what to say to students who asked, "What if they come forward—what will their consequence be?" She asked the principal. He wasn't sure either. He asked if the student discussion had generated any ideas on that topic.

Universal Support: Advisory

The above scenarios convey some of the uncertainty that educators encounter when we engage in the democratic, discussion-heavy, collaborative problem-solving that's part of restorative approaches to repairing harm. However, the stories convey with clarity that classrooms are places where the social-emotional muscles needed for restorative work are built—both in students and in adults.

The classroom is an important place where mutual understanding and belonging can be cultivated. Discussion structures that help students and adults develop deep listening skills and skills to respectfully talk about challenging topics are an essential social-emotional infrastructure for restorative practice.

Readers will note that the role of the school leader isn't pronounced in the above anecdotes. The role of the school leader is essential, but in these scenarios the presence of the principal was downplayed intentionally. This is because teachers play a primary role in carrying the work of universal support for restorative practice. It is through how and what teachers teach that students develop the awareness and skills necessary when the need for intensive interventions comes along. The role of the school leader is to value, model, support, and spread such practices. Imagine the strength of a school culture if some of the more isolated practices described in these stories were instead schoolwide pedagogical approaches, reaching across grade levels and subject areas. The impact could be profound.

The three scenarios shared above take place in third, fifth, and seventh grade settings. Discussion-based classrooms where personal and political topics are handled with care are an essential universal support for restorative practice at all grade levels. But additional universal supports are required as students move out of elementary grades. In the younger grades, students typically have fewer teachers, fewer groupings of peers, fewer classroom spaces to inhabit. As the number of teachers and classroom groupings multiplies in middle and high school, it can be more difficult to universally establish and maintain a sense of belonging and to have consistent approaches across teachers to fostering empathic interactions and mutual understanding.

A structure called Advisory is one way that middle schools and high schools can create an additional universal support for restorative practice—and much else besides. Advisory goes by other names, such "Crew" at Expeditionary Learning schools, and it takes many different forms, but the broadly accepted essence of the structure is that it provides a space for academic and social-emotional support for a small group of students who, over time, form trusting relationships with each other and an adult, their advisor.

The corps of advisors at a school is made up of the school faculty and staff. Sometimes administrators participate as well. Sometimes every adult in the school is asked to have an Advisory. Many of the staffing considerations depend on the size of the Advisory groups that are being established. The smaller the groups, the more advisors the school will need. When it comes to the "content" of Advisory, many schools develop or adopt a curriculum to ground the work of Advisory, but this is very hard to implement effectively at various grade levels and across a diverse group of advisors. Advisory needs routines, norms of interaction and tasks, more than it needs curriculum content.

When done well, Advisory creates a sense of belonging among students and helps develop mutual understanding. Advisory groups can mix students in ways that they might not otherwise mix socially or in academic classes. This is an important community-building function. When the pedagogy relies largely on facilitation of circle process or small group discussion, students develop the social-emotional skills needed when the normal tensions and conflicts of school life arise.

Restorative justice interventions can draw heavily on the skills and relationships developed in Advisory, as shown in some of the stories about conflict resolution at the beginning of this chapter. In the story about the fight among senior girls, and the process of restitution, advisors played an important role in supporting students through the turmoil and toward healing.

Above all, Advisory helps students feel that they belong to a community. This is a community that they want to help heal if it is harmed. It is a place they want to return to if they are asked to step away, and it is a space where people can believe in them when they struggle to believe in themselves.

Building and sustaining Advisory is hard work, and school leaders must believe in it and invest in it if it is to be the foundation of restorative practice and community life that it can be. There are matters of resources to be considered, including those resources most crucial to school life, like the people involved and the time given. Several essential elements of a well-designed advisory program include the following:

- Adequate time and size for well-bonded groups
- Meaningful tasks
- Skillful facilitation of even mundane matters
- Curriculum "content" that is the life of the child and the life of the school
- Faculty who can support advisors in the work

Advisory: Well-bonded Groups

At full maturity, Advisory should meet four or five times each week, for twenty to thirty minutes each meeting. Longer class times may also be needed occasionally when the work demands it. This may not be possible in the early years of developing an Advisory program, but it will be possible as investment in the structure increases over time.

A corollary to adequate time is small enough size. Ten students is about right; smaller is fine; twelve is about the upper limit. A simple reflection on what happens in a given day can show us why. Imagine a group of students whose desks or chairs are in a circle. It is Monday morning, and each student needs time enough to speak during the connecting and community-building activity, which can be as simple as reflecting on their weekend or sharing thoughts on the week ahead. If ten students and the advisor are each to speak—for only one or two minutes—the Advisory session needs to be at least twenty minutes long. There will also be daily announcements and other business to discuss. A twenty-minute period may even seem rushed.

Over the course of the week, this group should come together multiple times so that the routines, the ups and downs of a typical week, and the announcements and tasks that relate to the life of the school can channel through Advisory. Four or five meetings each week is ideal, and an outline of the work for a typical week will be shared below.

It is not just the completion of tasks that adequate time in the week allows. Bonding happens when people spend time together having basic discussions and simple daily interactions. Relationships and routines develop, and these create trust and stability. Ideally the Advisory group that meets multiple times each week will remain together over the course of multiple years. Such a structure helps students and families with major transitions that take place from semester to semester, from year to year, and across developmental changes. Families also build strong relationships with advisors if the Advisory group is together over time and if the program has the right tasks assigned to it.

Advisory: Meaningful Tasks

No matter how much time Advisory is given in the weekly or annual schedule, it needs to be given meaningful tasks to accomplish. Advisory will be dismissed by skeptics if it isn't given responsibilities that include important practical tasks in addition to the work of relationship building.

Advisory programs that have more time than they can use for the tasks they've been given will struggle to feel purposeful. In other words, you never want to have too much unstructured time, because it leads to a feeling that the time is not needed. Some would argue that Advisory should be asked to do only what it can handle, and this makes sense, but it is better to always be asking Advisory to reach and do more. This is true in terms of what we ask of ourselves, our colleagues, and our students as well. We all have a zone of proximal development and should be reaching for goals and that are hard to attain, but for which we will strive.

An Advisory class that meets for fifteen minutes to start the school day, for instance, like a traditional homeroom, will be perfectly capable of being the place where announcements are shared, and student input is gathered on various matters. Meaningful relationships could develop over time, especially if the group remains with their advisor for multiple years. It would be ambitious, but an Advisory program of this scope could also be asked to take on the task of organizing and preparing for student/parent/teacher conferences, which are also called student-led conferences. Expeditionary Learning endorses the structure as it functions in their Advisory model, called Crew:

> A student-led conference is a meeting with a student and his or her family and teachers during which the student shares his or her portfolio of work and discusses progress with family members. The student facilitates the meeting from start to finish. Student-led conferences can be implemented at all grade levels, K–12. Preparation for a conference creates an authentic purpose for good

organizational and communication skills. The structure builds students' sense of responsibility and accountability for their own learning.[4]

Substantial preparation is needed to conduct student-led conferences (SLCs) well. Advisors will need professional development time, modeling, and support for implementation. There needs to be coordination between administrators, advisors, and classroom teachers. It's a heavy lift, which is why it is mentioned here. It is an important task.

If Advisory is tasked with SLCs, in addition to the professional development required, the advisor would need to engage students and families in the practical tasks related to scheduling and preparing for conferences. These meetings are about how things are going in classes: current work, past-due assignments, skills, habits and knowledge being developed, relationships, assessments, grades, etc. Advisory will seem quite important if asked to focus on this, for the tasks it must accomplish are high-stakes. The advisors who want to do a good job will begin to advocate for more resources to support Advisory. Instead of fifteen minutes a day, some advisors will want—and need—twenty minutes or more. School leaders can leverage such moments to implement changes to make Advisory programs more robust.

SLCs are an ambitious task. Other meaningful but less-demanding tasks that Advisory programs can be asked to take on over the course of a school year include:

- Supporting school counselors with the course selection process
- Nominating or electing students to representative positions in student government
- Planning elements of community meetings, grade-level meetings, assemblies, field days, annual celebrations, rites of passage, local events
- Nominating students or faculty for annual awards
- Reading a schoolwide or grade-level text
- Assigning students to academic interventions, tutoring, office hours, or other flexible interventions where students benefit from help connecting with their teachers
- Supporting student preparations for presentations of learning
- Hosting group discussions of important community topics
- Hosting individual discussions (advisor and student) of discipline reports
- Hosting individual discussions (advisor and student) of report cards or grades

Completing these tasks can reinforce the relationships of people in the group who are working together to get an important task completed. For instance, student-led conferences, mentioned earlier, are meetings at which students share evidence of their learning, progress, and challenges with families at certain times of year. To ask the advisor and Advisory group to support this work places the system at the heart of very important conversations about the core of schooling. The same is true when the Advisory system is asked to support students in preparation for presentations of learning, such as a portfolio defense at the end of the school year. Such tasks have authentic audiences and bring the work of Advisory out into the public view. In less high-stakes ways, asking Advisories to contribute to assemblies or school spirit events is also a way to motivate a group to collaborate and create bonds thereby.

Simple or complex, none of the above tasks will be particularly meaningful without some contextualization and well-facilitated discussion to probe for purpose and relevance. An awards nomination process, for instance, could be a silent, individual task done with an online survey, or it could include a meaningful discussion of what the awards are for, why these qualities are to be lauded, and what a community gains by giving awards to some people and not others. It is the work of finding meaning in all matters of school life through discussion that brings us to our next essential element of a well-functioning Advisory system.

Advisory: Skillful Facilitation of Mundane Matters

Experience of—and willingness to experience—well-facilitated small group discussions is an essential element of a strong Advisory program. Skillful facilitation of even mundane matters is essential.

Imagine Monday morning. Advisory is beginning. Some teachers are excited and comfortable with the task of asking the question. Others are not, because they know it is sometimes not easy with their group—and they don't always know how to handle it when students resist or avoid. The question is a very simple one. The students sit in a circle and the advisor says, "Okay, let's do our Monday morning check-in. Who would like to go first? How was your weekend?"

Educators experienced with students of varied dispositions and student groups of different personalities know that this question, as it is passed around the circle, can yield a huge variety of responses: long, rambling reflections from loquacious kids; curt, one-word responses from others; withdrawn silence; sincere confessions of what the weekend was like; superficial evasions of how things really are; silly or performative offerings by those who prefer to entertain; defensive stances by those who have something inside to protect; defiance or refusal to contribute for a variety of reasons, if only because youthful challenge to adult expectations is developmentally appropriate at times.

Even a simple prompt can yield complex challenges for the facilitator. A strong Advisory program depends on skillful facilitation of questions like these, and others. Sometimes the questions are about matters extraordinary, but often the questions are about matters mundane. Skillful facilitation of simple questions and quotidian topics is especially important when leading Advisory.

For instance, Advisory is sometimes asked to provide homework support and structured study time, and to help students keep track of assignments and other academic expectations over the course of the term. This can be useful in middle school and early high school grades, as many students' executive functioning skills need support and students are typically working with multiple teachers. It is also in these grades that many students are taking courses in common. Academic support can happen in the circle or other discussion formats, as well as in individual meetings. In the circle, with the group gathered together, conversations can happen about expectations in classes, deadlines for assignments students have in common, the grading and reporting calendar, and more.

And if we want Advisory to provide academic support and also sustain interpersonal skills and relationships, then mundane questions like "What deadlines do we have coming up in classes this week?" will also require tactful approaches. A neutral question about deadlines connects to sensitive subjects, like a student's academic standing in the class. It requires the ability to help students be supportive of each other across their differences of ability and self-concepts as students. The student who is struggling in eighth grade math class may not want to talk about math class. She may not be comfortable telling the group that she's not sure what is due this week because she feels so far behind. Or some other student who is struggling in math, when asked about the work that is due that week, may say something negative about the teacher as a way to avoid focusing on their standing in the class.

Skillful facilitation of quotidian conversations in a group does not come naturally to all teachers, especially if the discussion isn't focused on what they feel is their content-area expertise. School leaders will need to prioritize professional development on how to lead simple conversations. This means gathering faculty together for learning in circle process and small group discussion at faculty meetings. Facilitating small group discussions can seem simple, but it requires practice, for even seemingly neutral questions will reveal complexities about individuals and spark group dynamics that are sometimes not easy to manage.

Advisory: The Curriculum Is the Life of Child and School

At the intersection of meaningful tasks and mundane matters is the notion that the curriculum content of Advisory is largely the life of the kids and the life of the school. This includes the topics on the menu of meaningful tasks shared above and even more simple tasks and weekly routines.

If the pedagogy of Monday morning is to facilitate a circle that allows for personal connection after the weekend apart, then the "content" of the curriculum that day is the life, thoughts, and emotions of the children. The skills being developed include a number of transferable skills or habits, such as public speaking, empathic listening, questioning, and paraphrasing.

Likewise, if the focus of Tuesday's Advisory is academic support, the pedagogy may again be the facilitation of discussion, and the curriculum "content" is the academic life of the school: what's going on in each class; what deadlines are coming up; what are some strategies for studying for the quiz; what office hours or tutoring is available; which teachers do students need to visit or email for clarification; what online resources can be consulted for the information needed. There is no scripted curriculum or off-the-shelf social-emotional-learning lesson needed for this to be a useful and meaningful Advisory session for all students involved. The best curriculum content for Advisory is the life of the child and the school.

Building on the Monday and Tuesday sessions described above, here is a sample weekly routine that can be effective in many school settings where there are multiple Advisory meetings each week, with time in the schedule for twenty- to thirty-minute sessions:

- Day 1: Personal Check-In
  - Students are greeted and acknowledged and welcomed back to school.
  - Attendance is taken, and school announcements are shared and discussed. For instance, there's a new club being announced. The group discusses who has interests in this area, who wants to know more, who might want to email the leader of the club and ask for more information.
  - Then there's a circle process or other protocol that allows each student to share about their weekend, or about some other topic if the weekend is a fraught subject. A simple protocol to follow is the "rose-thorn-bud" series of prompts, asking students for a good thing that happened, a negative thing that happened, and something hopeful they are looking forward to. Depending on the protocol, after each student shares, questions can be asked as a way to show curiosity, empathy, and active listening.
- Day 2: Academic Check-In

- School announcements are shared and discussed. For instance, there's an athletic event after school. The group discusses who from the Advisory is on the team or planning to attend the event, what they're looking forward to.
- Then the advisor or a student facilitates a review of what's going on in classes this week, surfacing the various deadlines, resources, supports. A calendar can hang on the wall and be updated with relevant information. Communication with teachers can happen by email in real time or noted for later. Even though much of the information probably exists in online grade books or school information systems, talking about it and writing it down on a common calendar can help many students in their organizational thinking. The students leave Advisory with a good sense of what is expected of them that week.
- Day 3: Circle Process
  - As on Monday and Tuesday, school announcements are shared and discussed. For instance, there may be a change relevant to the cafeteria functioning or library hours that students need to be sure to understand.
  - Then the advisor or a student facilitates a circle on a topic of interest to the individual, a current event, a getting-to-know-you topic, or a school-related concern. The book *Circle Forward* and other online resources offer a wide menu of topics to choose from. Keeping in mind that the curriculum content is the life of the children, and the school should allow topics to readily present themselves.
- Day 4: Various Possibilities
  - School announcements are shared and discussed. For instance, there's a change to school transportation that students need to understand, or an arts event that evening that some students in the Advisory are in and could promote to their peers.
  - It is good to have flexible time in the week that can be used for other meaningful tasks that may come up at school, or to have a celebratory event or day dedicated to fun. Sharing food and playing games can be good ways to build positive group dynamics. Meeting with other Advisories for such activities is also a good way to build bonds within the group and the wider community.

Advisory: Faculty Who Can Support It

On any given week, in any given Advisory, the adult in charge may need support to maintain a healthy group dynamic or to navigate tensions that may arise. Part of the purpose of Advisory is to build and maintain relationships, so interpersonal conflict must be tended to. In the role of advisor, a teacher doesn't have the same toolkit of incentives for managing behavior as the teacher does in the content-specific classroom. A social studies teacher, in his social studies classroom, has content about which he feels passionate, and his passion about the topic can help engage students in the work. He also has the incentive system of grades always in the background to inform student motivation. If the student disengages from social studies or disrupts class and has to leave, their knowledgeability of the subject matter, proficiency in skills, and their grades can suffer as a result. This same system isn't at work in Advisory.

In Advisory, it's not the grades but the relationships that are the point. The curriculum is the students and the school. If something isn't working well, if people aren't forming a healthy group, or if there is conflict, the adult must mobilize a very different set of incentives for engagement. The group can't be motivated to maintain a respectful atmosphere because the social studies test is next week and it carries a lot of weight. Rather, the group is maintaining healthy relationships because healthy relationships are important.

One argument for keeping an Advisory group together over several years is that it increases everyone's incentive to invest in keeping relationships healthy. If people aren't moved to a new Advisory at the end of the term, it is in their interest to work on building strong bonds and repairing the group dynamic whenever necessary. This isn't always easy. It's usually hard.

Sometimes advisors and the Advisory group need support from people outside the group in developing and maintaining healthy relationships. For this and other reasons, an Advisory system needs a team of capable folks who do not have Advisory who can offer strategy, mentorship, and restorative interventions as needed.

The group of faculty that supports Advisory should have experience in facilitation of small group discussions about topics heavy and light. This group could include administrators, counselors, and veteran teachers who don't have a dedicated Advisory group but have roles as advisory coordinator or some other leadership role during the Advisory period.

If an advisor needs someone else present in the room for a weighty discussion, a person from this group can be sent in. If there is a crisis in the community and Advisory is a place where concerns will be discussed and information shared, this group of support people can disburse throughout the school to groups that need them. These people can also lead professional learning and professional development for advisors, including orientation for new faculty who join the school each year.

As mentioned earlier, one hour a month of meeting time is a good minimum allocation of time if a particular role, structure, or initiative is a priority. For Advisory to function well, it should be a priority to allocate meeting time for people to gather together in their role as advisors. That said, if there is other work that the adults of the school are doing through meetings in small groups where there are discussions of personal and professional topics through simple but careful protocols, then this is also *de facto* training for Advisory.

A school leader should be a visible and active participant in supporting Advisory and modeling the facilitation of small group discussion. When there is conflict, in Advisory and in other domains of school life, the school leader should be visible and involved, modeling restorative practice and leading intensive interventions.

PRACTICALITIES, CONTINUED: INTENSIVE RESTORATIVE JUSTICE INTERVENTIONS

One of the ways school leaders learn how to do intensive restorative justice interventions is by designing and facilitating them. We also learn when other people take the lead, when we are part of a circle or other process that other people are facilitating. We learn from the modeling of others, as well as from the successes we achieve ourselves and the mistakes made along the way.

By intensive interventions, we are referring to how the school responds to specific incidents of harm between individuals or groups. It is intensive because it requires time in planning and implementation. Intensive interventions are necessarily grounded in the specific needs of particular people, and so they are always unique in some way. Even if the approach is familiar, we can never feel fully confident that it's going to work in a second situation. Traditional discipline isn't like this, on the surface. Legislating a mandatory consequence is not imbued with the same ambiguity. When you suspend a student from school and the child and family understand the expectations, you can be confident that you'll get the basic outcome you anticipate in the short term. The student will not be in school the next day. Anticipating the outcomes of a restorative justice intervention comes with much less certainty.

Uncertainty, and the trepidation that comes with it, will often be felt during an intensive intervention. This is appropriate, because the stakes are high. We have already described some interventions in response to violence and aggression between students. Restorative interventions can also be appropriate for incidents of racist speech, sexual harassment, and homophobia.

In practice, some of these interventions can be designed rather quickly. Once the needs of those involved are understood, sometimes choosing a script from a book like *Circle Forward* is all that's needed to get started. Other processes can be more complex and can take weeks or longer to plan and execute.

It's Worth the Time

What's true no matter the scale of the intensive intervention is that they become easier to implement the more the culture of the school reflects restorative practice, sustained by universal supports like Advisory and discussion-based classrooms, which help create a sense of belonging and mutual understanding.

A school with an effective Advisory system is a school where students are practicing empathic listening routinely. They have habits of sitting in a circle and considering the voices of others. A well-functioning Advisory system also means that there are other adults who can execute intensive interventions when needed. The same is true when discussion is a dominant pedagogy in classrooms. All of these people—teachers and students—become resources for each other when the need arises for intensive interventions.

In every community, as has been said, the people in the place possess the knowledge and skills needed to repair harm that occurs in the place. By people we include those who do harm, and by community we mean a place where people have a sense of belonging and mutual understanding—and are continually striving for such. The school leader is responsible for modeling the habits and skills needed for this kind of reparative problem-solving, and for creating the conditions so that others can develop those same skills and habits.

Restorative practice is worth the time. It is time-intensive and requires slowing the typical pace of work in schools, but the more that respectful dialogue and empathic listening are infused in standard classroom functioning, the more efficient and effective will be intensive interventions when need for them arises.

Grounding the work in the universal practices in the classroom also insulates the circle and other intensive listening processes from the stigma of being associated solely with punishment or the consequences for problematic behavior. This is an insight shared by Nancy Riestenberg, an expert in restorative practice in schools; she writes:

> If the Circle is used only to repair harm, then this simple yet profound communication process becomes associated with frustration, anger, and shame....
>
> For restorative measures to be really effective, they cannot be just another process to use when students get into trouble. Rather, they must become a regular part of the classroom experience and integrated into school policy and practice.[5]

If universal supports for restorative practice are in place, intensive interventions come to feel like less of an exceptional event. They feel more like an extension of the day-to-day efforts to listen to each other and respond to each other's needs.

Intensive Interventions: Some Key Ingredients

It is important that people be willing participants in a restorative intervention. Restorative practice, in general, operates on this principle. For instance, in a circle people are invited, not required, to share their thoughts, and people should be invited—not required—to share appreciations and apologies at a faculty meeting.

Nevertheless, positional power can be used to assert that restorative practice is the way we do things in this place. The school leader can convey this by taking the lead in the creative process of conducting these interventions. In so doing, leaders should keep in mind several ingredients needed for an effective intervention:

- Common understanding of what happened: There needs to be a truth that all see and acknowledge. If two parties strongly disagree about whether something happened or not, they will not be able to talk about it. It can be important for the school leader to conduct an adequate investigation first, and to ensure that there is common understanding of basic elements of what happened, even if there are differing interpretations of impact.
- Care for those who have been harmed: The needs of those who have been harmed must be at the center of a restorative process. But those who have experienced harm may not be willing to participate in a process that involves revisiting the incident, or revisiting it in the company of the person who did the harm. This must always be respected. And even when a young person who has been harmed is willing to come to the table, there are cases where it will not be advisable. That said, there are ways to arrange a restorative process involving the perpetrator of harm that help them see their impact, even if the victim of the harm isn't present.
- Support for those who harm: Some students and families will resist the restorative process as a means of reckoning with the harm a student has done. The public accounting feels too risky, too potentially shame-laden. Support for these people can be built into the process so that they are more ready to be involved. Adults and students whom the person trusts can be asked to join an intervention as an ally. Their role is not one of legalistic defense. The investigation is done, and the facts of what happened are clear. Their role can be to speak to the person's strengths, propose solutions in which the person can participate, and perhaps help them execute what commitments result from the intervention. In addition

to offering support to people participating in a restorative process, a school leader can also offer incentives. In the same way that court diversion processes in the criminal justice system can offer restorative justice and community service as an alternative to a traditional punishment, a school leader can offer restorative justice interventions as an alternative to suspensions or as a way to shorten the duration of a suspension. If a student has been in a fight, and punched another student in the face, it may be appropriate for them not to be walking the halls again the next day—thus a suspension for reasons of safety and deescalation, and to communicate no-tolerance for violence in the community. But the term of a suspension could be reduced if the student successfully participates in a rigorous restorative justice intervention. Some might perceive this as escaping punishment, but this is rarely the perception of the student involved. For most students, a restorative process is not easier than a suspension in terms of emotional accountability.

- Gestures of repair: The restorative process will result in outcomes or agreements or commitments. Sometimes those commitments can be substantial and require a great deal of those implicated. But the commitments needn't always require extraordinary effort if those involved agree it is adequate to achieve a degree of closure or repair. Furthermore, the work of repair can be shared by all of those involved in determining the commitments or gestures of repair. For some people, the import of the gesture is that it communicates an outward acknowledgment of the deeper work that has already been done to hold a person accountable. Sometimes it can be as simple as an apology. Whatever the gestures of repair, there should be a sense of accountability, not shame. There should be sincerity. It should authentically correspond to a need that resulted from the harm. And, while it is part of an unfinished journey of living together as a community, it should also bring some sense of closure.
- Respect—not reverence—for confidentiality: There is an important tension when it comes to confidentiality. On the one hand, it is important to respect people's privacy and the confidentiality of a student's school record. On the other hand, we mustn't let concerns about confidentiality create undue barriers to the collective problem-solving that is restorative justice. Some school faculty and parents might firmly argue that we're not supposed to engage students in conversations about other students' behavior. In some cases, this is true. But if confidentiality has a greater priority than community-building, restorative practice of any significance will be hard to do. In crafting an intervention, it is important to respect confidentiality of certain personal information and certain identity factors. It is also important that the people involved in the intervention respect the privacy of the conversation, and not share details about

what happened, unless there is an agreement to do so. This is true for more routine circle processes, too, as some of the books referenced in this chapter can explain. But while much that happens in a restorative process can remain confidential, we mustn't let excessive concerns about sharing information get in the way of work that draws from the strength and wisdom of a group of people living in community.

Personal Stories, Historical Facts

School is an ideal place for restorative practice to thrive because schools are swimming in personal stories and historical facts. As discussed in our chapter on racial justice reforms, personal stories and historical facts build our understanding of what is true—and such truths guide us toward what is right, holding us accountable for getting there. But what if someone doesn't want to tell their story, or might be further harmed in the telling? Howard Zehr reminds us that we are working within the constraints of what is "possible" in particular circumstances:

> Restorative justice is a process to involve, to the extent possible, those who have a stake in a specific offense and to collectively identify and address harms, needs and obligations, in order to heal and put things as right as possible.[6]

In putting things as right as possible, it is sometimes not possible, appropriate, or necessary for an individual harmed in a situation to be in contact with the person who hurt them. That doesn't mean that their stories and truths must be absent from the process of addressing the wrong.

There are many ways that restorative interventions can be designed to ensure personal stories are exchanged in such a way that the impact of the harm is understood, and the potential gestures of repair are designed to match the needs and obligations of the people involved.

There are ways, also, that historical context can be given such that a person comes to see the harm they've done has a lineage, an etymology, a historical record—all of which gives contemporary weight and meaning to the repair that is underway. Surrogate storytellers, as well as literature, film, and the published personal essays of young people, can augment the resources for an intervention and be very helpful in showing students how their actions reside in a broader interpersonal and historical context.

Surrogate Storytellers: When the Victim Doesn't Want to Be Involved

On his way to lunch, Carter walked down the eighth grade hallway and—again—touched Caroline's leg in a way she didn't like. She'd told him last week not to touch her in that way. She'd told him the same thing back in seventh grade. He wasn't respecting her boundaries.

At lunch, Caroline told her math teacher what happened and that she wasn't going to math class if Carter was going to be there. The teacher told the principal, who conducted an investigation after lunch, interviewing Caroline, Carter, and two others who were present when it happened. The principal interviewed the students at different times, in such a way that Caroline didn't have to be in the same classroom with Carter for the rest of the afternoon. Caroline also spent some time with the middle school counselor discussing further how it made her feel and what she needed.

After school, the principal and counselor talked. It was a clear instance of harassment, and it was clear that it felt like a significant violation to Caroline. It was also clear that Carter thought it was no big deal. They'd known each other for years, he said, and he was sure that they'd be friends again next week. But the counselor and principal felt Carter needed to better understand the harm such gestures and attitudes can cause. The principal asked the counselor if she thought Caroline would be interested in telling Carter directly about how she was feeling. The counselor had already explored this with Caroline, and the answer was no.

The principal and counselor met with Carter the next day and informed him that he was to serve an in-school suspension for the day, in part to give Caroline distance from him as she attended classes and walked the halls, and in part to give Carter time to meet with the counselor to prepare for an intervention they were going to have about respecting physical boundaries. The intervention was to be a conversation facilitated by the counselor, and it would include another adult whom Carter identified as a support. He identified his PE teacher. There would also be another student there, Serena.

Serena was an older student, enrolled in a Career and Technical Education (CTE) program on campus that Carter had plans to join when he was older. Serena was two years older than Carter and willing to tell him how it had made her feel when physical boundaries were not respected. She was more than willing to tell him why it was not okay to cross such boundaries.

When the meeting took place, Serena told her own story in a way that affirmed her voice and power, and, at the same time, allowed her to serve as a surrogate storyteller, a voice that could stand in to represent aspects of Caroline's experience. One outcome of this process was a commitment from Carter not to touch Caroline in any way at all in the future. It had been suggested by Serena that Carter apologize to Caroline, but the counselor said she'd need to talk to Caroline first, to see if that was a conversation Caroline wanted to have. Another outcome was an agreement that if such an incident were to occur again, Carter would need to meet with the director of the CTE program to discuss it, and that his entry into such programs might be in jeopardy. A final outcome of the meeting was a commitment from the PE teacher to check in with Carter each Wednesday before class to ask him how he was doing in adhering to the agreements decided at the meeting.

Caroline was informed of the outcomes of the meeting and was satisfied that Carter had understood and been held accountable for the kind of harm he had done. She told the counselor that she'd think about whether she wanted to hear an apology from him.

Surrogate storytellers, like Serena in this story, can be useful in helping those who perpetrate harm understand the impact of what they have done. There are other means to do this as well, strategies for putting harm in context so the person who harmed can understand the broader context and impact of their actions.

Harm in Context: Personal Stories

Youth Communication is an organization that publishes the stories and personal essays of young people. Their published compilations of youth writing, as well as their online blogs and magazines, comprise an extensive catalog. The books are worth acquiring in every school library, and the online resources are just a few clicks away. These youth voices can be useful in restorative interventions, as the following anecdote about a ninth grade boy will convey.

Coach Thomas reported to the athletic director that he'd heard one of his players on the soccer field use a homophobic slur in the locker room after a game. It wasn't said in reference to anyone on the team; rather it was in reference to the opposing team's goalkeeper.

The athletic director reported this to the principal that afternoon, and they met to discuss it the next day. They discussed various ways to respond, including group interventions with students who may have been present when the comment was made in the locker room, some of whom may have validated the use of the word, others of whom may have been impacted by it in a more harmful way. The principal ultimately decided that while a group intervention was possible, it was a better idea to intervene quickly with the individual who made the comment, a ninth grade boy named David.

The principal's goal was for David to understand the harm he did in using the word, even though the insult was directed toward someone who wasn't in the locker room, and was not even a student at the school. The students in the locker room may have had needs to be addressed, but in focusing on David's learning, rather than interview the many other students who were present to try to gauge the impact of the comment on each person in the room, the principal had a different strategy for integrating youth perspectives he thought David needed to hear. To help bring youth voice into the intervention, the principal searched the Youth Communication websites and found an essay written by a youth writer named Ash who identified as gay. In his essay, Ash recounted his struggle to accept and understand that aspect of his identity in middle school.

The principal and athletic director met with David and informed him of the reading and reflection he would be doing because of his use of a word that put down others based on their sexual identity. The boy would spend the first hour of the next practice in the athletic director's office doing the reading and reflection, which included these prompts:

- How did Ash feel while in middle school? What feelings does Ash name in the essay?
- Ash didn't stick up for his (straight) friend when he heard the friend being called "gay" or "fa-got." Why not?
- What made Ash's middle school years "some of the unhappiest" of his life so far?
- Did any of Ash's story connect to the statement you made or the language you used? Why or why not?
- Why does our school not want people to use the word you used, or use the words "gay" or "queer" in a negative way?
- Is there any repair or amends you might consider making based on what you said?
- Thank you for doing this reflection. It is not always easy to reflect and write about these topics. What other thoughts do you want to share on this topic or your actions?

David's responses revealed that he understood that people who heard the words he was using could feel the word was hurtful, even if they didn't show it. When it came to the final two questions, the boy said he didn't have any ideas about what gestures of repair might be appropriate.

When the athletic director and principal discussed David's reflection afterward, they were satisfied with aspects of the reflection, but they were unsure, like David, about whether any public gesture of repair or accounting was needed. They decided to get someone else's opinion, someone who was also implicated in what happened in the locker room. The next step was for the athletic director to talk with the coach of the team, share some of David's reflection, and ask him if he had any thoughts on what gestures of repair might be appropriate in this case, or if there were other actions that might bring appropriate closure to the intervention. The Athletic Director would also prompt the coach, if he'd not already done so, to remind the team of all norms for a respectful locker room, including that language that puts down a person's identity is not tolerated.

In this anecdote, the administrators decided to not interview the various members of the soccer team present in the locker room when David made his comment. But they still asserted that harm to others was inherent in the comment David made. They used a personal story written by another high school student to prompt David's reflection on this. There is always an interpersonal, relational context for the words we speak and for our actions. There is always historical context as well, as the next anecdote will explore.

Harm in Context: Historical Facts

A middle school teacher was on lunch duty in the cafeteria and overheard three boys using the word "retarded" as a teasing insult to each other. They were friends, often poking fun at each other in some way or another.

"I told you last week that I didn't want to hear you using that word," said the teacher.

The boys said they were sorry and wouldn't do it again. They were smiling and they continued to tease each other in other ways, about the food one was eating, about one of the boy's sneakers. The teacher didn't feel they were taking her concerns seriously. She didn't want to let it go and told them so.

"Wait, we're getting in trouble for this?" one of them asked. The teacher said they were and walked away. She had to teach immediately after lunch, so she sent a quick email to the principal including her conviction that "something needs to happen."

The principal met with the boys that afternoon, first as a group. The boys again apologized and said they just used the word as a substitute for "stupid" or "weird" and that they weren't trying to offend anybody. The principal wanted to go deeper with the boys, to help them understand that disrespecting people with disabilities is tied to a history of harm.

When they were together as a group, the boys were used to minimizing the importance of such matters, so the principal decided she'd ask the boys to engage in individual reflection and discussion, rather than continue their group conversation.

The principal informed the boys and their families that they'd probably be pulled from a class at least once over the next few days to do some reading and reflection on the word they'd been using to tease each other. The principal also asked their social studies teacher if she'd mind that the boys were asked to do this reflection during her class, and the principal told her that she'd be asking the boys to understand some of the historical context of their choice of words.

The social studies teacher said this was fine. The principal told her what she had in mind, which included a reading. She asked the teacher if she thought each of the boys could do the short reading independently. The teacher said one of them would need to read it with adult support to truly comprehend the text. The principal thanked her for the guidance and told her she'd share the boys' reflections afterward.

The prompt for the reflection was a short article about the eugenics movement in the United States and how people with intellectual disabilities were targeted for sterilization. This was paired with a short video from the *New York Times* called "The Nazi's First Victims Were the Disabled." The prompts for reflection—and the discussion that the principal had with the boys afterward—had several priorities: educating the boys about the painful historical context for negative attitudes about people with intellectual disabilities; enabling empathy for those who might feel insulted by the word; not shaming the boys; asking them to be accountable and commit to not using the word in the future. The prompts were:

- Read the article. Underline or highlight three passages or sentences that you think are important.
- Historical reflection: What are three things you learned about how people with disabilities were treated in the United States in the 1920s and 1930s?
- Historical reflection: After watching the video, what are three things you learned about how people with disabilities were treated in Germany in the 1920s and 1930s?
- Personal reflection: Have you ever been put down or talked about negatively by others? When has this happened, and how did you feel about it? How do you feel about it now?
- Personal reflection: When have you heard or used words that have negative meanings toward people with disabilities?
- Commitment: We have learned that discrimination against people with disabilities has a terrible history, including programs in our country to prevent them from having children, and worse, like in Germany, where people with disabilities were murdered in concentration camps. This history is one reason why schools take it so seriously when people with disabilities are put down. Another reason is that it could make someone in our school feel badly about themselves. This can make it hard for them to access their education, which is their right to have. In your own words, why is it important to respect people of all abilities, including people with disabilities?

In addition to meeting with the boys, first as a group and then individually, it had taken two hours of the principal's time to organize this intervention: to find the resources, talk with the social studies teacher, talk with the families, connect with a school counselor to ask her to read the text with one of the boys, to draft the prompts, print them on paper, and copy them. The principal thought the process was worthwhile, but it took a lot of time.

Given the time required, the principal decided to keep copies of the article and reflection prompts on file so that they'd be at the ready if this sort of thing happened again in future semesters, which, unfortunately, it probably would. And if it happened again, she'd probably involve some other adults in the work of meeting with the students, supporting their reading of the texts, and writing their short reflections. This was a school of several hundred students, so there were several other adults, who were not teachers busy in classrooms, who had skills in supporting behavioral interventions. The principal would delegate some of this work to them next time.

Harm in Context: Historical Facts—A Second Scenario

We can imagine many examples of how educators can put contemporary harm in historical context to help a student better understand the full weight of their words and attitudes. This can help repair harm that has happened, expand a student's capacity for empathy and self-control, and help prevent future harm from occurring.

Gerry was only a sixth grader, but he considered himself a "history buff." He especially liked to watch the History Channel documentaries about World War II with his uncle, who was a veteran of the first Iraq War. In fourth and fifth grade, when there were opportunities for student choice in reading books or research projects, Gerry would always focus on World War II.

Now in sixth grade, Gerry was at the middle school in a new building where the teachers were still getting to know him. The science teacher was taken off guard one morning during a lesson on renewable energy. She had just told the class they were going to study how Germany's efforts to reduce its use of nuclear power led to an increased use of wind power and coal. Gerry, who sat toward the front of the room, turned to his table partner and said, with an effort at a German accent, "Germany, yah. Heil Hitler." The teacher and Gerry's table partner heard it. She walked over to the table and asked him, "What did you say?"

"Nothing," said Gerry, who then got silent and didn't want to talk any more. The teacher said that it wasn't okay to make comments like that, and that she'd talk to him later about it. After class she spoke with Gerry.

"It just came out," Gerry said. "I watch a lot of videos about World War II, and the Nazis, and all that. It came into my mind and I said it." The teacher said again how it wasn't appropriate. Gerry said he was trying to be funny. The teacher asked him if he understood that it wasn't funny. He said he did. The teacher still felt that she needed to let others know, so she told the counselor, who told the principal.

The counselor and principal met with Gerry, who has nearly-white blond hair and radiant blue eyes. It was still early in the year, and neither of them knew him well yet. Their questions revealed that he spent a good deal of time with his uncle, that he felt he knew a lot about World War II, and that he was very concerned about whether the school would be telling his father about what happened.

He said his father reacted very severely if he ever got in trouble at school. When asked about the specific comment about Hitler, Gerry again said, "It just came out. I wasn't trying to offend anyone." The principal and counselor tended to believe Gerry about the impulsivity of comment, but they wanted to learn more about Gerry's understanding of Nazism and the beliefs he might have been exposed to in the home.

The principal told Gerry that she was undecided about calling home, that she might decide to give him the opportunity to tell his family about what happened first. She could see how afraid he was that his father would find out he'd "gotten in trouble at school." She didn't think there was any risk Gerry would say the words again in the coming days, and she felt calling home could wait at least another day, until she had more discussion with Gerry about what he'd said. She didn't want his fear of punishment to shut down their dialogue.

"I don't need to call home about this right now," she said. "But your job is to come into school tomorrow and come see me when I ask for you so we can continue our conversation, okay?" Gerry seemed relieved and readily agreed.

The principal decided to use science class time the following day to continue the conversation with Gerry. This would show Gerry's table partner, and others who might be aware of what happened, that an intervention was underway, even if they didn't know the details. Also that day the counselor would find time to check in with Gerry's table partner, and two others whom the teacher identified as close by, to learn how Gerry's statement might have impacted them.

After meeting again with Gerry and further probing his understanding of the Second World War, the principal and counselor decided it would be good to use Gerry's interest in history as a way to continue the dialogue with him about what he'd said in class.

After searching online resources from organizations she trusted, the principal found a short film about the war by the organization *Facing History and Ourselves*, which supports teachers in designing curriculum that centers on ethical questions throughout history and the implications of such lessons for society today.

The film was called *Confessions of a Hitler Youth*. Gerry and the principal and only watched the first half, because the second half contained graphic images of dead bodies that she didn't want to expose Gerry to without first informing the family, and they'd decided to wait on that part of the intervention.

The first part of the film focused on the interpersonal consequences of Nazi efforts to divide the people of a small town community by removing and resettling Jewish residents into camps. It is based on the recollections of a man named Alfons, who would become a member of the Hitler Youth organization and was a resident of the town at the time. Alfons recalled, as a child, seeing people he considered family friends and neighbors being forced to leave their homes.

The principal stopped the film along the way to clarify vocabulary and the events that were transpiring. Gerry had information to add based on all that he knew about the time. But he wasn't an expert, and he'd never seen a film before that featured the recollections of a boy who would have joined Hitler Youth at about Gerry's age.

The film shows how Alfons later came to see the terrible way that Nazism destroyed communities and ruined so many lives. After watching the film, the principal gave Gerry some prompts for written reflection:

- Opening reflection: Have you, or has someone you know, ever talked about one race of people being higher or better than another race? If yes, you don't need to give names, but please describe what you have heard.
- Teaching false "racial science": Alfons recalls being in school and what he was taught about different races in his "racial science" classes. What was he being taught about the race he belonged to? What was he being taught to believe about Jewish people?
- *Kristallnacht*: Alfons remembers what happened in his village on a night called "Kristallnacht." What happened in his village?
- Watching his neighbors being taken away: Alfons says that he watched his neighbors being taken away from his village. He tells us that his first childhood friend was a Jewish boy. He says he felt badly for them, but he also believed they needed to go. Why did he believe that his old friend and neighbors had to be taken away to concentration camps?
- "Master race": Alfons was taught to believe that he belonged to "the master race" and that this race was entitled to rule the world. These are beliefs that lead to conflict—and violence. How can such beliefs lead to conflict—in families, neighborhoods, schools, and towns?

- What is harassment? You are doing this reflection in part because of something you said. As we have discussed, what you said could be considered harassment based on race and religion. Do you understand why this is the case?
- Closing reflection: Thank you for taking the video and reflection seriously. What other thoughts do you want to share on this topic or your actions? Please write a couple of sentences at least.

Gerry and the principal discussed what Gerry had written. His responses included a statement about why it is not okay to say what he said, given the harm that Hitler had done. Gerry understood the Holocaust was a terrible thing. But he also shared over the course of their conversation that his uncle thought that "it was a long time ago" and people just needed to "get over it."

The principal made it clear to Gerry that the Holocaust wasn't something people could or should forget about. Gerry said that he understood. That afternoon the principal checked in with the counselor, who had spoken to other students and to the teacher. They discussed what their next steps should be.

The counselor shared that the science teacher thought that an apology to the class would be a good gesture of acknowledgment of responsibility. The guidance counselor said she could work with Gerry on writing or speaking it, and be there to support him if needed. The principal wasn't sure if this was the best plan. If only one or two people had heard the comment, would making an apology to the entire class potentially create further worry and harm in the community? Perhaps an apology just to the people who had heard the comment would be better. She wasn't sure.

The principal and counselor decided to meet with the teacher together to make the decision. And once the apology was made, the principal would tell Gerry she was going to call home and both report what had happened and share how Gerry had done a good job in accepting the consequences and following through.

Neither the school counselor nor the principal was sure what to do with the fact that the significance of the Holocaust was being minimized by adults in Gerry's family. They wondered about the content of the films and ideas he was being exposed to in the company of the uncle and others. This was cause for concern, but they were heartened that they had several more years to work with him and his family before he moved on to high school.

FIFTEEN CONCRETE ACTIONS
EVERY LEADER CAN TAKE

Whether it is an intensive intervention that happens in the principal's office, or a universal support that takes place in day-to-day classrooms, restorative practice can connect the work of healing in the present to harm that has interpersonal implications and historical roots. It can connect the story of the self with the stories of others, past and present. Schools can help right wrongs between people in the community, and schools can address wrongs that happened long ago and continue to impact lives today.

This work is possible when the needs of people are understood in a community in which they feel belonging. It is possible when school leaders believe that they and the people they work with have the knowledge and skills needed to create the community they desire. This is a good and empowering belief to hold. It means that if you are a leader who wants to deepen restorative practice in your school, you already have the resources you need to do it.

As noted above, deepening restorative practice doesn't involve jettisoning all traditional consequences and disciplinary interventions. It certainly can't take the place of investigations and processes required by policy, such as in incidents of harassment and bullying. But traditional consequences and restorative measures can be creatively intertwined.

We should also keep in mind that deepening restorative practice means that intensive interventions, which involve specific individuals repairing harm, are only one area of school life where the work must live. Cultivating universal supports for restorative practice is the foundational work, and it concerns how we learn and interact together every day. These universal supports and habits happen in classrooms, meetings, and other venues.

In the following list of concrete actions school leaders can take, readers will note some similarities between this chapter and the earlier two. Restorative practice, democratic practice, and anti-racist school reforms intersect in a multitude of ways.

- *Speak—in your words—about your place*: If your school doesn't have something written down describing what restorative practice looks like, write it. Consult resources and use the words of others as reference, if needed. But use your own language, too. Share your description of restorative practice as a draft with your leadership team, or publish it more widely as information to share, or for feedback. Use strongly stated values and concepts that motivate and unite people, like justice, democracy, accountability, trust, and fairness. Link restorative practice to the stated values of your school and school district. If your district mission is very broad, like, "all children can learn," use that language to explain why restorative practice is important. Describe practices that already exist in your school. If you are describing something you hope to put in place, that's useful, too, for it can set goals and be prophetic. Speaking it can help make it so. Envisioning it is a step toward making it be.

- *Make the circle*: Dispel the idea that sitting in a circle and talking about feelings is just for little kids. It's not an early childhood modality only. We are never too old for a circle to be the shape of how we interact with each other, including in the meetings you run. As discussed in our chapter on democratic practice, the school leader has a lot of power over the form and content of meetings. Do you gather in a room that's a bit crowded such that not everyone can see everyone else's faces? Change that. Don't have some people looking at the back of other people's heads. Use meetings as on-the-job training opportunities for faculty in how to use circle process and discussion protocols. Even large meetings involving scores of people, which will need to break out into smaller groups, you can start or end in a circle where everyone sees every other person. You can do this standing, if needed, in the library, or gym or outside. You won't have time to invite everyone's voice in a huge gathering, but you can see everyone and affirm everyone's belonging. If meeting in these modalities is new to the faculty, or new to you, be transparent about why you are doing it. The reason can be quite simple: We are a community that works best when we work together, and so it's important to see everyone's face and hear everyone's voice. Be open to feedback—some will say it takes too much time, for instance, to hear everyone's voice—but also be persistent. Remember the five-year rule. It can take a long time to develop new habits of interaction in a faculty community.
- *Invite appreciations and apologies*: Begin or end meetings with opportunities for people to affirm the web of human connection that structures community life. Asking people for appreciations or apologies is one ritual that can affirm a sense of community and belonging. If people are reluctant to speak, model the practice and the vulnerability and strength by doing it yourself and soliciting the contributions of others who can manage the same. Give it time and be persistent. Model it outside of meetings as well, in casual conversation, in email to individuals or groups. Eventually it will take hold as a norm and valued practice.
- *Allow for connections in the agenda*: Before beginning the task-oriented portion of any meeting, offer a moment for connecting with others. Simple prompts like "How are you doing today?" will work. Other prompts that are less personal are also useful, like "Are you a cat person or a dog person or none of the above—and why?" Silliness and playfulness can be good ice-breakers, connecting people to each other as

people. Allow people to pass, but come back at the end to check in to see if they'd now like to share. Don't forget about the person who passed. If you forget about them, they may feel they don't matter. Model what people need to see modeled, which sometimes is energy and optimism; sometimes is vulnerability or solemnity; sometimes is task-focused and other times is contemplative.
- *Slow down*: In the meetings you facilitate, if the agenda seems full and you have a sense you will not adequately have time for all items, take items off the agenda. Just as important, do the same with your annual professional learning plan and in-service agendas. Less is more. Pace matters. In addition to making space in the agenda for connections, and appreciations and apologies, make space for actual discussion of the topics on the agenda. Actual discussion means many voices are heard, protocols are used, facilitators are being intentional, norms and agreements are in place to ensure equity of voice. Give people time to collect and share their thoughts. Offer moments of mindfulness practice, such as inviting people to be quiet and breathe. Even a few minutes of such practice can be effective for the quality of the meeting, and it shows the value you place on slowing down and a degree of self-care and self-awareness.
- *Normalize norms, agreements, protocols*: Veteran educators, teachers who are career changers, and many other people in schools may not have the habit of running meetings or classroom discussions according to norms or agreements. If they've been involved in formal governance bodies, they may know Robert's Rules of Order, a procedure for deliberation, voting, and adopting resolutions. But they may not be comfortable with silence, with deeply listening, with the careful and empathic navigation of topics with personal and interpersonal importance. Norms, agreements, and protocols for discussion may not be familiar to many in your faculty and should be employed by the school leader in meetings, to model and spread the practice. The School Reform Initiative is a good place to go for discussion protocols. Many people also look to *Courageous Conversations About Race: A Field Guide for Achieving Equity in Schools* by Glenn Singleton as a resource for developing discussion agreements. Again, if there are teachers in your school already employing such practices, draw from their work first and amplify it in the meetings you lead and in the practices you ask or invite others to adopt.
- *Praise the pedagogy*: Which teachers are already comfortable arranging students in face-to-face conversations? If it's working well, take a picture or record a short video of such discussions and share it in some way. Who in the school is already facilitating discussions that allow students to build mutual understanding and foster a sense of trust, bonds,

and connection? Ask this teacher to facilitate a portion of a meeting with you. As we have noted in earlier chapters, in your school there are teachers already doing elements of what you envision becoming more common. There are teachers in your school who use some version of norms, agreements, or protocols for discussion that ensure students listen empathically to each other. Praise these teachers' work in tactful ways, and share it. Especially find ways to share this kind of practice with new teachers you hire. This kind of pedagogy is a universal support for restorative practice that is essential to expand across the school.

- *Teach or co-teach a class*: One way to broaden your school's commitment to restorative practice is for you, the school leader, to teach a unit of study or a class on it. This will show your own commitment to expanding the work, and it can provide venues for actually doing it. Teaching a class has a special accountability inherent. There is a group of children waiting for you, depending on you, face-to-face. You will dedicate time to it, and the class period itself will give you time in the day to do some of the actions in this list. You can use the time in class, in collaboration with students, to generate statements for the community about what restorative practice is, and where it's already at work in your school. You can engage the students in the class to educate others. You can give students in the class access to faculty meeting time, where students can present their ideas and understanding of why restorative justice interventions are important to schools—and to your school in particular. You and the students in your class could use the class time each week to become skilled facilitators of circles—and then you can use the class time later in the year to be a container for restorative practice. In other words, when ready, you and your students can use class time to host and facilitate interventions. As the school leader, you can decide which incidents of harm can be channeled toward the class. This kind of teaching reinforces the principle that the curriculum should correspond to needs of the community, and that teaching and learning should be conceived of as problem-solving. Students in such a course will be empowered by doing work that needs doing. As noted in earlier chapters, co-teaching—not solo teaching—is often a good way for an administrator to be a teacher during the school day, for it ensures another adult is in the room if you get called away. A counselor or other adult who is a skilled facilitator of small group discussion could be a co-teacher of such a course. For more on this concrete action, you could see an essay I wrote about teaching a class like this in the book *Teaching When the World's on Fire*, edited by Lisa Delpit.

- *Make small groups, and give them meaningful tasks*: Do you have small group meetings of students regularly each week in your school? In most schools, a group of six to twelve students would constitute a small group, and there are ways to allocate resources—staffing, time, space—to achieve those groupings. These are important to cultivating mutual understanding and a sense of belonging. Small groups are where bonds are made and trust is built over time. Small groups can cohere well when they have good facilitation, and a sense of purpose in meaningful tasks. In middle and high school, if you have an Advisory program or something like it, whatever the scope, give it meaningful tasks. Consider tasks like those listed in this chapter. Always give it just a bit more than it seems capable of achieving: its zone of proximal development. If Advisory is given meaningful tasks, people will be invested in the structure and will want to expand the structure to do the work well. Tasks take on deeper meaning when they correspond to a real need and when they have an audience, people who will see the tasks in completion. Consider asking for products, playful or serious, that need to be shared with others. As a general rule in school, if it matters, make it public. And when it becomes a public event, a visible object or demonstration of learning, it's bound to start mattering more. If you have no Advisory program, begin to investigate how it works. Look at the structure called Crew in Expeditionary Learning Schools. If you are working at the lower grades, many of the meaningful tasks that can be given to Advisory groups can be given to your elementary school classroom groups, contributing to the bonds that form when people work together on something important to the place where they are.

- *Let reforms mature with the children*: When students first arrive at your school, they have not yet experienced your school. Their parents may have certain expectations based on their own experience, or that of a child's older siblings. They may be resistant to changes. But every new cohort offers an opportunity to begin a reform that can take roots and last. "This is how we do things here" can be defined for the younger students in that first year, and then, for the sake of continuity, their experience can be made to follow them. This doesn't mean there will not be teacher resistance to reforms that move up from one grade to the next, but it can radically reduce student resistance to structural or pedagogical reforms, such as changes to the schedule, discussion norms, or common expectations for behavior. It may require creative scheduling, but an Advisory program can be started in the earliest middle school grade, and then be continued in the next grade above it once the students move from one year to the next. Likewise can discussion norms and protocols deepen their roots and power to produce positive school culture as they follow the students. Nurturing a new structure over the course of one whole year has the added benefit of giving you time to make

improvements before it is spread more widely in the school. It allows you to prove the concept to those who might have doubts and show your capacity for humility and openness to feedback to inform adjustments, responding to needs as they arise.
- *The One-Hour Rule*: If you are working with faculty to implement new discussion norms, circle process in classrooms, or a new Advisory structure, remember the one-hour rule. When it comes to major reforms and important roles that faculty take on, they need at least one hour of meeting time each month to meet with role-alike peers and engage in professional learning or problem-solving.
- *Offer support for implementation—including yourself*: Learning about something in a meeting of adults, and even experiencing it among adults, is important preparation for working with children in the same modality. But it is not the same as working with kids. Some people will need support during the implementation with children. Small group discussions about topics of meaning, which must include matters mundane as well as extraordinary, can be difficult. Even teachers who have experience bringing students together in a circle or hosting a whole-class discussion, may have developed strategies over time to deflect or avoid topics with personal, moral, or political importance. They may use their positional power to keep students from having a reasonable disagreement. They may feel pressure to move quickly to the next topic. Let teachers know that you and other faculty are available to help facilitate, or just be in the room for small group discussions, especially when you are asking them to discuss matters of importance. If there is a crisis in the community and there will need to be discussion and information shared, distribute the support people throughout the school to groups that need them. This group of support people could include administrators, counselors, and others. The support offered should definitely include the offer of your presence.
- *Learn by doing*: If you are not yet facilitating restorative justice interventions yourself, take the lead in some of them. Design them in collaboration with others and facilitate some of them yourself. Involve other adults in the interventions and debrief with them afterward. Doing this assumes you have some experience facilitating conversations where people are carefully listening to each other. If you have mentors or colleagues you respect for their facilitation skills, invite them to join you and offer you feedback. Build your own repertoire of circle prompts, protocols, and facilitation techniques. Revise and refine as you learn from your mistakes. Use scripts and structures provided by others, or design unique interventions of any shape or size based on the needs of the people involved. Guide yourself by keeping in mind that you are

striving for mutual understanding, a community of belonging, and you are empowering people to repair harm and solve problems relevant to their lives.
- *Cultivate teacher facilitators*: If you are already in the position of leading restorative interventions and need to expand the school's capacity, use your positional power to distribute the work to others. Create teacher-fueled engines for the work. Preparation for the work happens by being engaged in the work, learning by doing. Involve other adults in interventions with you, and then after exposure and modeling, ask them to try facilitating themselves. If they are teachers and they want to take a lead role, regularly throughout the year, support them by giving them time or stipends. If they are not teachers, help them in managing their priorities so they find the time for leading restorative justice interventions. If they are hesitant, include them in interventions you facilitate first, to learn from your example.
- *Invite the outsider's gaze sometimes*: Most of the actions on this list don't involve a purchase order or an invoice. There's no outside expert needed, no professional development package or consultant required. We are guided here by the idea that you and your school already have the resources—knowledge, skills, dispositions—that you need to do and deepen this work. However, sometimes spending money to bring in outside experts is helpful. Sometimes a professional development course of study for faculty is just what is needed to give everyone a common language and common point of departure. Sometimes money spent on books for the faculty is well worth the investment. Some of the authors and books mentioned in this chapter that can help teachers and administrators facilitate restorative processes are *Circle in the Square: Building Community and Repairing Harm in Schools*, by Nancy Riestenberg; *Circle Forward: Building a Restorative School Community*, by Carolyn Boyes-Watson and Kay Pranis; *The Little Book of Restorative Justice*, by Howard Zehr; and *Start Here, Start Now: A Guide to Antibias and Antiracist Work in Your School Community*, by Liz Kleinrock. Drawing from outside experts is worth doing, as long as you set aside the meeting time—in the short and long term—for teachers and administrators to digest their teachings and collectively operationalize them in your context.

UN-HIDING THE WEB OF CONNECTION

In *The Little Book of Restorative Justice*, Howard Zehr lists three core principles at work in a restorative approach to seeking justice. First, that there has been "a violation of people and of interpersonal relationships"; second, that these "violations create obligations"; and third, that "the central obligation is to put right the wrongs."[7] Zehr goes on to name the human interconnectedness at the heart of these ideas:

> Underlying this understanding of wrongdoing is an assumption about society: we are all interconnected. In the Hebrew scriptures, this is embedded in the concept of shalom, the vision of living in a sense of "all-rightness" with each other, the creator and the environment. Many cultures, however, have a word that represents this notion of the centrality of relationships: for the Maori, it is communicated by *whakapapa*; for the Navajo, *hozho*; for many Africans, the Bantu word *ubuntu*. Although the specific meanings of these words vary, they communicate a similar message: all things are connected to each other in a web of relationships.[8]

Schools, alas, can be very good at hiding the web of relationships. Schools are good at separating people into groups, putting them into rooms with the doors closed, moving us quickly through hallways to the next room and the next closed door. Behind those doors are often desks in rows, where most people look at the backs of most other people. And what those people discuss, read, and write about in one room is often disconnected from what is learned in other rooms. This is an elaborate academic fabrication of separateness. In our disconnected state, with the web of connection obscured, the science of global warming is disconnected from the history of the Industrial Revolution. Acquiring the skills to write powerfully is divorced from reasons to write powerfully. Sonnets and stories about love and heartbreak are read as texts to dissect in preparation for a computerized test rather than songs that touch our experience and that we may also need to sing.

Schools can mask interconnectedness, both the intersectionality of academic disciplines as well as intersections of identity and relationship. Restorative practice can help put relationships—to self, to others, to past and present—back at the center of schooling. It can help restore connections we've lost and make tangible the webs of needs and obligations that, whether we hide them or not, always connect us.

Chapter 4

Student Activism and Organizing

What relation should schools have to promoting social movements?
 Where is the line between supporting a social movement and creating a safe space?
 Does this kind of activism—flags, walkouts, etc.—actually make a difference?

—Youth Journalists, Underground Workshop, *VT Digger*[1]

Suddenly the principal didn't approve. It was 2017, and the senior class president and valedictorian, Peter Butera, was delivering a slightly different graduation speech from the one he'd submitted for the principal's review. Judging from the video of the ceremony, the opening of the speech seems to pose no problem to the principal, who is sitting not far from the podium. Peter discusses the opportunities that had been available to him and gives thanks those who had supported him:

> Throughout my time at Wyoming Area, I have pursued every leadership opportunity available to me. In addition to being a member of the student council since I was a freshman, my classmates have also elected me class president the past four years, which has been my greatest honor, and I would like to thank you all for that one final time, it really means a lot.

And then he departs from the approved remarks:

> However, at our school, the title of class president could more accurately be class party planner, and the student council's main obligation is to paint signs every week. Despite some of the outstanding people in this school, a lack of real student government and the authoritative attitude that a few teachers, administrators, and board members have, prevents students from truly developing as leaders. Hopefully, this will change. . . .[2]

A look of concern clouds the face of the principal as the class president describes the superficial work of student government at his school. At the mention of "authoritative attitudes," the principal turns and comments to someone, who then turns off the student's microphone. The words "hopefully this will change" echo into the audience as the student realizes his voice is no longer being amplified.

Even with his microphone off, the student continues to speak to his classmates and community. He reads a few more sentences about his hopes for the future before the principal stands up, approaches the podium, and motions for him to leave the stage in the middle of his remarks.

In June of the next year, on the other side of the country, another valedictorian, Lulabel Seitz, is silenced when her graduation remarks turn to an indictment of how her school responded to sexual harassment concerns. First she tells her community a bit of her family story, that she was the granddaughter of immigrants and the daughter of parents who left high school early and didn't attend college. She says to the applause of her classmates, "I didn't think I'd be standing here as your valedictorian." She then connects to her peers by saying that her story is not unique, that overcoming adversity is something they've done together, and that striving for "unlikely dreams" is something that her special classmates can also claim.

She describes the obstacles they have collectively faced, from climate change disasters, to teachers striking for a contract "they deserved," and other challenges. She appreciates the many dedicated and compassionate teachers, family members, and custodial and other school staff who have supported them. She then says, "This is why, when some people on our campus . . . " And the power to her mic is cut.

The school leadership must have seen a draft of her remarks and known what she might say, because the power is out before she can finish the phrase. A chant of "Let her speak!" rises from students and others in the crowd. She speaks, though many can't hear her, and when she is done, she resumes her seat to the cheers of her peers.

This student posted a video of the incident online, and shared a rendition of her entire speech. The opening frame of her YouTube video includes a further indictment of her school administrators: "In fear of the truth, the administration cut my microphone while I was speaking."

Judging from her video, when the power of her amplified voice was silenced, what she was about to say was that even when "some people defend perpetrators of sexual assault and silence their victims, we didn't let that drag us down." She also describes how the school's leadership showed a lack of support for funding the arts and other opportunities for "love of learning." In the final frame of her video, she tells her viewers that she had just one thing to say to her principal, quoting Malcom X: "A man who stands for nothing, falls for anything."[3]

WHAT IF YOU AGREE?

School leaders have the power to turn off the mic. It may not silence the student for long, indeed it may only serve to spread their message further, but school leaders have this power in the moment.

We can turn down or turn up the volume. We can go light or go heavy with consequences for breaking rules. Indeed, in many cases, we have discretionary power to determine what qualifies as the breaking of rules in the first place.

As school leaders, what would readers of this book have done in those the instances described above, when the student began to critique the school's lack of authentic student government, or when the other student began to critique the school's response to allegations of sexual assault? You've approved one version of the speech, but then the student delivers another. What to do?

There are other such stories. In 2021, Bryce Dershem, valedictorian at his New Jersey high school, was delivering a speech that included his story of coming out as queer and feeling "so alone." These courageous words are the last to be spoken before the mic is turned off. The principal approaches the podium, takes the speech that Dershem had brought to the stage, and indicates that he should read from the one on the podium instead. Then a new microphone is brought out. It seems to be a choreographed intervention, an effort to suggest to the audience that there were technical difficulties causing the interruption. Dershem decides to recite the rest of his speech from memory, delivering the version that the administration was trying to silence.

By what criteria should school leaders decide whether to silence a student or allow the student to speak? There have been court rulings, and their interpretations can guide administrators—and students. In a guide published during 2018 student protests against gun violence and school shootings, the American Civil Liberties Union (ACLU) advised students to "know their rights." The guide informs students that a "school can adopt reasonable rules that regulate the 'time, place, and manner' of exercising these free speech rights." The ACLU goes on to explain to students:

> The school is not allowed to prohibit or censor speech or press activities based on its content (what you are saying), unless it falls within one of these two exceptions:
>
> - It is foreseeable that the speech will cause substantial disruption to the operation of the school.

- It is too lewd or vulgar for the school audience.[4]

This is helpful for students and school leaders to know. It's especially important to note how much latitude a school has when it comes to defining categories of prohibited speech. What is "lewd or vulgar" or causes "disruption" in one school community may be very different from another. School leaders have significant discretion in determining what constitutes a disruption to the operation of the school, or what constitutes expression that is inappropriate.

What was the reason the school principal silenced Lulabel Seitz, the student who dared to express her disapproval of how the school responded to cases of sexual abuse? According to a local newspaper, the principal said that he was "trying to make sure our graduation ceremony was appropriate and beautiful."[5]

Why was power cut to the microphone of Bryce Dershem? The *New York Times* reports that the principal felt that remarks that focused on sexual identity and mental health weren't "broad enough" to correspond to the experiences of the many hundred other students in the graduating class.[6]

By what criteria would readers of this book decide whether to silence a student's expression of their story or belief? Appropriateness? Breadth of appeal? Beauty?

Whatever criteria we have for determining what is disruptive or inappropriate, it is essential that we intervene when speech or actions constitute an assault on protected categories of identity, including race, sex, religion, gender, national origin, disability, and sexual identity. As a school principal in rural New England, for instance, I became quite used to constraining the speech of students who displayed the Confederate flag.

"I Don't Matter"

"As long as you're flying that flag out there," the grandfather said, pointing out the window at the Black Lives Matter flag, "he's going to wear that hat to school."

Every fall, often after the county fairs, where students buy or win all kinds of stuff, from hats to knives to stuffed animals, there need to be interventions in response to a student wearing the Confederate flag on a shirt, belt buckle, or other article of clothing. This time the flag appeared on a baseball cap.

The boy was in middle school, living sometimes with his mom and sometimes with his grandpa, his mother's dad. And he lived sometimes with his father, too, in another town not far away. Mom understood why the school wouldn't allow the hat, but she didn't feel she had much influence over the grandpa's thinking. Grandpa was a man who held firm to his beliefs about right and wrong, some of those beliefs forged in his upbringing in rural Vermont, some of them forged in his several tours of duty in US wars abroad.

The boy had already accepted one suspension rather than take off his hat. He reluctantly came to school the next day without it but said that his grandfather wanted to talk. "My grandpa says that as long as you fly that Black Lives Matter flag, I'm allowed to wear my hat."

It was clear that this intervention wasn't finished and that it was indeed worth the school's time to meet with his grandfather to learn more about his perspective, see if the school could influence it, and convey the inflexibility of the school's position when it came to this kind of student expression.

Before his earlier suspension, with the support of a staff person who'd known him well since his elementary school, the boy had already discussed with me, his principal, his reasons for valuing the symbol.

He didn't entirely know what to say. He mentioned Southern heritage. But it was not clear, from discussions with his mother, that he had any heritage in the South. There were other reasons for valuing the symbol that he tried to re-create from what his grandfather had told him. But his wearing the hat was as much about allegiance to his grandfather and the family's broader distrust of schools, and other institutions, than it was about Southern roots or states' rights or other ideas often offered in defense of the symbol. It was also, directly or indirectly, a symbol of a system of belief that positions whiteness as having special rank and value.

The Confederate flag is a symbol cradled in a belief system that cradled the boy as a child, and which continued to cradle him still. How did it feel to be carried along in this belief? In part, it felt like the rough-yet-caring hands of men in his family, like his grandfather, who saw notions of "white privilege" as laughable as the family struggled with the hard life of the working poor in the richest nation in the world. And his grandfather was a man who believed he'd fought well for that nation at war, and he'd come home with PTSD, with which he also struggled by his own admission. And "When I see that BLM flag" he said when we finally sat down face-to-face, "it tells me that I don't matter."

(More will be shared about the special meaning the grandfather saw in the Confederate flag in the next chapter, which considers a school's responsibility to confront the dangers of white supremacist extremism, as well as the more insidious dangers of the mainstream manifestations of those ideas and symbols.)

Several hours were spent with the grandfather over the course of the next few months, and many more with his grandson. As a means of preventing the symbol of hate from reentering the school, and of preventing the harm that came with it, the school felt that it was important that the boy and the man had the chance to explain their thinking, that they were important members of the school, and that their importance to the school was not tied to the symbol of the Confederate flag.

"He won't be allowed in classrooms if he wears that hat," his grandfather was told. "We know you don't want that for him."

"We'll see," he said. "I can tell you aren't going to change your mind."

He was right. This was a form of student expression that the school would silence. It disrupted the learning environment and was a symbol of harassment regardless of intent. A school leader need not feel ambivalence about it.

The conversations with the family were laborious and difficult, but it was not a difficult decision to prohibit this form of expression. It's more difficult when students disrupt school for causes we believe in. In those cases, it's harder to know what to do. Paradoxically, the school leader can both be an ally of students who organize disruption in their advocacy for justice while still being the one who enforces the rules.

THE PARADOX: YOU CAN BE AN ALLY AND STILL ENFORCE RULES

According to the newspaper, "Schools in the Randolph area were closed and all after-school and extracurricular activities were cancelled on Tuesday, after a threat to 'shoot up the school' was reported to the Randolph Police Department, late Monday night."

The paper went on to explain: "The threat, which stemmed from an altercation between two middle school students—whose identities have not been released—was reported by the mother of one of the students. She called police at approximately 11 p.m. on May 21, police said."[7]

According to my own recollection, the police chief called me, the principal, a little after midnight, and then the superintendent called around 4 a.m. to say that school was going to be closed. It was May 2018, and just a few days since ten people were assassinated in a Texas high school.

There was a meeting the next morning with the superintendent to determine the roles various people would play in the investigations. Even when the police have their process, there's a school-level process as well. It would involve reviewing video-camera footage, interviewing students, and managing communications with families, faculty, and the wider school community.

Outside the school, the clouds sat and rain fell, and reporters from local television stations and newspapers came to capture images of empty parking lots, a few police cars, an officer checking to make sure all doors were locked. The TV stations would pair the images with paraphrasings of the police press release and run the stories that evening.

A local reporter sent an email to school leaders later that day: "Sorry that I'm introducing myself under these circumstances," she wrote. "I hate having to ask these questions over and over again as these threats come to our schools. Are we doing enough? Too much? Where do you go from here? Would like to hear your thoughts. Wishing you all the very best."

Something about this reporter's tone and questions conveyed that she was interested in more than a surface-level story.

The district's facilities director stopped by the office. He was the only other person around. He'd been watching the video-camera footage of the previous day, a role the superintendent had given him as part of our investigation, looking to see whom the boy who'd allegedly made the threat was talking to at the time.

By that afternoon, the police had concluded their investigation, determining there would be no charges pressed, there was no credible threat, and it was safe for students to return to school the next day.

Now it was up to the school to decide if the statement about shooting up the school was indeed made by this student. There were already some reports that it might have been someone else. And if the accused boy had indeed made the remark, what was his reason? Was there sincere rage behind the threat, or just a dark playfulness or exaggeration? Either way, if he'd said it, it had provoked a major disruption to the lives of hundreds of students and families.

There was plenty to continue to look into the following day, when students were back and we could interview them to see what we could learn. Back at my desk, an empty response to the reporter's email was waiting. What to say to her?

"Are we doing enough?" she'd asked, "Where do you go from here? Would like to hear your thoughts." It was the "we" in her first question that was significant. It meant that she was implicating herself, another concerned citizen, perhaps a concerned parent. She seemed to be an ally.

Between responding to other emails from parents, faculty, and staff, and sending the emails about plans for schoolwide Advisory discussions with students the next day, I took a break from my desk and walked the empty halls. Just two months ago I'd written a letter to the faculty when the news broke that seventeen students at a high school in Parkland, Florida, had been killed by a former student. It had been the deadliest school shooting since the rampage at the elementary school in Newtown, Connecticut, in 2012, when twenty-six people were killed. I came back to my desk and wrote to the reporter:

> The reason why we're closed today is in no way like what has happened in other schools recently. But there was an alleged threat, and now there are fears and visions and memories of violence.

I'd be glad to talk by phone if you like or in person—and I may say more here than I'd typically say to the press via email, but I assume you won't print without confirming such with me—and I sense a sincerity and humanity in your open questions which compel me to stop what I'm doing and reflect on this with you. Here's what comes to mind:

When children are killed—by adults or by other children—it is a sign that the family, community, or society has a problem. Killing the community's children isn't in accord with how the life cycle is supposed to turn.

In very recent headlines, one can too easily find stories of parents killing their own children, police killing a child, soldiers shooting children at a nation's border, one nation's army with my nation's support bringing war, cholera, and other plagues to the children of a third nation. And then there are the stories of kids killing other kids in schools, and of threats, or alleged threats.

What is troubling in all of this, and what also gives me hope, is this terrible notion: that police and armies—for all that they protect and "us"—have been killing other people's children throughout the history of human civilization. And sick and desperate parents have killed their children throughout time. And one nation has helped another nation kill the civilians of a third nation—such grim alliances—since the dawn of nations. I don't mean to be complacent about such bloodshed. I simply mean to note it seems part of a terrible inheritance or human tradition.

In contrast, what is new and perhaps more preventable is this phenomenon of children killing other children in our country's schools. By my reading of history: This is new. By my reading of contemporary society and politics: It is preventable. And that prevention will require martyrdom.

But those martyrs will not be children: They will be politicians and other adults willing to self-sacrifice, to lose an election or career, for what they know in their hearts is right, for the trust of the child they cannot abide knowing they've betrayed.

The school's investigation would wrap up in a couple of days. It was found credible that the boy had made a statement about a shooting, but that it had been made provocatively, an exaggeration, without intent to harm anyone. But the disruption had been real, and the work of reintegration and repair—with both students and families involved—was to be a long process. The spring of 2018 was a long spring, even for those school communities removed from the actual bloodshed of the shootings across the nation. There were many hours of worry about violence, palpable anxiety in the air, and, in the midst of it all, dilemmas for school leaders about how to handle the organizing of student activists.

Freedom through Resistance

Our nation's dominant culture abhors suffering of the self, even in mild forms, from a slight fever or cough to the discomforts of seeing oneself get older. Rather than be a source of meaning, pain of any degree is killed. Painkillers of countless types, from pills to creams to syrups, overflow the shelves of pharmacies, while cosmetics pack the shelves the next aisle over, and in the next we find potato chips, soda, and racks of magazines celebrating celebrity. "It is a culture," writes Chris Hedges, a journalist, pastor, and student of totalitarianism and war, "based on self-absorption, medical procedures to mask aging, and narcissism. Any form of suffering . . . is to be avoided."[8]

Of course we do not want people to suffer, or for students to be in danger, but we do want our students to feel the discomfort of moral dilemmas and the clarity that comes with action on the other side of choosing.

"I do not mean to be sentimental about suffering . . . " wrote James Baldwin many years before Hedges, in a similar vein, "but people who cannot suffer can never grow up, can never discover who they are."[9]

We want our students to struggle with difficult choices in the name of what's right. When students are energized and organizing for a cause in which they believe—and one in which we adults may also believe—what is the best way to support them? If they are planning an action that disrupts the normal functioning of school, this question becomes even more complicated. Should we make it easier for them—and for us? What is gained or lost if we change the rules and accommodate their disruption? What is lost if we allow student protest and resistance to be without hardship and ethical dilemma?

A certain quality of freedom is lost.

"In every act of rebellion we are free," says Hedges about political resistance, artistic expression, and other assertions of humanity in the face of oppression.[10] He's right. It is in speaking, dancing, or singing a personal, spiritual, or political truth to power that one finds freedom and feels the strength of one's moral core.

Getting in Trouble

Earlier that spring, after the Florida school massacre, students across the nation were organizing public demonstrations against gun violence. It was only two days before the walkout that student organizers approached school leaders to inform us. It was to be a local action, in alliance with a national action, at a common hour across the country.

In different schools, school leaders were responding to the student organizing in different ways. Some schools were adjusting the expectations that students be in class, so students wouldn't have to walk out of a lesson. Others were hosting assemblies for those who chose to participate in the demonstration. These were reasonable approaches.

Schedules and staffing assignments can be changed by school leaders to help amplify the student voices without a rule being broken. School leaders can help students with the tech support needed for the microphone, and get the custodians to pull out the bleachers in the gym, or move the theater class so the auditorium is free. We can put out cones and deploy staff to the parking lot to redirect traffic if the students are going to do their demonstration outside.

But at our school, the student leaders didn't ask permission and we didn't ask them if they'd like to have it. Whom would it have served if we'd said we'd help them by making this a school event? Who then would be doing the making?

We told them we supported their cause and that we supported the nonviolent civil disobedience that they were planning. They were planning to peacefully break a rule for something they believed in.

The student leaders came back the next day to ask for clarification. They were getting questions from their peers. It was clear that the small group of organizers was going to do the walkout no matter the consequences. But would others join them if they were going to get in trouble? And what kind of trouble would they be in?

Many of the students considering the walkout had never been in any kind of conventional "trouble" in school before. Maybe they'd been late to class, but most had never made a trip to the principal's office or been given a suspension. These students were worried about what their families would say, what their school record would say, and whether their chances of admission to future high school programs, early college, and beyond would be compromised. There were also kids considering joining in who had been in trouble before and their families had told them in no uncertain terms that they never wanted to get a call from the principal again. Those students also felt some risk at the idea of breaking the rules and getting in trouble by walking out of class without permission.

Child's Play with Grown-Up Meanings

On any spectrum of civil disobedience and danger, the actions planned by the students for this walkout were relatively minor in risk. One might even call it child's play. But school is a site for children at play, and this play is often very serious. A school is a site for experimenting with ways and tools of the adult world, including machines like computers and skills like persuasive writing.

School should be a place where the lines between child's play and grown-up work are blurred. People of every age need to feel needed and to be building competency in important skills in the company of mentors and teachers. People of every age have a need to wield tools toward the completion of tasks that need doing—in the classroom, in the sandbox, in the home, in the arts, on athletic fields, in the wider community.

Schools should be a gray area where there are real-world risks, adult tools, and authentic experiences with emotional meaning and identity implications attached—all under an umbrella of extra care and safekeeping. When students break rules for the causes they believe in, they find themselves, just like adults, upon a testing ground for moral courage.

And how the adults respond to their rebellion can enable learning experiences for them and others in the community. We can help them place their actions in a tradition of civil disobedience that has made our nation stronger. It's a learning opportunity.

Consequences

Normally, when a student leaves class or school without permission, there's an immediate effort to find the child, and to inform the parents if needed. We must find them and ensure they're safe. In the following hours or days, there would normally be a meeting between an administrator and the student, to discuss the importance of not leaving school without permission, which can be unsafe and can disrupt the learning and work of many people. If there were a pattern of such behavior, there would be additional consequences. There might be a need for a restorative process, if there was a particular relationship problem that was motivating their leaving school, or some particular harm being done. There'd be paperwork and data entry to be completed by several people in the main office: a discipline referral written, entered into the computer system, mailed home, with copies to the mailboxes of various faculty who might be involved or need to know.

What disciplinary consequences would be in place for students who engaged in the walkout? Minimally, we told the student organizers, there'd be a discipline referral and a meeting with school administration. This was a typical, baseline response. Whether other consequences were in order would depend on how the event transpired, and whether the disruption was nonviolent. Much depended on how it unfolded.

We were putting the ball back in their court. It was for now the student organizers to decide what shape they wanted this event to take. It was their work now, as organizers, to determine how many people they wanted there, or could persuade to be involved, and how they could get those people to follow their lead. What if the student action moved from the school out into the street? That wasn't their plan, but it might happen. What if there was disrespectful speech, for instance about students who chose not to join? What if there was vandalism? Whenever large groups of people congregate, behavior becomes unpredictable and can become aggressive. Whether the school administrators and faculty intervened, and what scale the consequences would be, now depended the student leaders' actions and the actions of others.

Learning through and about Civil Disobedience

The students' flyers described the event as a "Safety & Solidarity Walkout" with the purpose of "promoting safety in our school and standing in solidarity with victims of school violence." The posting of flyers was one area where the rules were allowed to be broken. The flyers were hung in the school without the formal permission typically required, and they were allowed to stay up.

It is worth reflecting on what would have happened if school leaders had taken them down. This could have been another opportunity to enforce rules and see what acts of resistance students might take. Were the students using school photocopiers to make the flyers? Should the school force them to be more creative in their advocacy for an unsanctioned event?

It was all happening so quickly, being organized just days after the school shooting in Florida, that these questions didn't come up. But it's worth considering, as school leaders, all the various choices we have to make, and the choices we want to push student leaders to confront. Some of the choices they'd have to confront would only arise as the event unfolded. Depending on how many students were involved, they'd have to decide where to gather and how to manage the behavior of their peers as the walkout was underway.

The students didn't need to know—though the superintendent and other administrators did—that we'd informed local law enforcement of the event and asked them to be ready to support public safety if needed. A protest about gun violence is also a protest that many will cast as a protest about gun control and the Second Amendment. Strong emotions can follow. Many people in the towns and surrounding hillsides would know of the event. Many people would disapprove.

We made sure to share our thoughts about the event with local police officers we trusted. We told them we didn't expect the group to leave school grounds, but we'd let them know if it was moving in that direction. Several nonteaching faculty were also instructed to go outside and be in touch with the main office if any concerns arose.

Ultimately, it was a large event for the size of the school. Forty percent of the ideologically diverse, rural, and small-town student population participated in the walkout, well over one hundred students.

On the inside, teachers were asked to note the names of students who left class without permission. Many teachers had asked if they could take their classes outside to participate in the event. They were told that they had to remain inside with any students who chose not to participate. This was another way of forcing students to wrestle with their political and moral conscience and make decisions for themselves. Students would need to be held responsible for making up any work they missed. If the entire class were to leave, the teachers were told, then they had a responsibility to follow them out, to be in their company and help ensure safety and respect while they are on campus.

The students gathered in front of the school, in the parking lot, as the snow fell on a wintry March day. The mass of students followed the guidance and example of the leaders, who held megaphones and spoke with conviction to the crowd. They did as their flyers had said and observed a long moment of silence. They spoke prepared remarks. It felt somber, important, and powerful.

Based on the emails, phone calls, and in-person conversations with students, families, and teachers before and after the event, it was confusing for many that the school administration didn't grant permission for the walkout. Some parents were upset that students would be "punished" with disciplinary consequences for standing up for their beliefs. There were more than a few angry emails. But the power of students using civil disobedience to break rules for a cause of importance to them was undeniable.

Neither the student leaders nor school administration had envisioned it in advance, but so many students participated in the walkout that it was not feasible for the school to process the infractions in the normal way. As one social studies teacher told the students afterward, "Through your mass action, you broke the school's discipline system." Given the number of students involved, it would have taken countless hours for the secretarial staff and others to just move the paper and do the mailing. Instead a simple entry was made into the online system, and a letter was sent home, with a copy given to each student. There wasn't time enough for individual meetings with school administration. The students were given their letters in one large meeting with school leadership in a large circle in the high school gym. The letter said:

> Last week, a large segment of our student community engaged in a student-organized "Safety & Solidarity Walkout." The students who spoke delivered a message of sympathy and compassion for the seventeen victims of the recent school shooting in Florida, and expressed solidarity with students across the country who are engaging in similar walkouts. The students shared a letter to school administration containing a list of concerns and requests related to school safety and security. The student organizers also implored the student community to be generous with each other, to connect to seventeen new people on this day in an effort to build a strong and kind community. The walkout was documented on the school website, and by local print and television news.
>
> The administration of the school was proud to watch and listen. We were proud to be part of a school community with student activists who organized

a public demonstration of dissatisfaction with the status quo, demanding that their school and country become a safer place for all. We were also proud that students were willing to become part of a long tradition of civil disobedience by nonviolently breaking a rule for a cause they believe in.

The student organizers did not ask permission for this event. They did not ask the school to set aside time and space for an assembly in the auditorium. They asked their peers to show their convictions by walking out of class. What this means is that the students organized an act of peaceful and courageous civil disobedience, joining a tradition strong with names like Rosa Parks, Henry David Thoreau, Martin Luther King, and Gandhi. Such citizens chose to courageously break rules to draw attention to a cause they believed in, and they accepted the short-term consequences, including arrest and greater hardship. But in the long-term, they did not accept the status quo. Their courageous acts of peacefully breaking a rule drew attention to their larger cause and helped make the world more safe and just. The students at our school who chose to participate in the walkout are now part of this tradition.

Why didn't the school give official permission to walk out? If the school had granted permission for the walkout, it would be impossible for the action to be part of this tradition of civil disobedience. Nor would students have had to weigh the short-term consequences of breaking a rule with the potential long-term impact of being part of "student-led change." This decision was consistent with guidance from the state secretary of education, the Principals' Association, and the National Association of Secondary School Principals, which told principals to "make it clear to students that a walkout protest is an act of civil disobedience and, by definition, a violation of rules."

We know that students and families do not take breaking rules lightly. It is for this reason that, as soon as we knew what was being planned—just two school days prior—we made sure to write to all students to convey that "students who choose to leave classes or school grounds without permission will have their choices documented with a disciplinary referral." We will not be assigning a detention for this instance of leaving class, but we will be following our procedure of noting it in the log in the student information system, and having a conversation with the student. Because of the number of students participating—over one hundred —we will have group conversations, and we will not be asking the office to process the normal paperwork. What the log will say is this: "On 3.13.18, this student left class and joined peers in a student-organized walkout to 'promote safety in our school and stand in solidarity with victims of school violence.' The walkout was peaceful and students returned to class after seventeen minutes."

These students' actions were not only part of a tradition of adult actions of nonviolent civil disobedience, but youth-led civil disobedience, including: the 1963 Children's Crusade in Birmingham, Alabama; the 2014 protests of students at Garfield High School in Seattle, who joined teachers united against standardized testing and budget cuts; the students in Arizona who, in 2011, chained themselves to chairs at a Tucson school board meeting to protest the banning of Mexican American studies; the youth who have led Black Lives Matter protests for years across the country, including the girls in Chicago who, in 2016, led a thousand people in peaceful protest, shutting down city streets, in outcry against the deaths of Alton Sterling and Philando Castile, each a Black man killed by police officers, one while being detained on the ground, the other while in his car at a traffic stop.

Common Cause, Different Roles

The ideals and causes about which school leaders may find themselves feeling solidarity with student leaders, activists, and organizers are many. But when protest is an element of the student activism, school leaders may feel that the daily schedules, norms, and various responsibilities of administrators are inherently misaligned with the moment.

Our schedules, routines, expectations for comportment, responsibilities for supervision, and other duties are designed to contain and channel the electric energies of youth down orderly pathways, into and out of countless boxes, rooms, rubrics, and graphic organizers, efficient and orderly containers of thoughts and bodies. Our school system's rules and roles have evolved to minimize disruption and maximize order and supervision, down to the minute. This is even more true for the teacher's day than it is for the school administrator, and so there are parallel questions that can arise for teachers when it comes to showing support for student activists.

What should teachers do when they feel common cause with the activists and organizers in the student body? What if the students plan a walkout and all but two students leave the room? The teacher holds beliefs aligned with the student protesters—but what about the teacher's responsibility to the student who chooses to stay behind and continue with the lesson? These questions are not only for the teachers to consider. School leaders have a responsibility to help manage these conflicting interests in a way that is fair and consistent with the teachers' contractual responsibilities and job description.

In the case of the student walkout to protest gun violence, teachers were explicitly told that they were not to leave their classrooms. They were told this both to preserve the quality of civil disobedience of the student action, and to ensure that those students staying behind couldn't say that their learning that day had been compromised by a teacher walking away from the lesson. In the days leading up to the walkout, teachers were reminded of their responsibilities:

> School faculty and staff should not give students permission to leave class or school unless the normal protocols are followed—for field trips, health office

visits, etc. School faculty and staff do not have the right to walk out of school when they have other assigned duties, such as teaching, preparing for class, team meetings, etc. If students leave the building, our normal protocol is to ensure the students are accounted for, supervised, and re-integrated into the school appropriately. This will be the responsibility of employees in the event of a walkout.

The letter sent to students and the wider community after the walkout included a note about teacher involvement, with an allusion to the power that teachers have in their own right as a collective of workers. This note was added partially in response to parents and faculty who had asked if teachers who were outside with students on that day had been breaking a rule as well. The response was that no, some teachers and faculty had been assigned to go outside to monitor the event on school grounds as a duty during their preparation period. It was noted, furthermore: "Teachers across the country are a powerful political force, and have their own means of protest, including rule-breaking, which are ways for them to draw attention to a cause. But in this case, the acts of courageous civil disobedience were on the part of the students, not the teachers."

Several years later, at another student protest to demand action to combat climate change, some teachers in fact decided to leave their posts in the middle of the day. Their intention was to accept risk and consequences in solidarity with the students.

Again feeling common cause, school administrators worked with these teachers, just as had been done with the students, to craft a response that validated their stance, while also maintaining the normal constraints of their contractual obligations. Without such constraints, their action would not have been of the same kind of solidarity with the students.

Each teacher who left school to participate in the climate change protest received a letter of reprimand, sent to their personnel file at the district office, documenting their choice to leave their duties without permission. The letter was gentle in tone, and acknowledged that these teachers had taken responsibility to make arrangements with colleagues to ensure that their classes were supervised and that the lesson plan was intact for the students who remained.

The risk to these teachers' professional standing was not acute, but neither was it nonexistent. Principals come and go, as do superintendents and human resource managers. To have a letter of reprimand in one's file, which typically doesn't go away, comes with the risk that a future supervisor will not view it in the same sympathetic light as a current supervisor. The teachers felt this degree of risk, but it was important to these educators that they assume this risk in solidarity with students.

THE PRINCIPLE: THE ACTIONS OF A FEW CAN LEVERAGE THE LEARNING OF ALL

Rules can be upheld even while you support those who are breaking them. This paradox becomes easier to navigate, and even more worth embracing, when we find ways to leverage the moral courage of a few for the learning of all. School leaders have access to a variety of means for doing this. We have means for sharing information with the entire school community, opportunities to engage students and other stakeholders in discussions, and we have flexibility to permit others access to the same resources for dialogue and learning.

In the wake of the Florida school shooting, in conjunction with the student organizing discussed above, and in addition to the schoolwide communications already mentioned, several other actions were taken by school leaders to enable the activism of a few students to contribute to the learning of many more.

As events unfolded, the school administration shared information with the community about local and national events that were happening in the wake of the Parkland High School massacre. The local events listed included information about what was happening in other towns as well as what local students were planning at the school level.

In addition, student organizers were allowed to visit every Advisory class to share information about the walkout they were planning. The students were thus given the opportunity to inform all students about the purpose of the walkout and the consequences that they would face if they engaged in the civil disobedience. This ensured there was clarity and uniformity of information being shared, and no rumors about what would or wouldn't happen to people participating. This information sharing could have been done by the administration, but instead students were given access to venues for doing it.

The school leaders also asked teachers to engage in discussions with students in Advisory. Despite the horror of the school shootings, many teachers and students at the school had strong positive associations with gun ownership, in part because many were hunters. The discussion prompts were developed with these people in mind, as well as students who had favorable views of expanded gun control regulation. There were two discussion activities that faculty were asked to choose from for an Advisory lesson.

One of the activities focused very specifically on the school site, and what could be done to make the school be and feel safer. Teachers were given a script to read at the beginning of the conversation:

> Today we're going to be having a conversation about school safety, and exploring some of the different perspectives on this issue both within our school and

across the country. Some of you may have heard about the student walkouts and marches that are being planned across the country, including at this school. And some of you may have really strong opinions on this issue, which might be different from the strong opinions of your peers. But you all deserve to feel safe, and you all deserve to have the chance to share your perspective on what makes us safe here.

There were four prompts to which students were invited to respond:

- On a scale of 1 to 10, how well is our school doing at making sure every student and adult feels safe?
- What changes would you like to see in this school, or in schools or society in general, to make you feel safer?
- What ideas about making schools safer have you heard that you strongly disagree with—and why?
- What would it take for people with different opinions about this issue to find common ground?

Student responses were collected and shared with administration. A second activity was to listen to a short discussion from a local public radio program with gun owners about open-carry laws, gun registration regulations, and gun violence. One caller, named Dwight, identified as hunter of sixty years, with experience with high-capacity weapons. He was a hunter who felt strong emotions about the topic, but he was comfortable advocating that all semiautomatic weapons be out of civilian hands. There were again four prompts to which students were invited to respond:

- How did you feel listening to Dwight's comment during the show? What did it make you think about?
- What ideas did you hear expressed in the show that you strongly agreed or disagreed with?
- Should people who want more gun control listen to people who own guns? Why?
- Why do you think this issue divides people so much? Is it possible to find common ground?

In addition to administrators, there were two teachers involved in creating these activities. One was a teacher who favored expanded gun control measures and held strong views about the positive power of activism and protest. The other teacher was less vocal about her views but was sensitive to the backgrounds of kids from families with guns. She herself hunted deer each fall and turkey in the spring.

THE PRACTICALITIES: SUPPORT FOR STUDENT ORGANIZING AND LEARNING

In times of unrest and protest, sharing information universally across the school and creating structures and supports for discussion are ways that school leaders can use the activist actions of a few to leverage the learning of all people in the community. As we have discussed in other chapters, the support that is offered should go beyond how-to guidelines; it should include hands-on, in-person support.

Faculty who are not ready, or student groupings in which there is volatility, deserve to have additional help to facilitate conversations that are heavy with personal and political content. Administrators, school counselors, and others can be deployed from offices to classrooms to help. If student groups are small enough, one teacher who is uneasy with the conversation can ask to join a colleague who is more comfortable. Or, the teacher who is outwardly resistant to hosting the conversation can be invited to play a secondary role. In the best-case scenario, teachers of contrasting views would be involved in shaping the form and content of the discussion or learning activity. Sometimes time will allow this, and sometimes not. In the case of 2018 student protests, the timeline was weeks, not months. Sometimes, however, the learning that attends the activism and organizing can and should unfold over a longer period of time. People need time for the interrogation of assumptions, and for sharing and learning from personal stories and historical facts.

One School Sparks Citywide Solidarity

The actions of a few can quickly catalyze the learning of many, but the more resources dedicated to that learning, the more enduring will be the understanding that is gained. "How One Elementary School Sparked a Citywide Movement to Make Black Students' Lives Matter" is the title of an essay by Wayne Au and Jesse Hagopian in the Rethinking Schools' book *Teaching for Black Lives*. Au and Hagopian tell the story of how, in just a few weeks during the fall of 2016, one elementary school's mid-September celebration, and the related controversy and press coverage, sparked a massive "Black Lives Matter at School Day" at every school across the city.

Au and Hagopian conclude this inspiring account of community organizing and individual courage with a section on "lessons learned," which illuminates a contrast between the work being done at the school that sparked the citywide demonstrations, and the work happening at other schools that joined later in solidarity.

> [W]ith more time and resources, we could have done better organizing. For instance, we had to grapple with the fact that when the John Muir Elementary staff made the decision to wear their #BlackLivesMatter T-shirts, it was after being part of sustained discussion and professional development that took place over multiple years. Ideally, all schools should have had the opportunity to have similar discussions as part of their typical professional development so that, when a moment like this happens, all school staff have a stronger basic understanding of racial justice to guide their decision making.[11]

The language that Au and Hagopian use to write about these events blurs the lines between the concepts of activism, organizing, professional development, and student learning. This is appropriate. Schools are places where activism, organizing, and the learning of all community members can intertwine. The role of the school leader is to allocate the resources to allow for the learning and organizing to take place in peaceful, sustained, and meaningful ways. Sometimes this requires quick action in response to sudden changes in circumstances; sometimes it requires long-term planning and a slower pace.

The slow-moving organizing and the processes for deeper learning can be harder to implement. It can require channeling activism and idealism that call for immediate change into forums and processes that take more time. But when those slower processes work well, they can help even more people find the understanding needed to stand strong in their convictions for the welfare of the community.

"Impatience with the Preliminaries"

The controversial Chicago community organizer of the mid-twentieth century, Saul Alinsky, observed in the 1970s that "youth are impatient with the preliminaries that are essential to purposeful action." He goes on to say, "Effective organization is thwarted by the desire for instant and dramatic change."[12]

This invocation to patience in organizing is not a relic of activist decades gone by. When journalist Chris Hedges visited the Standing Rock tribal national encampment in North Dakota in 2016, where people were gathered in resistance to the Dakota Access oil pipeline, he spoke to the Native American activist Tom B. K. Goldtooth. Goldtooth emphasized the importance of not jumping too quickly into action. "'I talk about the need for young people to have patience,' said Goldtooth, 'to put the prayer first, rather than just jumping out there and putting their energy into action.'"[13]

Sometimes it is astounding how much patience and time are needed for organizing. At the opening of her account of the unionization efforts at an automobile factory in Mississippi, Heather McGee makes note of the years spent in the effort:

> On August 4, 2017, a group of workers at a Nissan auto factory in Canton, Mississippi, held a historic vote about whether they should join the United Auto Workers (UAW), a move that would bring their wages, job security, and benefits closer to those of the unionized factories in the Midwest. Pro-union activists had spent ten years organizing and campaigning.[14]

Ten years can seem like a long time to be teaching and organizing. But the worthiness of the goal demanded enduring effort. These organizers were building the understanding necessary for courageous action to thwart the dehumanizing impacts of racial divisions in the workforce. The unionization efforts in this case were not successful. Hierarchies and divisions that had endured for hundreds of years were not to be unmade even in a decade of organizing.

In schools we are certainly not used to thinking of change in terms of decades. The seasons of change in the life of a school are typically much shorter. We plan in terms of one year to the next, and most school principals are not even in their roles for more than a few years before leaving that position for another. Still, without being complacent about status-quo inequities, we must keep in mind the importance of patience and long-term strategy in working for liberatory schooling. Even when status-quo injustice seems unlikely to be undone in the short term, there is hope to be found in solidarity forged with other people in the enduring struggle toward the goal.

A Second-Time "No"

Sometimes saying "no" in the moment can help achieve a future "yes" to our objectives. This is especially true when saying "no," "not now," or "not yet" is actually a way of saying "let us bring the learning to more people," or "let us raise the awareness of our allies," or "let us make sure we know our various roles," or "let us take a breath and gather the strength we ourselves will need to stand up."

The second time I said "no" to raising the Black Lives Matter flag at the school where I was principal was a cold, wet morning in late winter. A district colleague on the facilities team—who also worked in law enforcement—walked into my office just seconds after I arrived. He knocked, walked through the open door, and told me that while he didn't question my authority, he'd heard that I approved of students raising the Black Lives Matter flag, and he wanted me to know that if that flag flew there it would offend every law enforcement officer in the state—from country sheriff, to state police, to local PD, including him.

He then made a few observations about the origins of the Black Lives Matter movement, which he believed was started by a "cop killer." He reiterated again that he did not question my authority. "It's your school," he said.

"I wouldn't say it's *my* school," I told him.

"You're the principal," he said, reminding me that the school's position on such matters is certainly connected to my position. I acknowledged this, but I said I didn't understand why he was speaking to me about it at that moment.

He walked past me, past my desk, and pointed out my window. "Look," he said, and then he walked out.

I looked, saw it, sat, and took a breath. A Black Lives Matter flag was draped across the school's marquee sign at the front of the driveway. I'd driven in on the other side and hadn't seen it. It covered up the welcome message for the day. I felt the dilemma settle into my gut.

The First-Time "No"

One student had already been told a version of "no" some weeks prior, when he'd emailed to ask if the school could raise the flag. He'd written with reference to the work of students at another school to our north, "I'm not sure if you were aware, but Montpelier High School is putting up a Black Lives Matter flag for the month of February. A few of my friends and I thought that it would be a good idea for our school to do this too. Let me know your thoughts about this! Thanks!"

After meeting with him and a friend and sharing resources used by students in the other school in their organizing for the same cause, they were encouraged to broaden their dialogue to include more students and student groups, to get their support and engagement.

The advisors of various student leadership groups were told that they might be approached about the idea. There was cause for optimism that this was the beginning of a new effort in learning, organizing, and coalition building at the school. The conversation about racism in schools—and in our school specifically—had been explicitly going on for some time. Small faculty working-groups, faculty-wide summer readings, and faculty-wide professional learning were happening in parallel with whole-school dialogue involving students.

One catalyst for the work in those years had been a graduating senior's letter to the school administration denouncing the racism she'd encountered as a student of color. Parts of the letter had been shared—with her permission—with students in an end-year assembly, along with a commitment from school leadership that the school do better to become a safer place. In the last paragraph of her letter, she wrote:

> I am moving on from this place, hopefully prepared for this world by the efforts of a few teachers and the encouragement of my family. I am writing this letter to let you know that there are students in your school that do not feel safe. I feel things need to change to really educate the students you have entrusted to you. The world is changing, and you need to help the school to keep up.

Her words were a wakeup call for many, or a call to keep waking. There were teachers in the middle and high school grades who had been working for years to make their curriculum a place for courageous confrontation of hard truths about our nation's past and present racism. But much more work was needed.

The following year, school leaders invited an educator with experience helping schools start a Racial Justice Alliance to visit the school to discuss the learning and leverage for change that can come with such groups. She met with faculty, staff, students, and families. The school had also been using assemblies as an important forum for schoolwide dialogue. Faculty, staff, and students had spoken about their identities in assemblies, as a way of claiming strength in identities often put down in the dominant culture. Explicit invitations had been shared with the school community to confront our challenges and speak to the change needed.

In making these invitations, information was shared about harmful incidents that had happened at the school. Information needed to be shared, and school leadership decided to be explicit with the community about what had happened or had been reported, including instances when symbols of white supremacy had surfaced in the school within the last year:

- Outside: joking about being an immigrant by someone who is not an immigrant.
- Hallway: comment to student of color about monkey mask on Halloween, comparing to student's family.
- PE class: student casually using the N-word.
- Classroom: comments that put down students for being of Asian heritage.
- Swastika drawn by friend on hand other student.
- "KKK" drawn by friend on hand of another student.
- Classroom: comments comparing the speech of African Americans to gibberish.
- Classroom: comments about throwing people of Mexican heritage over a wall.
- Lobby: comment about killing people from another country.
- Cafeteria: swastika on tray.

Each incident had been met with disciplinary responses and consequences, but collective, community-wide responses were also needed. So it was encouraging that some white students were now talking about raising the Black Lives Matter flag, as one important symbol of standing with students of color against the racism being seen in the community. Indeed, students had been stepping up and stepping in all year. Most of the incidents that had come to the attention of administration had been reported by concerned students. Many of the responses relied on restorative practice where student-to-student dialogue was essential. There were allies. There were those who refused to be bystanders. There were activists, and there were softer moral voices. There were students who spoke at assemblies, and quieter students who sent emails.

The increased incidents of white supremacist expression at the school were part of a nationwide trend that some called the Trump Effect, an emboldening of people by the divisive and derogatory rhetoric of the 2016 presidential campaign and its aftermath, which correlated to "an increase in bullying, harassment and intimidation of students whose races, religions or nationalities have been the verbal targets."[15] People were emulating the harmful model of their leaders. Racism and xenophobia were becoming more visible to more people.

Hands Shaking

When the Black Lives Matter flag was anonymously hung on the school's marquee, a painful professional and personal dilemma arose. It had happened by surprise, without the dialogue and coalition building that we'd been encouraging. And with no name attached, if a school leader chose to leave it up in that moment, the gesture would in large part become the school leader's gesture, rather than the outcome of organizing among the hundreds of students and the scores of faculty and staff who worked with those students every day.

Without the work of collective dialogue, learning and coalition building, the action would be vulnerable to undoing. Indeed, if the gesture were seen as belonging to the leader, it could very well undermine the more grassroots, movement-building foundations that were being built—and that needed more building still.

I went outside, took the flag down, came back inside, carefully folded the flag with shaking hands, and then typed a note to teachers to share with all students. The community was informed that a Black Lives Matter flag was hung, anonymously, and without approval, and taken down. The community was reminded of the school leadership's support for starting a Racial Justice Alliance, and reminded of the public work that students were doing at other schools. The words of the students at Montpelier High School were shared again, to provide a model and inspiration. "Raising this flag," they wrote, "is a part of a wider campaign to grow awareness and make changes in our curriculum, climate, and shared understanding of the need for racial justice." They went on to say:

> Over the past year there have been many steps forward in our community including some direct curricular choices, administrative trainings, faculty in-service, a schoolwide assembly, and the Race Against Racism. And yet, we need to do more to raise our predominantly white community's collective consciousness to better recognize white privilege and implicit bias. The Racial Justice Alliance believes putting up a Black Lives Matter flag is imperative for both demonstrating our school's fight for equitable education for our Black students, and modeling a brave and appropriate challenge to the status quo impeding public institutions across the country.[16]

With the flag sitting there folded on the table, I wondered: Why wouldn't people in our school make more than episodic or anonymous calls to raise this flag? The reason why the dialogue hadn't happened was precisely why it needed to be further encouraged and supported: because reckoning and repair aren't easy. One reason for taking it down was not to allow the process to be easy, to prompt the local movement to grow stronger through wider conviction-seeking, dialogue, and organizing.

A Third-Time "No"

The flag had been taken down from the school marquee in February. March, April, May, and June came and went. No Racial Justice Alliance was formed, no wider public BLM dialogue occurred, and no student groups took up the flag on their agendas. Four students did come forward to claim the flag they'd hung up that one morning. They were basketball players, two of them students of color, two of them white, and they'd been inspired by stances NBA athletes were taking in response to police brutality. One of them was the boy who'd emailed weeks before. They were given their flag and again given the message about how important it was to find ways to engage the community in dialogue and to say why raising it was important to them and the community. They didn't show any enthusiasm for this process or stay long in the office to talk about it.

Yet the conversation had continued in other ways that spring, in forums large and small. For instance, in private settings, there were follow-up conversations with my colleague on the facilities team about his assumptions about the origins of the BLM movement. In a much larger forum, the whole school gathered to hear an invigorating speaker and community organizer, sponsored by the school's National Honor Society, with support from the superintendent. This was a visit that sparked further dialogue, in groups large and small, about race, violence, and identity. Another important moment came at an assembly on the last day of school, when students again stepped forward to take the mic.

An eleventh grade boy named Zeb was the last student on the list. Before him had come an eighth grader of Abenaki heritage, a girl who identified as pansexual, a boy who identified as autistic, and several others. A community member who'd been present remarked afterward that "you could have heard a pin drop" as the entire school listened to students claim these identities as strengths. Each of the students also shared a hope for the school next year.

When Zeb spoke, he discussed his multi-racial parentage, and when he concluded he offered what he called a "challenge" to "the faculty." He said, "I challenge you to start the next school year with the Black Lives Matter flag flying." There was applause, even cheering by many. There was excitement in the room as the school year came to a close.

But there was also some cause for disappointment. Zeb had said "you" in making his challenge to "the faculty" to raise the flag. It was again being cast as a gesture to be undertaken without more intentional organizing and collective learning. Not flying the flag in response to Zeb's challenge was the third time I said "no." The community would not see it flying at the start of the next school year. But momentum for collective action was building.

Resources to Support for Student Organizing

The next year, key resources—time, people, space—were allocated to expand the community organizing, dialogue, and learning needed for a broad coalition of people to express their conviction that the Black Lives Matter flag should fly at the school. Readers may be reminded of a scenario shared in this book's first chapter about resources needed for the work of anti-racist reforms.

Between the applause of Zeb's peers at that final whole school assembly and the first day of school the next fall, an important allocation of resources took place. An English teacher and a special educator proposed to teach a class called Racial Justice that would be the vessel for the work of a Racial Justice Alliance. This class was given space in the course catalogue, space in the daily, weekly, and yearly schedule, and the additional support of an administrator responsible for cultivating project-based learning in the school, including summer professional development and on-the-job support throughout the year.

There were certainly pressures to allocate those teacher resources differently, such as making another section of tenth grade English, or additional special education interventions in math classrooms. But the school decided that this Racial Justice class would have its place as a yearlong, multi-grade class with a mission to respond to increasing concerns about racial injustice in the local and national community.

Space was also reserved on the faculty meeting calendar for the students of this class to work with the adults of the school to conduct professional development or present a proposal or demand. The teachers of the class were also told that they and their students could access classroom groups and Advisories across the school if and when they needed time and space for schoolwide learning and dialogue. The class took advantage of all these resources and soon strong public voices of students and faculty were vocally leading the work.

"We Have Been Educating . . . "

It is hard to see and quantify the quieter measures that members of a community undertake in any movement toward making their community more just. For every individual public gesture, there are quiet moments of deliberation. For every public gesture of institutional change, there are countless smaller—and no less significant—gestures that lay the foundation for the more visible moment.

Before and after Zeb voiced his challenge, momentum was building with the weight of many individual actions. There were teachers who had been reading about white privilege of their own accord in a voluntary reading group. There was the boy who emailed to say we should fly the flag, the basketball players who hung the flag at dawn, and the youth who spoke at assemblies with dignity. There were the many students who said something when they saw something in the halls, on the bus, in a classroom. There were the teachers who spoke at the assemblies, and the teachers who for years might not have spoken at assemblies but were doing the crucial and quieter work of writing curriculum with racial justice and the whole child at the core. All these people were now poised to be public allies as the new Racial Justice Alliance got to work that fall.

After five months of work, in January the Racial Justice Alliance sent a proposal to raise the BLM flag to the school's leadership. They discussed some of what they had learned, including topics about which they'd also been educating others:

> Raising the Black Lives Matter flag is a clear statement that students of color are safe in our school. Black lives historically haven't mattered in our country; from chattel slavery, to convict leasing, to Jim Crow, to the War on Drugs, to mass incarceration, black lives have not been valued in the same way as other lives.

They provided contemporary statistics and historical facts to support their assertion "that black lives continue to matter less" in our communities. They spoke of the message they intended the school to send to the wider community:

> Raising the Black Lives Matter flag also sends an important message to our greater community: that we recognize the systemic racial inequality in our society, and that we are committed to healing the racial divide that continues to plague our country. It is particularly important for us as an educational institution to take action when we see inequality in our society and to educate our community about issues of social justice.

They wrote about their work to educate students, faculty, and staff:

> [W]e have been educating Advisories to increase students' understanding of the Black Lives Matter Movement. We have also organized circle discussions with faculty to begin conversations about race in our school and society. Both of these educational efforts have given students and faculty members opportunities to share their perspectives, ask questions, and learn more about this topic.

They specifically proposed when and where the flag should be raised, and they closed with a commitment to ongoing learning and community building: "We are committed to further dialogue and continued educational efforts within both our school and the larger community." Their work indeed continued, including, in the months to come, the first of its kind student-led statewide conference about racism in schools, at which hundreds of students and educators from around the state were in attendance.

Amidst all this, there was backlash. The task of confronting and channeling that backlash—which took many different forms—also became the work of the students, faculty, and school leadership. But the backlash didn't derail the work.

In the years to follow, the teachers of the class would expand their work to include a Racial Justice Alliance class offered to students at the local Career and Technical Education (CTE) Center, which serves students from many more towns. With pressure from the two teachers leading the Alliance, the school revised its hiring process to include questions focused on a candidate's experience learning from and about matters of inequity in schools.

In addition, pressure from people near and far mounted to change the mascot of the school because of racist associations with the image.[17] Public pressure also began to influence the adoption of anti-racism policies at the board level, and to influence professional development at the elementary schools in the district. Following the work of one of the teacher leaders, the school's instructional leadership team adapted and then adopted the Social

Justice Standards from Learning for Justice as a lens for curriculum reform across every discipline, centering topics of identity and power. It wasn't yet 2021, and so nationwide public debates about Critical Race Theory hadn't yet begun to inflame school board meetings and social media forums—but when that time came, a coalition had been built at the school that would make it less vulnerable than others to the efforts to silence teaching about race in school.

Authentic Learning or Theatrics?

Readers may object that the stories recounted in this chapter are not stories of genuine student protest, activism, or organizing. The positional power of school leadership is always in operation. There is coordination with student leaders, and efforts by people with power to support student organizing in ways that may seem like choreography designed to look like grassroots movement. Some might question the very possibility of an institution's leadership doing anything other than sustaining the status quo, an arrangement upon which that leader's power and position are built. Some might see only superficial efforts to structural reform cloaked in talk of social justice and liberatory change.

In his frightening analysis of how liberal democratic institutions have failed to counter the destructive effects of increasing wealth inequality, Chris Hedges interviews Michael Gecan, codirector of the Industrial Areas Foundation, a network of community-based organizations. They discuss how people with power manipulate protest movements to ensure they do not yield substantive reform:

> The corporate state, [Gecan] said, has learned how to manipulate protests and render them impotent. He dismissed as meaningless political theater the boutique activism in which demonstrators coordinate and even choreograph protests with the police. Activists spend a few hours, maybe a night, in jail and are "credentialed" as dissidents. Gecan called these "fake arrests." "Everyone looks like they've had an action," he said. "They haven't." These protests, he said, were sterile reenactments of the protests of the 1960s. Genuine protest, he said, has to defy the rules. It cannot be predictable. It has to disrupt power. It has to surprise those in authority.[18]

This notion could be discouraging to school leaders who want to use their position and authority to be allies of activists working for justice, including institutional reforms at the very schools where they wield that authority. There certainly would be truth in an assertion that the student actions discussed in this chapter were coordinated with the people with positional power. But that doesn't necessarily remove all the high stakes from the actions those students have undertaken, nor does it negate other aspects of the liberatory work that is taking place.

Michael Gecan, in the same Hedges interview, goes on to contrast the value of episodic protests in the street with sustained organizing and learning in communities. When people are in the streets demonstrating, people are generally not in sustained dialogue with other people sharing stories, learning historical facts, and building common understanding. The public action is important, but so, too, is the work inside communities and institutions to help people relate to each other:

> "Three things have to be happening in great organizations; people have to be relating, people have to be learning, people have to be acting," [Gecan] said. "In . . . a lot of activism, there's a lot of acting but there's not much relating or learning."[19]

Relating, learning, and acting are ways of being that schools can embody. There will always need to be efforts by adults to help guide whatever good anger-at-injustice is being expressed by students. There may be elements of theater in this. School leaders will naturally work to limit surprises and disruptions, and we must always tend to the emotional, intellectual, and physical safety of the children in our care. We can't let young people be in psychological or bodily danger. But we can find ways to shine lights on injustice, or give the microphone to those who will name it, and we can help channel in productive directions the anger that people awake to injustice appropriately feel. School leaders—with all our necessary allegiance to rules and routines—can yet do good work with people who are ready to change their world, including the world that, for a time, is the place called school, where they come for learning.

FIFTEEN CONCRETE ACTIONS EVERY LEADER CAN TAKE

The actions of a few can leverage the learning of many when they are given the right mix of quiet and public support, as well as access to the basic resources that structure school community life, such as time, space, and staffing. The school leader is in a position to allocate those resources and help enable the activists to engage others in the learning, relating, and coalition building that can lead to lasting change. Leadership will change, teachers will come and go, and so the institutional habits of allocating resources toward liberatory schooling need to be put in place.

Part of the allocation of resources is the justification for the allocation of those resources. This justification comes from the truths born of personal stories and historical facts, including the history that happened just yesterday. How the leader speaks, and what information the leader shares both matter. It also matters how the leader models commitment to quiet relationship building, vulnerable self-reflection in moments of moral or ethical dilemma, and, occasionally, the capacity for visible public risk-taking.

No matter where your school is in your efforts to engage students in making the world a better place, there are youth activists and leaders in your community who will benefit from any number of the following concrete actions that every leader can take.

- *Find grounding in state and national standards*: Being grounded in national teaching standards can help you explain how learning about civil disobedience and popular protest is consistent with the learning objectives you are responsible for as a school. Many states have, for instance, social studies standards aligned with the College, Career, and Civic Life (C3) Framework for Social Studies State Standards, standards which are themselves aligned with Common Core ELA standards. One of the K–12 C3 standards asserts that, by fifth grade, students can "apply civic virtues and democratic principles in school settings." By grade eight the standards assert students should be applying those virtues and principles in "school and community settings."[20] Which standards are guiding teaching, learning, and assessment in your state, district, and school? Know and inform others, as needed, of the standards that support learning about and from organizing and public action in support of democratic society.
- *Find grounding in federal law*: Federal law prohibits the harassment of people based on race, national origin, color, sex, sexual orientation, gender identity, age, disability, or religion. There will be certain symbols, statements, policy positions, organizing, and advocacy that will constitute harassment and that you will not tolerate in school. The actions of students who organize their peers, during school, in support of victims of gun violence or racial discrimination have their place, as we have discussed in this chapter. But the organizing of students in support of anti-Semitic, white nationalist organizations could not be tolerated. Not all activism can be equally accepted in school.
- *Find grounding in experience*: Activism, organizing, and the related risk-taking will be familiar to some readers from personal experience, and perhaps not as familiar to others. Each of us is better able to be strategic in our support for student activists and organizers if we understand what they are going through. Even if you are not participating

directly in activism and organizing, you can still attend events, rallies, information sessions, and webinars to listen and observe. Go close, as safely as appropriate, and listen to your own body and thoughts as you observe or engage in public actions. How are you feeling in your limbs, your chest, your head? How is your heartbeat and breathing affected? What thoughts are you having about your welfare and the welfare of others? Our support for students who are advocating for justice in their communities will be stronger if it comes from a place of empathy, an understanding of what activism, organizing, and risk-taking feel like.

- *Inform students of their rights*: The American Civil Liberties Union and other organizations, like the Southern Poverty Law Center or the National Association for the Advancement of Colored People (NAACP), offer resources to young people to help them know their rights when it comes to permitted and prohibited speech, assembly in public, and actions in school and out, including interactions with the police and other authorities. Find appropriate opportunities to share this information with students and invite discussion. This could happen in a social studies classroom, or in a forum like an assembly or Advisory session created because of actions taking place in your community. Compare this information about legal rights with what is in the student handbook or school or district policy. Be transparent with students about your positional power, your interpretations of policy, and your ability to use discretion in certain cases.
- *Subscribe*: Your email is probably so busy that you'd rather not add anything else to your inbox, but one way to stay conversant with the organizing and activism happening in your community and across the country is to subscribe for updates from organizations that will let you know what organizing is happening. Many of these organizations will come and go as crises and causes shift and fade over time, but some probably won't. Your local chapter of the NAACP, which is an organization that has endured for more than one hundred years, may have an email update that could keep you informed about certain actions and organizing happening in your region. A newer organization that will have an urgent agenda for the foreseeable future is Extinction Rebellion, a group focused on the climate emergency. The Western States Center, based in Portland, Oregon, also has a weekly digest that highlights prodemocracy actions as well as threats from antidemocratic actors. Find news that tells stories of resistance and solidarity, as well as the dangers being confronted.
- *Share information about activism and organizing*: Given the way that social media is curated toward individual interests, many people in your community may not know about prodemocracy actions, coalition

building, and organizing for justice in your region. There are teachers in your school, student organizations, and other entities that may be interested to know about actions and organizing in the world today. Just as we say that to understand is not to condone, to know about an event is not to endorse an event. You can share information about prodemocracy and antibias coalition building events, which may have a connection with a unit of study, or with the focus of an extracurricular club, without necessarily asking people to participate in it.

- *Share biographies about courage in community*: Ask your librarian what books are in the library about everyday people acting courageously in their communities. There are books like this for very early readers and more sophisticated readers. For instance, a book for younger readers is the picture book, *Separate Is Never Equal: Sylvia Mendez and Her Family's Fight for Desegregation*, by Duncan Tonatiuh. Read some of the books your librarian has acquired and let people know about them, or find opportunities to discuss the character and the story. Encourage teachers to use such resources and related questions, like, what compelled the person to act on their convictions? Where did those convictions come from? What connections can we find between the text and our own lives and circumstances?

- *Follow your moral compass*: Your own moral compass is already pointing you in a direction toward doing something about something you know isn't right in your school, your district, or your community. Voice the expectation that something be done about it. Say that you are ready to work with others to address the problem. Be strategic about it, and enlist allies in advance, or inform a supervisor of your plans to start the conversation. Taking action in the direction where your moral compass points can be as simple as asking a question, sharing data, telling a story, or helping others to tell a story. Publicly model for students and teachers that you are willing to take a risk or make a sacrifice for something you believe will make your school a better place. Ask others to take action in their sphere as you take action in yours and find solidarity at the intersections.

- *Appreciate the power of organized labor*: This can be difficult for some administrators, given what often seem to be opposed interests of a unionized workforce and people who are in supervisory and management positions, but we need to value the push and pull between powers in the workplace that lead to benefits for the working class and middle class. Unions, like any organization, can be subject to corruption and mismanagement. But overall, if we chart the rise and decline of unionization in the United States, we chart the rise and fall of the middle class and wages that make ends meet.[21] It is important that all members of the

school community—teachers, students, administrators—understand the powerful collective action that people in unions can achieve, and how it differs from the collective action of a public protest. The former is sustained over time; the later is episodic and sometimes quickly fades without lasting institutional impact.
- *Derive relevance from need*: As noted in chapter 1, often teachers concerned with student engagement ask themselves—and their students—what students might be "interested in" or "want." This can result in superficial projects and allow people to avoid difficult topics. Rather than interest, frame relevance as derived from "need": the developmental needs of kids, their families, and the local needs of the school and community. When supporting teachers with curriculum design, backward design, and essential questions, ask how the framing of the work can be grounded in needs.
- *Describe teaching and learning as problem-solving*: From whole class syllabi to units of study and particular assignments, validate, encourage, and support teachers in designing curriculum that is focused on solving problems in the school, the community, the wider society. Doing this can open the door to conversations about how people go about solving problems—from grassroots actions and organizing to lobbying and legislative solutions. It will open the door to discussions of student activism and organizing.
- *Praise the pedagogy*: As noted in chapter 2, there are teachers in your school who support students' skill development in public speaking and debate. There are teachers who engage students and community members in projects that require collaborative problem-solving and organizing of people, time, and resources. Praise these teachers' work in tactful ways and share it. Especially find ways to share this kind of practice with the new teachers you hire.
- *Meet with leaders and first-followers*: Being the first person to follow the leader may require just as much courage, and be just as important, as being the actual leader of something. In a short TED Talk, a thinker named Derek Sivers explains that "the first follower transforms a lone nut into a leader. If the leader is the flint, the first follower is the spark that makes the fire." He goes on to say that the second follower is the "turning point," for it's proof the other two are worth emulating.[22] With this in mind, when there are student activists mobilizing in your school, meet with a small group of them to talk, strategize, coordinate actions, or express support. The group, not one leader alone, is where the power of the few resides, and they will need each other for support when they encounter obstacles.

- *Support the arts and public performance*: Many leaders of past and present civil rights reforms have had childhood experiences in church communities where there are strong traditions of performance and public speaking aligned with moral and spiritual conviction. Traditions of religious and artistic expression can lay a strong foundation for courageous expression and advocacy in any community. In the wake of the murders at their school, many of the Parkland, Florida, students who became leaders of the youth-driven movement against gun violence were students who took courses in the arts, like theater and chorus. These kinds of classes, and related forums for the public exhibition of voice and student work, can help students develop skills and confidence they will need to be effective organizers in their communities when their moral compass points them in such directions.
- *Embrace your inner/outer intellectual*: Whether or not you think of yourself as a public intellectual, you are one. You are an intellectual—since you lead a school, how could it be otherwise?—and you are also a public figure, among the most important in the community. Embrace these two aspects of your professional identity and speak, write, and act in ways that model an understanding of the intellectual project of school in a public policy and historical context. When communicating with the wider community—in email updates, or letters to the editor, press releases, or otherwise—situate the work of school in broader sociopolitical, economic, and cultural contexts. Many people will say that schooling is about basic skills and that contemporary political matters are not relevant to the project. This flawed understanding can be challenged by school leaders who help people see the work of schooling as a real-time enterprise situated in broader contexts. If you are communicating with the community to discuss a free breakfast program, consider combining that information with reference to the fact that our country is one of few wealthy nations that allows so many children to go hungry. If you are communicating about school safety measures, put that information in a broader public policy context about what makes communities safe and unsafe. You can do this with a lot or a little advocacy in your stance. Sometimes simply sharing information will inspire some people to brand you as "too political." But school leaders are in a position to educate others through our thoughtful public positions on important matters. And there's no escaping that the role is inherently political. School life—from the books we read, to our funding formulas, to the daily routes the buses follow—is wholly shaped by political forces, past and present.

THE FUTURE FACE-TO-FACE

"Have you ever met anyone that's killed somebody?" This is a question Liz asks her boss in season 3 of the comedy television show *30 Rock*. She doesn't wait for a reply. She says, "I think my grandpa may have—but he never liked to talk about what happened . . ."

There's a short pause.

In this brief pause, one might imagine that she is about say, "in Vietnam." For she's communicating something about regret, or guilt, and she's talking about someone—her grandfather—who feels conflicted about the violence he committed in the past. Feeling guilt about the violence committed in war is not uncommon. But it wasn't Vietnam that her grandfather didn't like to talk about. What she instead says is that her grampa, who once killed someone, "never liked to talk about what happened . . . at Kent State."[23]

It's one of the darker jokes among countless others in the episode. The story quickly moves on, and there's no return to the topic. But the topic is one that our nation will never fully leave behind.

Lethal Force against Unarmed Civilians

The National Guard killings of four student protesters at Kent State University in Ohio was a moment that, in the words of Professor Richard M. Perloff, "marked the end of the 1960s and the beginning of our era of political polarization."[24] It was 1970, and the National Guard had been called in by the governor in response to demonstrations at the university, property damage in the town, and unrest that had included setting fire to a building used for US Army recruitment.

According to Perloff, "Student activists had long been at the forefront of the antiwar movement, and Kent State, with some 21,000 students, boasted a long tradition of radical protest, partly because of its proximity to Cleveland, then a stronghold of progressive labor." These students planned to protest the presence of the National Guard on campus, but the university wouldn't permit it. "The students gathered anyway, facing off across a hilly green against a phalanx of guard soldiers."[25]

These were certainly not the first young people to stand in protest, face-to-face, with agents of the state who would kill them. Perloff notes the importance of seeing these events through a critical lens informed by race:

> The students shot on May 4, all white, became martyrs; most people have forgotten that less than two weeks later, Phillip Lafayette Gibbs and James Earl Green, two students in Mississippi, were killed by police officers in the wake of a false rumor about the death of a civil rights leader. And while Kent State stands

out as an exception—National Guardsmen killing white college students—over the years, state authorities have killed far more African-American protesters than whites. Seen through that lens, Kent State was not an aberration at all, but a dramatic continuation of national afflictions—above all the willingness by the state to use force to quash dissent.[26]

Perloff argues that these national afflictions persist. The polarized responses to the killings at Kent State, with some saying the students deserved to be shot while others holding them up as martyrs, continues today in how people view such incidents. And the use of lethal force against unarmed civilians—abroad and at home—continues as well. So, too, continues the resistance to injustice.

The students in your school today are living in an era that will continue to see public protest, activism, organizing, and the push and pull—sometimes violent—between forces on opposing sides of public debates, picket lines, and police barricades. What experiences do you want them to have in their youth to prepare them for these events in their future? Every person in such a situation, on whatever side of a divide, will have choices about how to wield their power, and with what tools to have an impact. It's worth considering this future as relevant to our work now in schools.

The Future Face-to-Face

Athletics and physical education were not always activities students did in school. Nor was theater. Nor was student government. Nor was debate. Nor were many other domains of learning we take for granted today, from scientific experimentation to the visual arts. Nor did most people in our country come to school for most of their childhood and into their early adult years.

The broad scope of all that schools do now, from a person's pre-K days through adulthood, is a development that took place within the last hundred years. Schools today have an extraordinarily broad mandate to prepare young people for the vast worlds of work and democratic life that await them in adulthood.

People will readily frame the purpose of schooling as preparation for college and career in the future. But political protest and unrest awaits them in that future too. There are skills and dispositions that people need in order to be able to participate in these experiences with nonviolence and the welfare of democracy in mind. Rare would be the school that thought it part of their curriculum to prepare kids with skills to navigate a world that includes protest, nonviolent civil disobedience, and volatile confrontations. But we should consider it.

Imagine the future police officers and National Guard members who are now students in your school. What experiences and exposure, skills and knowledge do these people need in order to do their future jobs with allegiance to democracy, not authoritarian figureheads? What experiences could prepare them for the moment of tension, face-to-face with their fellow Americans, such that they do not pull the trigger and kill an unarmed civilian? And what experiences do those advocating for change need in order to be effective at making change without bringing about bloodshed?

As noted in the first pages of this book, it is our job to imagine the worst, and to then work to prevent it. We must also imagine more hopeful scenes, and work toward such visions.

In more hopeful visions, we can see some of our students becoming public servants and agents of the state—some of them armed in their roles—who pledge allegiance to the flag, not with blind obedience but with a eye for the responsible use of the powers they've been granted by the communities they serve.

We can envision multiracial coalitions of working-poor and middle-class people who advocate for and achieve reforms for a more just society. And we can teach students about past coalitions and help them to build new ones, face-to-face, in our classrooms and broader communities. We can teach students about people who question authority in powerful but nonviolent ways. We can be those people ourselves.

We can be school leaders who are transparent about the authority we have to constrain, restrict, enable, and foster. We can be transparent about rules, consequences, and our own relationships with police and others who have state-sanctioned access to force. In a time of political polarization and, indeed, extremism, we can model courageous conviction and take public actions in commitment to the welfare of the children in our care.

Chapter 5

Counter-Extremism

> Our job now is to create and hold enough time and space for the generation coming up, the generation that does not dispute Black Lives Matter, to get its chance.
>
> —Eric K. Ward[1]

"Fuck a Nazi," said Talia Lavin, "I don't care about them. I don't care about their lives. I want them to die. I have no patience. The more we socially marginalize their views, the more we make them unacceptable, the fewer people will join."

This was in response to a question from Briahna Joy Gray on the "Bad Faith" podcast in 2021. The episode description explains Lavin's work and the questions Gray was pursuing in the interview:

> As the Trump era brought spiking hate crimes, white supremacist rallies, and a renewed interest in racist online communities, journalist Talia Lavin began a fascinating social experiment aimed at understanding and exposing the white nationalist movement: She went undercover as an idealized Aryan date on whites-only dating sites. To disguise her own Jewish roots, Talia used images of an anonymous European huntress to set a trap for lonely white supremacists. The result of her investigation into the alt-right was 2020's acclaimed book, *Culture Warlords*. Nearly a year after its publication, Brie asked Talia about what drove her to want to enter the belly of the beast, what she learned, and whether her direct experiences with white supremacy have made her doubt the possibility of a broad, multiracial coalition. To what extent, if at all, is deprogramming Nazis a useful goal? Is Nazi punching as scalable as addressing the social and economic marginalization endemic to some of her targets? Why not both?[2]

Gray never finishes her interview with Lavin, who leaves the conversation in frustration. Lavin is tired of being asked questions about the value of deradicalizing or in any way building relationships with people who wish violence upon her and others. Lavin, whose career has been in investigative reporting, has endured years of anti-Semitic, misogynistic, gruesome, and hateful speech from people with such views.

Gray, who is Black, and claims just as full a right to be angry at white supremacists, is, however, still interested in the potential to pull people from the far-right into the political center or further left, where coalitions can be built across differences to advocate for policies that improve life for all people.

Gray reflects on the interview with her producer in the final minutes of the podcast. She says, "I have personally experienced that even the most racist, radical, insane people in the world when confronted with my own humanity sometimes make a different choice." She expresses the hope that she'll never "have such little faith in humanity" that she wouldn't want to interrogate white supremacist belief systems, the people who adhere to them, and attempt to see if there are any doubts, hesitations, or cracks through which might be perceived glimmers of common cause. She also acknowledges that this approach to the work may not be for everybody.[3]

PUNCH A NAZI OR COALITION-BUILD?

School leaders must both vigilantly forbid hate speech and engage those who speak it. Without using violence, we must silence white supremacist expressions in our schools, and make these beliefs "unacceptable," as Talia Levin asserts. We must also coalition-build, engaging young people in dialogue and experiences that confront the dehumanization of others with the humanity of others. As Briahna Joy Gray asserts, sometimes this can make a difference. When confronted with the humanity of the previously dehumanized other, a person holding racist views can sometimes, as Gray notes, "make a different choice."[4]

This is not to say that every educator must be ready or willing to engage in dialogue with those who express hateful ideas. The various members of any prodemocracy coalition—whether it's in a school or other organization—can have different roles. Based on positional power, racial identity, past trauma, present disposition—and countless other, often shifting, factors—different people can bring different strengths to bear. And those of us who are school leaders can sometimes find ourselves taking on roles and stances that might appear contradictory.

In the first pages of this book, I told a story about the aftermath of a soccer game, when a visiting player and his mother got out of their truck in the parking lot and harassed students of color with a racist slur. In addition to lengthy collaboration with the other school's principal and athletic director about the details of the incident and consequences for the student involved, I also issued a no-trespass order to the mother. Her son might be on the basketball team later in the winter, but she would not be allowed to attend. She was no longer allowed on campus. At the same time that I issued the no-trespass order, I sent her a letter to ask if we might talk. This was not to validate her racism. This was to learn what I could learn about what cracks there might be in the walls that she'd built to exclude and dehumanize others.

This effort at dialogue was not an effort to give a platform to racist thinking, but to understand it and hopefully make a connection with the woman, a connection that might lead to the prevention of harm in the future, whether it be harm to students from my school, or harm to other people whose paths she crossed, or harm even to herself. The mother of the son who goes into the world with racist beliefs and commits an atrocity is also going to be hurt when her son goes to live with the hard walls of his belief behind the hard walls of a prison.

In my efforts to engage this woman in dialogue, I was not attempting to bring her into a discussion with the students she had harmed. They were not asking to play that role in the process. It was, however, a role I was ready to play, based on my identity and belief in what would make the broader community more safe. In the same way, and with a similar goal of future harm reduction, I have found myself ready to engage my own students and their family members in dialogue about their racist or flawed thinking and to interrogate my own.

Not every school leader should feel obliged to talk to those who speak racist thoughts, but someone in the school should be prepared to, for a paradox at the heart of this work, especially with young people, is that to counter and silence extremism, we must listen to it.

PARADOX: TO SILENCE EXTREMISM, WE MUST LISTEN

In the previous chapter I told a story about the grandfather who said that when he looked upon the Black Lives Matter flag, it told him that he didn't matter. *What meaning did he see in the other flag?* I wondered. When my student's grandfather finally explained to me what meaning he saw in the Confederate flag, I was astounded.

"This flag," he said, "was a battle flag carried by American soldiers in a war that freed the slaves." I'd never heard such an explanation before. I didn't know what to say at first. All of it was true. And all of it was false.

The intellectual contortions and emotional gymnastics that this man was engaged in to preserve a positive sense of self in the symbol was extraordinary.

He was a war veteran who knew what it meant to fight beneath a banner in battle. He was a man whose value and valor in war was linked to pride in his country. But he also probably felt abused by his country for being tossed three times abroad to fight in war without end or any clarity of objective. The nation for which he fought was in some ways not worth his devotion.

And so he'd invested in this symbol a story that preserved white supremacy, valorized the military, brought freedom to the enslaved, and enabled both devotion to and rebellion against the nation. It was an identity cocktail of white supremacy, Black liberation, national pride, and antigovernment anger all in one. I was alarmed and fascinated.

I was also an educator. Over the course of several separate conversations, we covered a lot of ground. I shared a story with him of Confederate soldiers, flying the very flag he was asking his grandson to wear, crossing the Northern border into Canada and reentering the United States into our state, where our banks were robbed, buildings burned, and people assaulted. I'd shared the same story with his grandson, and the newspaper article in which I'd read it. I asked him what he thought about this flag being flown during assaults on our state. And I told him what I understood the Confederacy to stand for.

And to explain the importance of the other flag we were discussing, I showed him simple sketches I'd once drawn to illustrate the violence I understood to have taken place against students of color in our school. He needed to hear both historical facts and more contemporary and personal stories.

The pictures were actually ones I'd drawn for a student with whom I'd once had similar conversations. I was not being condescending; I was being concrete. Sometimes an image—even a stick figure—can illustrate reality better than words. By drawing just a few lines on the paper, I showed him the bathroom stall where hateful words were written. With a few other lines, a hand and a swastika drawn upon it. In another image, one stick figure is kicking smaller figure, and a speech bubble contains the first letter "N" of the slur. In another, the same word from two people in a truck, with stick figures standing in front of it. And there were other images as well.

I'd been listening to him, so he was willing to listen to me. I explained to him that this was why the BLM flag was flying, and it was not flying to make him feel shame or that he didn't matter. It was flying to tell the students of color that the verbal, physical, and emotional violence against them has no place here under that flag.

He asked what would happen if his grandson continued to wear the hat. I said he'd not be allowed back into classrooms. He said, "We'll see. It's up to him. But he's got my permission to wear it." His position had softened slightly. He'd shifted from asserting that his grandson would wear the hat to leaving it up to his grandson to decide. The grandson was in the room. I said that I hoped he'd choose to leave the hat at home because we valued his being in our classrooms.

I pointed to an archaic metal panel in the wall of the office, behind which was a strange mechanism that was a relic of an old public announcement system in the school. His grandson had expressed curiosity about it once when he'd spent some time in my office for another incident in his first year at the school. I'd promised his grandson that someday we'd get the custodial engineer to come meet with us to take off the panel and look inside. I told the grandfather and the boy that I valued his curiosity about how things worked. I truly did want him in our school so we could continue to learn together—about everything from how the old contraption in the wall used to function, to how systemic racism infects our lives today.

Validate—Challenge—Request

Over the course of my conversations with the grandson and the grandfather, we passed through three phases that are important to working with people who have felt devalued, what Dr. Kenneth Hardy and Dr. Tracy Laszloffy would call VCR: Validate, Challenge, Request. In their book, *Teens Who Hurt: Clinical Interventions to Break the Cycle of Adolescent Violence*, they define *validation*: "Validation consists of sending a message that acknowledges a strength or a goodness in the young person in question. It is important to note that validation is not synonymous with agreement."[5]

Hardy and Laszloffy are focused on youth who do violence to others, and sometimes to themselves. They go on to note, "After adults have appropriately and adequately validated adolescents, it then becomes possible to go on to challenge all those troubling teen thoughts and/or behaviors."[6]

In my interventions, I validated the grandfather's service in the military under the Stars and Stripes as something that must have been profoundly important for him, and I validated the grandson's curiosity about the workings of tools and machines. I did not validate their choice to wear the image of the Confederate flag, but I didn't shame them for it either.

That's not to say they might not have felt some degree of shame. It may have arrived as they wrestled with the historical facts and contemporary stories we were discussing. I don't know if they did or not. My job was to assert the school's boundaries, listen to their reactions, and engage in VCR: find ways to validate their humanity, challenge their thinking with alternative perspectives and stories, and then request that the boy return to school without his hat.

In the short term, it worked. He returned to school without his hat. In the long term, I'm not so sure. His mother, grandfather, and father all lived in different towns, not far from each other, but far enough to mean that the boy lived a transient kind of life week to week, year to year, moving here to there. In the years that followed this interaction in my office, I visited another school in the region, in the town where the boy's father lives. It was my first time visiting that school, and it was, coincidentally, this boy's first day at the school. He was standing outside when I passed him at the entrance wearing a sweatshirt with the bars and stars of the Confederate flag on his back.

Extreme or Mainstream?

We have an obligation to listen to young people who are expressing extremist or far-right beliefs, says Dr. Cynthia Miller-Idriss, expert in counter-extremism: "[T]he hardest words to listen to are, I believe, the most important ones," she writes. "It is my strongest belief that we need to understand as much as possible how young people are thinking in order to develop effective strategies to address this kind of hatred."[7]

Our nation has experienced the mass violence that can result from not listening to, understanding, and neutralizing this kind of hatred. In 2019, a white supremacist's mass shooting in El Paso, Texas, killed twenty-two people. This event and the mass murder the following day in Dayton, Ohio, excited extremists across the globe. Miller-Idriss explains that those who were yearning for race war and social disintegration "were celebrating on social media with phrases like 'it's happening' and 'the fire rises!'" According to Miller-Idriss, they were not wrong to see fires of hatred rising:

> These shootings came nearly two years after the world was stunned by scenes from the University of Virginia showing scores of white men in polo shirts marching across campus, bearing flaming tiki torches and chanting "white lives matter" and "Jews will not replace us." The following afternoon the governor of Virginia declared a state of emergency in response to the violence at the Unite the Right rally, downtown. Shortly thereafter a twenty-two-year-old neo-Nazi drove his car into a crowd of counter protesters, injuring at least nineteen people and killing thirty-two-year-old Heather Heyer. All of that came on the heels of an increase in violent hate crimes. Dylann Roof had recently received a death penalty sentence for murdering nine African American worshippers in a South Carolina church, amid a wave of incidents in schools, college campuses, and public spaces across the country. In short, the events at Charlottesville catapulted the modern far right into the public eye and helped cement a growing realization: white-supremacist and far-right movements were unquestionably on the rise in the United States. In the months that followed, a steady stream of hate confirmed that Charlottesville was not an exception. In 2018, the number of hate groups in the United States reached an all time high, with white-nationalist groups alone experiencing a nearly 50 percent increase. That same year, right-wing extremists killed at least fifty people in the United States,

outnumbering all other terrorist- and extremists-related deaths. Meanwhile, hate incidents have surfaced in local communities nationwide.[8]

Schools are within those local communities. The danger is ours to recognize, understand, and counter. This does not mean, however, that extremely violent expressions of white-supremacist thinking necessarily threaten your particular school community.

The next Dylann Roof or El Paso shooter is now being radicalized, to be sure. While not likely that he is a member of your particular school community, we can be sure that some young people in school communities across the nation are becoming adherents to far-right ideologies. These ideologies are dangerous in the mainstream, even if no mass shooting event is the outcome. Indeed, it may be that the mainstream expressions white-supremacist thinking are even more dangerous than the episodic extremist violence that they catalyze occasionally—and yet all too frequently.

Consider the death toll of the El Paso shooting in 2019: twenty-two people. Or consider the grim tally Miller-Idriss registers for the previous year, 2018: at least fifty people killed by right-wing extremists. This number is troubling. But fifty is smaller than the number of unarmed people killed by police in a given year. Of the more than 6,500 fatal police shootings between 2015 and 2021, there were more than four hundred unarmed people killed.[9] The El Paso shooter killed many unarmed people, but our police are killing more in a given year, and those killed are disproportionately people of color.

Terror is too often something that our dominant culture thinks of in the extreme rather than mainstream, or as a foreign threat rather than a domestic state of affairs. But hate is a formidable force in day-to-day life here at home—sometimes requiring formidable force in response. People of color know this well. It behooves all of us to consider it carefully.

Most readers will recall that in 2021, awash in concern about violence from groups like ISIS and the Taliban, about 6,000 US military troops were deployed to Afghanistan to help get 15,000 people out of Kabul. That was a significant surge in soldiers deployed to provide safe passage out of the country. Let us also recall that in 1962, more than 30,000 National Guard—five times as many soldiers—were deployed to provide safe passage for just one Black man into the University of Mississippi.

THE PRINCIPLE: QUESTIONS ARE AS STRONG AS ANSWERS

Combating white supremacy and extremist ideas in mainstream institutions and individual minds is as formidable a task as confronting or eliminating violence at the extremes. But this is not a matter of either/or. There is a continuum—a range of actions, expressions, and beliefs—along which young people can find themselves on the landscape of white supremacist or white nationalist ideology.

On the one end, there is accidental exposure to such ideas. A boy may come across an edgy meme or a racist joke in a video game chat. On the other end of the continuum is far-right radicalization, which can include planning for violence against those who have been dehumanized. Many of our students' lives intersect with this continuum at some point, some as victims of harm, others as perpetrators or potential perpetrators. Intersecting with potential adherents to the beliefs and perpetrators of the harm is certainly the intention of those who hope to convert young people to extremism.

Targeting Youth

The Western States Center (WSC) is a civil rights organization based in the Pacific Northwest dedicated to inclusive democracy. They support prodemocracy efforts in many different sectors of the society, including schools. In their "Toolkit for Confronting White Nationalism in Schools," the WSC includes a quote from a neo-Nazi on the opening page that parents and educators will find chilling: "'My site is mainly designed to target children' for radicalization, the editor of neo-Nazi site The Daily Stormer, Andrew Anglin, said on a radio show in 2018. '[Age] 11 through teenage years. . . . Young adults, pubescents.'"[10]

The toolkit goes on to explain why adults working with teenagers should be concerned about this targeting. Because what white nationalist ideologies offer white youth is what most adolescents are, in various ways, seeking:

> All teenagers seek a sense of identity and belonging. White nationalist organizations know this and look for ways to connect with young people in order to grow their base. It takes vigilance on the part of teachers, administrators and parents to ensure that all members of a school community feel connected in positive ways and are not left vulnerable to extremist rhetoric or recruitment.[11]

The vulnerability of adolescents to recruitment to extreme or totalizing ideological belief systems is not new. Erik Erikson, writing in the mid-twentieth century—a time of world war, totalitarian regimes, and great bloodshed—was particularly focused on the role young adults can play in the development of radical political movements. He asserts that there is an underlying need that young people have for strong ideological commitments—on the political left and right, from the radical demands of socialism to the radical terror of Nazism. Erikson points out that, even though some ideologies are fanatical oversimplifications with many dangerous implications, this does not invalidate the underlying need for them:

> Ideologies, then, seem to provide meaningful combinations of the oldest and the newest in a group's ideals. They thus channel the forceful earnestness, the sincere asceticism, and the eager indignation of youth toward that social frontier where the struggle between conservatism and radicalism is most alive. On that frontier, fanatic ideologists do their busy work and psychopathic leaders their dirty work; but there, also, true leaders create significant solidarities.[12]

The uncompromising commitments to absolute values and rigid constructs that ideologies entail have appeal to adolescents. Childhood is a time when self-centered and family-centered beliefs provide a foundation of ideological certainty about what is right and good. One might say that this is the protective "hood" of childhood. Adulthood, later in life, typically includes settled routines and strong commitments—like childrearing—that likewise offer protective hoods of strong belief and certainty about what is right.

In between the two life phases of childhood and adulthood is adolescence, or the teenage years. There's no "adolescent-hood," however, to describe it. Even our lexicon offers no protective "hood" to people of this age. It is a time of tremendous change and uncertainty, in body, in mind, in worldview, in the array of life's pathways that present themselves. Sources of certainty and stability are needed and explored, some beautiful and good, others ugly and evil, such as the ideological falsehoods and literal white hoods of the Ku Klux Klan.

White supremacy and white nationalism and the various ideological ingredients of those belief systems can offer young people—especially, of course, young white people—a sense of certainty during developmental uncertainty in a changing world that only amplifies the need for stability. In its extreme, this need for stability becomes fanaticism.

Erikson reminds us of the special dangers we face when fanaticism takes hold in an era when people have access to tools and technologies of great force, including weapons of mass destruction, the means of mass communication, and systems for mass transportation, incarceration, and extermination: "Technological centralization today can give small groups of such fanatic ideologists the concrete power of totalitarian state machines, and of small and secret or large and open machineries of extermination."[13]

The danger is clear, but so, too, is the potential for a healthy school community to help young people articulate strong beliefs about right and wrong without nurturing fanaticism and extremism. We do this by building relationships across differences and in spite of polarizing forces in the wider culture.

Schools can offer children and youth positive ways to feel belonging and connection. Schools can help students find expressions of identity that do not depend on the denigration of others, but are rather derived from affirming cultural communities, a sense of competence in skillsets valued by the society, ideals grounded in justice and fairness, and a sense of belonging in groups of various dimensions and types. But even healthy school communities and families today cannot fully eliminate potential exposure to the ideological tenets of far-right extremism.

The Ingredients of Far-Right Extremism

Professor Miller-Idriss offers a definition of the various ingredients of far-right extremism, which she describes as "four separate but overlapping categories" of belief and practice:

- Antigovernment and antidemocratic practices and ideals
- Existential threats and conspiracies
- Apocalyptic fantasies
- Exclusionary beliefs[14]

White nationalism is an example of exclusionary beliefs that typically overlap with existential threats and conspiracies. White nationalists aspire to a nation-state for white people only and are often animated by a fear that white people are being replaced by other racial groups, including Jewish people, who are often believed to be conspiratorially orchestrating the replacement. This dangerous belief system is at the center of the toolkit mentioned above, published by the Western States Center.

This toolkit is an important resource, and it should be read on its own in its entirety. There are useful definitions—such as the distinction between white supremacy and white nationalism—as well as practical guidance for educators who are faced with various expressions of white nationalism in schools.

Another important toolkit for educators has been produced by the Polarization and Extremism Research Innovation Lab (PERIL), at American University, in collaboration with the Southern Poverty Law Center (SPLC). "Building Resilience and Confronting Risk: A Parents and Caregivers Guide to Online Radicalization" was produced during the first year of the coronavirus outbreak and focused on the dangers of online radicalization at a time when more and more children were spending more and more time online, many of them isolated from positive peer and adult influences. After asking "What Is Online Radicalization?" and "Why Should You Care?" the authors answer:

Online radicalization occurs when someone's online activities—reading, watching videos, or socializing—help lead them to adopt politically or religiously extremist views. Extremist beliefs say that one group of people is in dire conflict with other groups who don't share the same racial or ethnic, gender or sexual, religious, or political identity. Extremists believe that this imagined conflict can only be resolved through separation, domination, or violence between groups. This frequently leads to antidemocratic opinions and goals, such as a desire for dictatorship, civil war, or an end to the rule of law.[15]

This toolkit, like that by the Western States Center, should be explored for all of its useful information and guidance. One theme that arises in both resources is the importance of questions and curiosity. Another theme is the importance of not scolding, shaming, or isolating young people in our responses to their problematic behaviors.

Feeling ashamed and isolated, like feeling confusion and insecurity, are emotional states that make people vulnerable to indoctrination or integration into far-right groups where they can find: simple answers to complex questions, the dehumanization of others as an outlet for grievances, forums for playful and dangerous rebellion, and a sense of belonging and purpose.

In their guidance to parents and caregivers, PERIL and SPLC advise us to listen and ask questions:

- "Listen to what young people are saying. If they begin to repeat themes or vocabulary associated with extremists and conspiracy theories, try not to ridicule or punish them. Ridicule and scolding have actually been shown to strengthen problematic belief systems."
- "Ask questions about what children are doing online, what they are learning, and what kinds of websites and platforms they spend time on. Approach these questions from a place of curiosity rather than monitoring."[16]

This guidance goes hand in hand with taking expressions of hate seriously and with vigilance. The dehumanization of others is a very serious danger, both to the young people who are adhering to the ideas and especially to the targets or victims. A young man who is expressing misogyny is doing harm to himself and doing worse harm to others; a person expressing antisemitism is doing the same. Curiosity and listening must be coupled with firm stances about what is and is not okay. When it comes to what to do in response to seeing harassing or hateful expressions in online or other spaces, PERIL and SPCL include the guidance to document and report what we see and share it with school officials or with other organizations that can help.

The Western States Center's toolkit provides several scenarios to illustrate how to respond with direct action to stop whatever harmful behavior is occurring, support those who may be harmed, and maintain a stance that does not lead to isolation of the young person who may be expressing these dangerous ideas.

One scenario involves the anonymous posting of hate speech in a school community. Guidance on how to respond includes acting swiftly to remove the content, involving other adults in the response, and "depending on the extent or severity, consider opening a community-wide conversation for other stakeholders to get information and ask questions."[17] The list of "what not to do" includes not ignoring or dismissing even minor or anonymous incidents, and not responding with undue severity or punishment: "Don't overreact. Punishing the study body as a whole or fixating on identifying the perpetrator may shut down dialogue and render stakeholders reluctant to come forward with future concerns."[18]

When it comes to expressions of white nationalist ideas that are traceable to students, overt and explicit, the guidance on how to respond likewise includes swift and firm measures to stop the harm, such as treating it as hate speech and harassment. In addition to such responses, the toolkit also advises adults to "open and continue a conversation with the student(s) involved, including wellness staff members when appropriate, to address underlying issues and support students on all sides."[19]

Another scenario in this toolkit describes students who have begun to advocate for explicitly Euro-centric or white nationalist or white-only spaces or curriculum. Sometimes white youth may believe they are a marginalized or victimized group. The fears of being replaced or demoted in status are emotional flames constantly being fanned by white nationalist actors. Included in the guidance on how to respond is a firm "no" when it comes to white pride spaces and content. Given how white supremacy functions in apportioning power and privilege in this country, the guide asserts that it is not possible to validate white-only spaces in the same way a school would validate an affinity group space for students of color. At the same time, the guide advises school leaders to "meet with" and "listen to everything they want to say, record their requests, take supporting information from them, and ask thoughtful questions."[20] The guidance goes on to explain:

> Often these students have little more than dogma to offer, but some students may have impassioned and intricate stances that have led them to this point. They will likely not listen to an administrative response if they feel they have not been heard, which may further cast them as victims of racial discrimination—the misguided perception that drives these requests.[21]

One must answer actions and expressions that dehumanize others with unambivalent refusal to allow it. Schools have a range of options to communicate zero ambivalence and zero tolerance for such. But the work doesn't end with erasing the graffiti or suspending the student. Some schools—private schools, charter schools, and others—have the option of expelling students from the school. But most schools can't do this for every incident of hate speech that occurs. The young people of a community attend the school of the community by law, including those who express hateful ideas.

The work with these students must continue all the while we answer hate with a refusal to tolerate it. This includes preventive measures as well as responses to harmful acts. It must include questions and listening. It also requires that school leaders focus on the readiness and resilience of the teachers and other adults who interact with these students every day.

PRACTICALITIES: CURIOSITY, TRANSPARENCY, VIGILANCE

In terms of far-right, white supremacist, or white nationalist extremism, most school leaders do not have a lot of practice integrating a focus on this danger into our professional development forums or our work with teachers to develop curriculum. Organizations like those mentioned already in this chapter are providing resources of extraordinary value, but how those resources are adapted for particular school settings will take creativity and the willingness to experiment and to make mistakes.

This is especially true in an era when communication and social media technologies are rapidly evolving. While the danger isn't new, the communication technology is rapidly shifting to produce new avenues for dissemination and indoctrination. We need to be ready to feel surprised and off-balance at times. We need to take a stance of curiosity combined with vigilance. We need to be transparent with our community about our concerns and our responsibilities. We also need to be learners, ready to learn from others and by doing with others.

The paradox we have named is that to silence extremism we must listen. A principle to guide us through the paradox is that questions are as strong as answers. Our curiosity is as important a force as our conviction. This leads us to consider forums for professional learning, community dialogue, and student engagement—the forums where we must hold these various stances of vigilance, transparency, and curiosity.

As with each section in this book focused on the practicalities, we are concerned with resources over which the school leader has control or influence. This includes the time given to meetings and classroom interactions; the content of those interactions, including historical facts and personal stories; the pedagogies and protocols we employ; and the staffing resources allocated to support the work.

Professional Learning

In the fall of 2020, my superintendent contacted me to ask to see my slides. Some faculty had come to him with a complaint about my presentation, which was focused on topics we are discussing in this chapter.

As school leaders will do, and as mentioned in the introduction of this book, I was imagining the worst. I imagined that we might miss a sign, that we might neglect to ask a question. I was imagining that a student—a boy, a white boy—would be lost, seeking meaning and purpose, and that he'd be seeing models of how to have impact in the media, and that he'd come to believe that violence was the way, that he was willing to copycat, and that he would be armed.

We were several months into the COVID-19 pandemic, back at school with new protocols, some students fully remote, others masked and on campus, everyone feeling off-balance, and some people feeling more isolated and anxious than when the pandemic started just the spring before. Meanwhile, the national headlines included frequent accounts of gun violence and posturing with guns throughout the ongoing racial justice protests and counterprotests.

The presentation, just fifteen slides, was called "Online Risks, Resources, Reflections." I told my colleagues at the start that this was a more presentation-heavy meeting than we were used to having, with less time for break-out groups and smaller conversations. But I hoped we'd be able to return to such formats in the near future. And, as I said to myself, I was doing more of the speaking because I wanted them to hear my voice and conviction about such matters clearly.

Slide 1 named the topics to be touched upon in the presentation:

- Youth & Exposure to Extremist Content
- Educator Stance: Curious
- Educator Stance: Transparent
- Educator Stance: Vigilant
- Educator Stance: Learning
- Reason for Concern & Reason for Hope

Slide 2 introduced a resource: the PERIL/SPLC guide for parents and caregivers on online radicalization in the COVID era.

Slide 3 drew from the PERIL/SPLC guide to name the increased risks related to online radicalization in the COVID era, which are reduced support from trusted adults; distracted adults and caregivers; new extremist content circulating; isolation from others who might challenge thinking; uncertainty and loss; and scapegoating and simplistic answers.

Slide 4, titled "Times of Uncertainty," included a quote from the PERIL/SPLC guide:

> Extremist groups exploit tragedy and loss by pushing blame onto scapegoats whom they claim are responsible for the virus and its broader impacts. Such groups thrive during times of uncertainty by offering simplistic answers and easy targets to blame.[22]

Slide 5 was a screenshot of a recent google search using the terms: "blaming Jews for covid." The purpose was to show that the conspiracy theories are easy to find and numerous.

Slide 6 was a photo, taken with my phone, looking down on my desk. There were papers, a pen, my laptop, and the printed manifesto of the "Unabomber," which a student had been reading and given to me when I was meeting with him to discuss a conversation he was having about race with another student at lunch the previous year. The picture also included a paper swastika that had been made by a student and found at school a couple of years prior. The slide included this text: *Adolescence is a time of extremes, of searching for answers and seeking belonging—to groups, to ideals, to ideas that help answer the questions "why?" and "who am I?"*

Slide 7 was titled "Intentional Outreach to Youth," and included a quote from the Western States Center toolkit, which I've already mentioned in this chapter.

Slide 8 was titled "Educator Stance: Curious," and it advised: *If you see a symbol, image, or phrase you don't recognize, or think may have racist or bigoted meaning, ask questions about it. Learn what it means to the student. And share the information with me and others if you have concerns.*

Slide 9 was titled "Educator Stance: Vigilant," and it included instructions on what to do if teachers see or hear prejudice, bias, or stereotype in the moment. This slide reminded faculty of the "Speak Up at School" resource from Learning for Justice (formerly Teaching Tolerance).

Slide 10 was titled "Educator Stance: Transparent," and included the instructions: *Remind students of our expectations for respectful interaction, that incidents of harassment are to be reported to an adult in the school—to a counselor or administrator.*

Slide 11 continued to focus on transparency, providing faculty with a statement to share with students in online classrooms, written by the social worker in the school's student services department. Faculty were told that they should reach out to our student services department for tips or support on communicating this message to students:

> In person and online, faculty and staff are dedicated to your education and social-emotional welfare. . . . This means that if we notice anything of concern, we will share it with the administration (i.e., drug use/paraphernalia, bullying behaviors, etc.) Mandated Reporting standards also remain the same. This means that if we observe anything that suggests harm to self or others we will report it to the appropriate people.

Slide 12 was titled "Educator Stance: Learning," and it reminded people of the resources named earlier in the presentation. The slide also included this assertion: *We are all learning about what it means to be committed to a pluralistic democracy in the current era of our nation's evolution. We have a responsibility to meet the needs of the individual student, and the broader society.*

Slide 13, "Reminder: Reason for Concern," noted that violent vigilantism and armed confrontation with fellow citizens was being celebrated, modeled, and enacted with murderous effect across the country, including close to home. The slide included four photos, mostly young white men, who had recently taken up arms. Also included were the dates of the related incidents—the last of which was not far away from the school and very recent:

- 06.28.20. A picture of Mark and Patricia McCloskey holding a semi-automatic rifle and pistol outside their home as Black Lives Matter protesters march on their street outside of St. Louis, Missouri.
- 08.25.20. A picture of Kyle Rittenhouse posing with a semi-automatic weapon in the woods. At seventeen years old, he killed two people at a Black Lives Matter protest in Kenosha, Wisconsin.
- 08.29.20. A picture of Aaron Danielson, a member of Patriot Prayer, a Portland-based, far-right group, who was killed by gunshot at a protest.
- 09.02.20. A picture of Jordan Atwood, a young man arrested for violating conditions of parole when he approached Black Lives Matter protesters with a semi-automatic weapon in a town not far from the school.

Slide 14, titled "Reason for Hope," shared a message related to the importance of dialogue and bridging differences as a means for undermining belief systems that dehumanize others. It included a statement by former neo-Nazi Christian Picciolini about how human connection with people he'd previously demonized helped crack the hard walls of hatred he had built around him.

I never learned what the complaints to the superintendent were about this presentation. I imagine they came from teachers who were personally sympathetic to some of the people whose pictures I'd included. The couple from St. Louis were seen as heroic defenders of private property by some. Many people across the country felt the same way about the boy, Kyle Rittenhouse, who'd come out to join law enforcement and other people ostensibly to protect private property in a climate of unrest. The pictures included three people who were menacing or had killed Black Lives Matter protesters, and one picture of a far-right counterprotestor who'd himself been killed.

Community Communication

School leaders routinely share information and resources with faculty in professional learning forums. School leaders also routinely share information and resources with students and families. Unfortunately, in years to come, there are likely to be many opportunities for school leaders to share thoughts with families and the wider community on the topic of violent extremism and the importance of nonviolence in schools and the broader society.

The days following the January 6th insurrection at the US Capitol provided such an opportunity. It was widely publicized that the FBI and local police across the country were making special preparations for possible armed rallies, as the power of the presidency continued its troubled transition from President Trump to President-Elect Biden. In my own letter to the school community with which I worked at the time, I noted this contemporary context and went on to discuss the importance of leaving weapons at home.

> Unlike other recent nationwide protests, this week the FBI and local police are making special preparations for possible armed rallies across the nation over the next few days, as the power of the presidency transitions from President Trump to President-Elect Biden.
>
> These concerns make this a good time to remind ourselves about why weapons and violence are prohibited in schools and in so many other places.
>
> We do not allow weapons and violence in schools, nor do we permit intimidating or harassing words. This is because it makes people feel fear, sadness, and other negative emotions—and children don't learn well when they feel this way.
>
> The only time I invite someone who carries a weapon into our school is when I, as principal, call upon local law enforcement to help us address a problem that could become seriously dangerous to the safety of students.
>
> I know that some principals in other places don't feel the same way, but I trust our local law enforcement officers, and we work well together to help keep students safe. That said, I feel the need to call law enforcement to school grounds very rarely. This is because we are a school community that finds ways to address problems without physical confrontation or extreme escalation. I'm speaking about all of us, adults and students.

The community was reminded of our nonviolent means for solving conflicts and building relationships, including Advisory classes, discussion-based classrooms, and restorative practice. Not knowing whether any members of the community were contemplating armed protest in the days to come, I decided to be transparent with the question:

> Will school community members carry weapons as part of protests over the next few days? Will our neighbors or family members? I do not know. I do know that weapons are not allowed on school grounds and that suspension or expulsion from school follows such incidents.
>
> I also know that our School Board's policy against bullying and harassment requires us to respond to incidents that happen both in and outside of school. This is about words as well as actions. If something is said or done outside of school, including on social media, we have to consider it a school concern if it interferes with any student's education. Let us all keep this in mind as we speak our minds and express our values, ideals, and hopes over the next few days, and all days.

It can also be valuable, in such moments, to remind people of our better selves, the ways we behave when we do good work and feel pride in ourselves:

> Our students belong to a place that stands for critical thinking, a strong work ethic, and striving for justice without resort to violence. This is how our students reach their goals and make their lives better—whether it's through extracurriculars or the classroom; whether it's at the Technical and Career Center, working in the community, or later in life at college and beyond. Students who embody these values and actions go far. Students who don't often struggle to meet their goals for schooling, college, and employment. This is true for adults, too.

Students—and all of us—sometimes need reminders about what the consequences are when norms or rules are broken. Such reminders can help people place their actions and emotions in context, envision future outcomes, and practice self-control. This moment was an opportunity for that as well:

> When there's concern about violence in the community, it's good for us to remind each other of consequences for behaviors that disturb the peace or harm others.
>
> Some of us may have heard of Sergeant Lucas Hall. He is a police officer in our state who was just suspended without pay from his job because he expressed support for the criminal acts that happened at the US Capitol last week.
>
> Or we may have heard of twenty-five-year-old Ty Garbin, who was once an airplane mechanic. He is no longer an airplane mechanic. He's in jail, because

he allegedly decided that violence was the way to solve problems and plotted to kidnap the governor of Michigan. He faces up to life in prison.

The lives of individuals and families can be ruined when we consider violence or intimidation the way to address our concerns.

I hope that the employers in our community—including my own employer—remind the people who belong to their organization what they stand for. I hope that our town officers, business executives, leaders of police and fire departments, and local business owners do the same. Let us ask our colleagues, neighbors, family members, and friends to leave out talk of weapons during this period of political transition. It will make our streets, schools, and neighborhoods safer for our children.

The letter concluded with a reminder of the kind of work that was happening at school and childrearing work done in collaboration with the parents and other caregivers of the community:

Meanwhile, here at school, we will continue to focus on the physical, emotional, and intellectual welfare of the community's young people. We will greet them in person with kind words each day as they enter for their health screenings. We will deliver school meals to them in their classrooms at lunchtime. We will play kickball and take walks with them at recess for a breath of fresh air every day. We will teach and model norms for respectful discussion and debate about topics of personal and political significance. These are priorities that will only gain in their importance in the days and months that lie ahead. We do this out of care for our students and the wider democratic society.

In addition to being emailed home, this letter was read to students in Advisory groups that same week. The spirit of this communication was less about curiosity and learning and more about vigilance and transparency: providing clarity to the young people and broader community as to what the values and policies of the school were in a time when there was talk of bringing weapons to the public square.

If people had breached the US Capitol, there was no reason to think that people inspired by their example might not emulate the same in a more local context. Vigilance and clarity were in order. In other communications with students during that period, the stance taken was more aligned with curiosity and inquiry.

Student Engagement

On Wednesday evening, January 6th, I wrote to social studies and English teachers to ask if they had anything planned for the following day. It was late in the afternoon, and certainly many people were immersed in following the unfolding events, including the Senatorial election in Georgia as well as the violence in Washington, DC. Not getting replies from teachers to my email, I decided to write a prompt that any teacher could use the following day to engage students in reflection on the historical events through which they were living. Because the school had altered much of its schedule during the COVID pandemic, to allow for ease of moving in and out of in-person and remote modalities, we didn't have our traditional Advisory structure in place that year, which is where such discussions would typically have taken place:

> If we had Advisory classes in place this year, I would probably be asking us to engage in a schoolwide discussion of Wednesday's national political events in Washington, DC, and in Georgia. Since we don't have Advisory, I am offering English and Social Studies—or any other teacher—a simple lesson plan that you can use to (1) acknowledge what took place on Wednesday and (2) begin to invite student reflection on the events.
>
> I'm not suggesting you necessarily jump into a discussion with students if you're not ready, but you could use the prompts I'm providing to engage students in reflection, collect some of their responses, and perhaps plan for a discussion next week. As always, when we discuss matters of significant personal or political importance, if you'd like an extra adult in the room to help facilitate or be there to step out with a student should the need arise, please reach out.

Various teachers chose to share the prompts with students the next day or adapt them to the needs of their particular class, and some coordinated with other teachers on their grade level teams. The prompts allowed for responses regardless of whether the student had seen the news the previous afternoon or not. One of the prompts allowed a purely personal response; others invited commentary or analysis of the recent events. The title of the lesson was "Unheard and Angry—*Then What*?"

First, information was shared so that every student and teacher had access to the same facts about what had transpired the day before:

> On Wednesday 1.6.20, there were two very significant events in national history and politics:
>
> 1. An election in Georgia resulted in two Democrats winning two Senate seats, which means there will be a Democratic majority in the Senate as well as the House. This means that the Democratic party has a better chance of passing laws that it feels are important in the next two years. It was also very significant that one of the new Senators from Georgia was a Black man, Raphael Warnock, the first Black Senator ever in the state of Georgia. Warnock's election victory is said to be due to the efforts of people like Stacy Abrams, who lost in an earlier Georgia election for

governor, in part because of efforts by state officials to make it harder for Black people to vote and have their voices heard.

2. Meanwhile, in Washington, DC, the final steps in Joe Biden's being declared president were taking place in the Capitol building. While this was happening, a large group of supporters of President Trump came to the Capitol building and forced their entry into the House of Representatives and Senate chambers. At least one person was killed, and there was a great deal of damage done to the building. After a few hours, President Trump told his supporters to be peaceful and go home, and he also said he loved them, that he felt their pain and saw that they were hurting inside because he was not declared the winner of the presidential election.

The assignment then invited students to think about the emotional drivers of these two significant historical events. A quote was shared from Martin Luther King Jr., who once said that "a riot is the language of the unheard."[23] In other words, sometimes people lash out in anger and with force when they feel they are not being heard. This framing allowed for several prompts to follow:

a. What do you do when you are feeling unheard? What do you feel, and what do you do?
b. The extreme Trump supporters acted with violence and force by storming the US Capitol. Based on what you know, do you think this was a riot because they were feeling unheard? Why or why not? How do you explain what happened?
c. Black voters and many others in Georgia felt unheard and silenced when the Black candidate for governor lost in an election marked by voter intimidation. They were angry and felt unheard. They channeled their anger into actions that got more and more people to vote in the next election, which resulted in their candidate winning the Senate seat. Have you ever seen people channel their anger or sense of injustice into positive action for their community? Please explain.

Teachers adapted this activity to their setting and grade level, but the generic task for students was, "Please write a short response to one of the above questions and submit it to your teacher." The students were told that the teacher would review the responses and determine next steps, such as creating a forum for discussion in the days to come.

One teacher at the 11/12 grade level reached out to say that she'd invited the students to write a written response to the questions, but she was not ready to engage them in discussion about their thinking. She sent copies of the students' writing. There was indeed the potential for a challenging discussion.

These older students had all chosen to weigh in on the events at the Capitol, and there were views on the left and right of the political spectrum, with one student sympathetic to the pro-Trump extremists clearly including references to Q-anon conspiracy theories about pedophilia in her response.

The teacher was in her first year, and it was understandable that she'd be asking for support. I was appreciative that she'd been willing to engage students in reflection in the first place.

After discussing several options with her, we decided that the best course of action was to share the student's writing with her colleague, a veteran US History teacher, who was teaching most of the same students in a US History class. He would be able to use the student's writing to inform his preparations for classroom discussion of the events, something he had years of related experience in doing.

Symbols with Multiple Meanings

Offering support to teachers who need it, and differentiating our expectations of teachers based on readiness and experience, is something school leaders can keep in mind when asking the community to confront challenging personal and political topics in the classroom. Another strategy is to pilot lessons or activities with teachers who are willing and ready to engage, and then learn from that experience before making it more universal. This was the approach colleagues and I took when we decided to raise awareness about a symbol of white supremacy, the upside-down okay symbol.

When turned upside down, the fingers of the hand making the okay symbol can appear to make the letters W.P., which stands for white power. The gesture is also one used in a "caught-you-looking" game that kids in certain places have played for many decades. This history allows for a double meaning and allows a person to assert plausible deniability when confronted with concerns. This is what happened after a middle school social studies teacher noticed an eighth grade boy making the symbol during an assembly on Martin Luther King Jr. Day.

Community members and students had been invited to speak to the legacy of King's stances on various issues, from his anti-war stance to advocacy for public transportation and jobs. A local pastor was speaking to the school about the power of love as an extreme force for good, and making reference to the evils of the Holocaust, when the eighth grade boy made the symbol, gaining the attention of his friends. The teacher met with him after the assembly to discuss it, and the boy denied knowing it was a symbol for white power. A few weeks later, we had developed a lesson for Advisories on the symbol.

Because this topic focused on an emotionally charged contemporary concern, we decided to pilot the Advisory lesson with a couple of experienced advisors. Their experience and feedback would allow us to revise the lesson if needed, or tailor it differently for other groups and grade levels.

The title of the lesson was "Symbols with Multiple Meanings: Confusion about Right and Wrong." Faculty were reminded, as was standard practice at the school, to ask for support with facilitation, if needed, or to ask for another adult to be in the room, in case additional support for students was in order. There were three "essential questions" grounding the lesson:

1. When symbols have multiple meanings, how do you choose what to believe in?
2. What kinds of experiences cause us to question our values and beliefs?
3. What can we do to challenge unkind and hurtful belief systems?

Advisors were provided with links to additional resources, including tools already discussed in this chapter. Advisors were also reminded of several commonly used discussion norms that would be useful for this discussion, and an introductory script was provided, framing the topic:

Sometimes symbols we see have multiple meanings. In fact, this is almost always true. The meanings of symbols also change over time. Two years ago, one of the most successful businesses in our region, with whom our school has a close partnership, decided not to publish a photo on their website. They didn't publish the photo because it included students making the upside-down OK symbol. The company's marketing and communications executives decided to not publish the photo because the meaning of the symbol was changing.

The story of how this symbol's meaning has changed is documented in an article from the *New York Times*, "When the OK Sign Is No Longer OK." The change began in 2017 as a hoax. Some people were trying to play a trick by taking a symbol with a harmless meaning and lying about it being a secret racist symbol.

However, as noted in the article, this trick has stopped being a joke, and this symbol is now associated with white supremacy. That doesn't mean the person using it necessarily intends to make a racist gesture that harms others. Sometimes it is done to be playful, rebellious, or provocative without intent to harm. But it can do harm because of the new meaning, and that is why the local business didn't allow the upside-down OK symbol in the photo, and it is why we don't allow students to use it in our school.

The lesson then asked that the group read the article, with pauses along the way to clarify meaning, and then move into discussion. The script conveyed that the group was not discussing whether the upside-down OK symbol is acceptable in school; the focus was on why and how this symbol changed over time, and what can happen when we become confused about what is right and what is wrong. There were three discussion questions, which advisors were encouraged to pose in a simple circle process, where each person is invited to speak:

1. In your parents' childhood years, the upside-down OK symbol used to be a game people would play. One person makes the gesture and tries to get another person to look, or the other person tries to jab their finger through the circle. Since it used to be a game, this means that someone could make the symbol today intending to mean "White Power," but when confronted they could say, "It's just a game." This is called "plausible deniability": You can mean one thing, but easily deny it. Jokes can be used in a similar way. Can you think of any time when someone did something that could be hurtful to some people, but when confronted by it said, "But it's only a joke"? Without sharing names, or repeating slurs/jokes, describe what you heard or observed.
2. Joking about something that could be harmful to others is dangerous because it means we are not taking seriously harm that others face. What can you do or say if you hear someone joking in a way that could be harmful to others?
3. What did the article tell us about how the OK symbol's meaning changed? Who might benefit from the confusion about the symbol's meaning? Who might be harmed, and how?

There was another chunk of script that teachers could read before a closing discussion question. The script was provided in part because many teachers are not used to planning lessons on such topics and can benefit from help framing them. But one of the lessons we learned from piloting this reading and discussion was that there was far too much content for the time allotted.

What we'd allocated to a couple of Advisory sessions, really needed days or weeks of work. These topics demand integration into the classes that meet every day, every week. Conspiracy theories that disavow the findings of science demand time in science classes. Social studies and English classes are grounded in standards that invite discussions of symbols, multiple meanings, plausible deniability. Health classes and discussions led by school counselors can be home to topics like boundaries, predation, and the vulnerabilities of youth. The final part of the lesson included a script to be read that touched on such topics:

> Sometimes it is good to question our beliefs and assumptions. Important learning can result. But in other cases, it can be dangerous. For instance, cult leaders often ask young followers to disavow their former beliefs, their families, and their community. This creates distance between the person and adults they would normally trust. Predators also do this. They create distance between a young person and trusted adults by demanding secrecy. They convince you something is good when in your heart you know it is bad. This is something that extremist groups also do. They create confusion. Using jokes, playful memes, false history, and conspiracy theories, they create uncertainty about what is true,

right and wrong. This makes a person vulnerable to being groomed or recruited to a new belief system.

It was silly to think that the various personal and political topics, as well as the readings and discussion prompts, could all be contained in a few Advisory sessions—even with experienced teachers and students who felt comfortable in their presence and with their peers.

But this is why we piloted the lesson: to be able to make some mistakes and learn from the process. Unfortunately, we were engaged in this work in the spring of 2020 and soon the COVID-19 pandemic would disrupt schooling for many months to come. This disruption made it harder to continue the work, and it made it all the more urgent to do so.

The disruption of the pandemic was like an earthquake that shook communities along fault lines that were already there, deep in the bedrock. The failings of our profit-centered healthcare system were there, and the pandemic revealed those failings more clearly. The systems that produce income inequality, channeling wealth produced by working people upward to the billionaires, only operated more effectively and cruelly, making billionaires more wealthy by billions. The uncertainty, loss, and pain that so many people felt already, only grew. A polarized society became more polarized. It became more challenging and therefore even more important for school leaders to intentionally work—in our schools where children gather—to counteract the forces that try to divide us.

FIFTEEN CONCRETE ACTIONS EVERY LEADER CAN TAKE

In the closing portion of the activity on the OK symbol, students were told, in clear terms, not to joke about or use symbols or words that have negative meaning toward other people's identity. They were reminded that it can be considered harassment and that if they hear it coming from others, they should speak up and say that they don't want to hear it and report it to an adult whom they trust.

In the same closing script, teachers were likewise reminded: "Educators, report what you hear to an administrator or counselor. Do the same when you hear someone talking about sadness, aggression, or feeling lost or hopeless."

There had been various stances taken in the activity, including vigilance about the dangers of symbols with harmful meanings, as well as transparency about the potential for harassment allegations and related consequences. There was also a stance of curiosity, questions that mined the children's own experiences and understandings. The session ended with the question: "What is one thing you can do this week to help you or someone else feel a sense of purpose and belonging?"

This last question centers a core need that all people have, including young people, and that some people fulfill through allegiance to ideologies and membership in groups that dehumanize others. A school community that cultivates a sense of purpose and belonging in young people, and does so without dehumanizing others, is a far-right-extremism-prevention machine. With this in mind, this chapter's list of actions every school leader can take includes references to actions suggested in previous chapters on democratic practice, restorative practice, and anti-racist school reforms. These actions help create healthy, bonded communities, which helps prevent violence and keeps people from seeking belonging in ideologies that dehumanize others.

- *Model the stances of vigilance and transparency*: Whenever there are concerns about far-right extremist ideology, including white nationalist ideology, or violence as a means of solving problems, express your intolerance and validate other means of expressing anger or the need for belonging. Explain what the consequences will be if people express hate or the dehumanization of others.
- *Model the learning stance*: In communication with faculty, share from the toolkits that PERIL, SPLC, and WSC have offered to schools. Explain that you are learning from these or other resources and that you are asking others to engage in this learning with you. Explore these resources with colleagues and with families. Simple questions can get things started, like, "What do you notice and wonder?" and "What connections do we see to our school context?"
- *Be in the know*: Your school has processes for reporting concerns related to bullying and harassment. Even if you have other faculty whose role it is to first receive such concerns, or respond to them, bring yourself into the process. It is important that you know the nature, quality, and quantity of concerns arising in your setting.
- *Build networks of solidarity*: Reach out to the organizations listed in this chapter and connect with the people there. These are national organizations, but they will have knowledge of resources local to you as well. Build a network of people who can listen to you and support you when you have questions about how to navigate challenging circumstances.
- *Create divisions of labor*: Since listening is one of the tools we use when youth express dangerous ideologies, determine who are the right people in your school community to take this stance. It involves curiosity, and it involves not shaming, all the while maintaining firm expectations for what is and is not acceptable. It involves validating the humanity of the person expressing dehumanizing ideas. This may or may not be a role

that is right for you, personally, to play. This is where coalition-building, allyship, and divisions of labor are important. Gather faculty, staff, and others from the community and come to know who is the best person to take the lead in certain situations. If a boy is expressing misogynist thinking, who is the right person on your team to work with him? If a young person has drawn a swastika on the inside of their notebook, who is the right person to ask him why, and ask him many other questions besides? It may not be you, and that's okay.

- *It's a community—tell stories*: Invite and tell stories—including your own story. You may not think of yourself as a storyteller, but you have a story to tell. If you are a white school leader, you have a story to tell about being white. Model the sharing of personal stories and integrate stories into your work with students and adults. Storytelling and sharing includes literature, drama, and the visual arts. If you are not ready to tell your own story, or not ready to invite the same from colleagues or students, a poem or short story can be a powerful entry point into conversations about complex topics. If you do not feel ready to facilitate a discussion about a text, there are teachers at your school who could do it. At some point, telling stories from your own life is important. This can happen at meetings, in classrooms, in the media, in letters to the local paper, or at assemblies. You do not need to tell everything, of course, but model the mix of power and vulnerability that comes with the telling of a personal story.
- *It's a school—be scholarly*: Model an appreciation for research, evidence-based arguments, and historical facts—including the history that was just yesterday in the newspaper and in contemporary policy debates. There are strong anti-intellectual forces and inclinations in our nation, as dangerous today as ever. Reject this and embrace your role as a public intellectual. Put the work you and others are doing in historical context.
- *Ask hiring questions with democracy in mind*: Schools are among those local institutions, often governed by democratically elected school boards, that will come increasingly under attack by people worried by conspiracy theories and a lack of trust in democratic process. In times of uncertainty, people can gravitate toward authoritarian leaders who convey simple stories in response to complex problems. In this context, it is important to remind people of the role of schools in civil society. Pick a quote about the democratic purpose of schools and ask a question about it in your hiring interviews. Make it one of the first questions, so that you let it make a first impression.
- *Lead through distributed leadership, representative governance, and collaborative problem-solving*: As discussed in chapter 2, democracy is a cultural way of life, but it is also a matter of formal processes and

structures for collaborative decision-making. The adults of the school should be engaged, through distributed leadership opportunities and representative structures, in routine opportunities for collaborative problem-solving in areas where they have agency and investment. The size of the school will determine how complex or simple these governance systems should be to allow adequate time and space for the work. The people who facilitate these meetings should have training and support in simple processes for deliberation and consensus-seeking.
- *Cultivate teacher facilitators*: Create teacher-fueled engines for the work. Preparation for the work happens by being engaged in the work. Involve other adults in conversations about antidemocratic extremism and violence, and after exposure and modeling, ask them to facilitate the same, in small break-out groups at a faculty meeting, for instance. If they are teachers stepping up to the plate to be facilitators, support them by giving them time or stipends for doing this work.
- *Normalize norms, agreements, and protocols*: Veteran educators, teachers who are career changers, and many other people in schools may not have the habit of running meetings according to norms or agreements. If they've been involved in formal governance bodies, they may know Robert's Rules of Order, a procedure for deliberation, voting, and adopting resolutions or policies. But they may not be comfortable with silence, with deeply listening, with the careful and empathic navigation of topics with personal and interpersonal importance. Norms, agreements, and protocols for discussion may not be familiar to many in your faculty, and they should be employed by the school leader in meetings, to model and spread the practice. Discussion of topics like those covered in this chapter will require norms, agreements, and protocols.
- *Make the circle*: Dispel the idea that sitting in a circle and talking about feelings is just for kids. We are never too old for a circle to be how we relate to each other, including in the meetings you plan. As discussed in chapter 2, the school leader has a lot of power over how meetings are run. Do you gather in a room that's a bit crowded such that not everyone can see everyone else's face? Change that. Use meetings as on-the-job training opportunities for faculty in circle process and discussion protocols. In the meetings that you facilitate, bring people together in circles.
- *Inform students of their rights*: The American Civil Liberties Union and other organizations like the Southern Poverty Law Center and NAACP offer resources to young people to help them know their rights when it comes to permitted and prohibited speech, assembly in public, and actions in school and out, including interactions with the police and other authorities. Find venues when it makes sense to share this information with students.

- *Find grounding in federal law*: Federal law prohibits the harassment of people based on protected identity categories. There will be certain symbols, statements, policy positions, organizing, and advocacy that will constitute harassment and that you will not tolerate in school.
- *Share good news*: Your email is probably so busy that you'd rather not add anything else to your inbox, but one way to stay conversant with the organizing and activism happening in your community and across the country is to subscribe for updates from organizations that will let you know what organizing is going on around the country and around the world. It is especially important to read and share stories of pro-democracy actions. The Western States Center communicates about pro-democracy actions as well as threats from antidemocratic actors. Find news that tells stories of resistance and solidarity, as well as stories of the dangers being confronted. Share the stories of solidarity.
- *Be devoted to dialogue*: Make time for one-on-one and small group conversations. When the need or opportunity arises, invite or accept requests for dialogue with people in the community who hold beliefs that may pose a danger to inclusivity and democracy. Find common ground through dialogue with people who hold views different from your own. To be in dialogue with someone allows you to validate their humanity, but doesn't mean you validate their delusions. Spending time together with someone in the same room, even if the time is spent in disagreement, can still build a degree of trust, a small foundation upon which you may later be able to challenge their ideas and make requests. This may help prevent them from doing harm or allow them to make positive contributions to the community. It's not contradictory to communicate to someone that "your ideas are worthy of my resistance, but you as a person are worth my time."

IDEAS OLD AND NEW

In schools where there are democratic and restorative modes of interaction, and where young people develop competence with skills and tools needed to complete meaningful tasks, purpose and belonging are being nurtured and violence is being prevented.

What is daunting about counter-extremism work in our online world is that the symbols and tactics of these harmful ideas and their predatory purveyors are constantly shifting. This is daunting for law enforcement and families as much as it is for educators. What is especially challenging for educators is that the lessons and materials for classroom instruction are still in development and will need to be developed by us—and shared among us—as we go.

In other chapters in this book, readers are told where to go for resources ready and waiting to help us in our work. There is no need to reinvent the wheel. There is curriculum already written to help us study racism and resistance to it in the United States. There are books with circle prompts for reparative interventions already written and well-suited to your setting. There are protocols and models of democratic governance and interaction already tried and true, waiting on the shelf in books and online. There are norms and agreements well-suited to discussing bias in your community that you do not need to invent.

But the lesson plans still need to be written on those like Dylann Roof, the young white man who became radicalized, in part, online, and who came to believe in the necessity of race war and intended to catalyze it with his murders of Black worshipers at the Mother Emanuel AME Church in Charleston, South Carolina.

There are school counselors practiced in talking about boundaries and consent when it comes to sexual assault or abuse prevention; families are familiar with concerns about sexual harassment and predation. We have less experience in understanding and responding to the threat of neo-Nazi predators who lurk behind video game interfaces as our children chat online.

There are many, many teachers who are practiced in developing curriculum for elementary, middle, and high school students that teach courageously about systemic white supremacy and the never-ending resistance to it by people of color and their white allies. For those school leaders willing to allocate the time, there are resources at the ready, which our teacher colleagues can be adapting right now to their social studies, English, science, and math classes at every grade level. But even educators practiced in doing the hard work to teach about oppression and resistance, from the seventeenth through the twentieth century, may need to invent new lessons to address twenty-first-century paranoias about white genocide. These paranoias pulse just under the skin of the body politic today. More and more we see them break through. We need new vaccines for such delusions.

The list of what we know and have done—and how inadequate those efforts are to some of today's challenges—could go on. Many schools have civics classes as graduation requirements. We need a very new orientation to civic understanding and civic engagement if we are to counter the ongoing erosion of trust that makes people hostile to their local systems of representative democracy and self-governance.

Many schools have science classes that teach about the chemical and biological mechanics of disease transmission. We need new lessons that teach this scientific story in the context of a polarized society where public health is a sometimes violent space of contested beliefs. We need new resources for teaching the science of contemporary pandemics in a polarized and paranoid culture. The same has been true, for a few decades, of climate change, a scientific reality that is met with denials both politically and religiously charged. We need additional resources, now, to teach about climate change and climate disaster in the context of extremism. Just as Dylann Roof thought a race war was necessary to open the door to a new social order, some extremists welcome environmental disaster as a precipitant of social disintegration. Professional development plans for these topics still need to be written.

Daunting is the work we have cut out for us. Educators have access to curriculum to teach about the Holocaust. But we will need new lessons to teach about how anti-Semitism and age-old myths about the sacrifice of children intersect with contemporary conspiracy theories about pedophilia and world domination by Jews. As such ideas or allusions to them become more mainstream, we need mainstream resources to confront them. Thankfully, while much of what we need has still to be created, much of what will ground us in the work is simple and already known.

The Courage to Try Old Ways

Audre Lorde wrote an essay to women about the necessity of poetry called "Poetry Is Not a Luxury." Speaking to women, but with assertions relevant to others as well, Lorde rejects the notion that our brains can be called upon to invent new ideas and tools to see and chart the path toward freedom.

> Sometimes we drug ourselves with dreams of new ideas. The head will save us. The brain alone will set us free. But there are no new ideas still waiting in the wings to save us as women, as humans. There are only old and forgotten ones, new combinations, extrapolations, and recognitions from within ourselves, along with the renewed courage to try them out.[24]

Just so, as educators approach the new challenges of teaching today in the name of freedom, for democracy, and against extremist dehumanization, much of what we need are old ideas and the courage to try them out. We need to make time for dialogue, for gathering in circles, exchanging stories, and building relationships that foster trust and belonging. This is about collaboratively solving the problems we hold with others in our community. This is about doing work that corresponds to the needs of the people of the place where we live together. Schools can be places where such needs are met and where such stories come true.

Conclusion

Pathways to Power

"I'm not powerful," she said, "I'm a bitch."

Vanessa and another girl, normally friends, were feuding. It was becoming loud, disrespectful, and very public. There were threats, insults, vulgar accusations between them, online and now in the hallways.

One of their teachers, Diana, had just pulled them into my office from the hall where they were shouting at each other on their way back from the cafeteria.

I opened the conversation by remarking their power. "You're acting powerfully this morning. Insulting each other with powerful words. Getting people's attention."

Vanessa rejected the idea.

I again noted the impact the two of them were having. "You are making a difference this morning. You're having an impact on others. We could even hear you in the office. You are having an impact on your environment. There are probably younger students who are feeling uneasy because of your words right now. We are all noticing you."

With help from Diana, we eventually began discussing other ways a person can have power and how our school was dedicated to helping them cultivate it. Now in ninth grade, both girls had struggled with engagement in school for years. Diana was a special educator who worked closely with each of them and their families.

The girls had brought their cafeteria orange juice and bagels with them into the office. "Let's pretend this is a crystal ball," I said, taking Vanessa's unopened clear plastic orange juice container, turning it, looking into it. "It's going to help us see the future." I was being silly and serious at the same time.

I told them something that my dad used to say: "We are and we become as we see ourselves being and becoming." I said that envisioning the future is part of making it come true. I envisioned three years into the future:

The two girls, friends again, are coming back from "Instant-Decision Day" at a local college, which is when an interview and transcript review both happen within a couple of hours, and an admissions decision can happen on the same day. They arrive back at school, run off the bus, and hurry down the hallway to knock on Diana's door. She says she's in a meeting and shoos them away, but the girls are so excited they won't leave. Diana steps into the hall, and then she hugs them when they tell her that they've just been accepted to college.

This brief look to the future helped change the vibe that morning. The girls began to feel less angry. Soon the four of us we were talking about what was happening in classes that day.

Vanessa was supposed to participate in a seminar discussion in social studies. I told her I was having another vision: that she was going to speak, and that she was going to say something powerful.

Three hours later, I stopped in to visit her classroom. Vanessa was at a table in the middle of the room with five other students. Peers were seated around them, taking notes on the conversation. They were discussing policing, race, and criminal justice reform. Vanessa was saying nothing.

An expectation of the seminar is that participants ask open-ended questions of each other. When a boy asked about the death penalty, Vanessa finally spoke.

She argued for rehabilitation and forgiveness. She took a stand. She didn't mention him, but she was probably thinking of her father, and the years he'd spent away from her in prison before he died.

Vanessa is a person who has lived a lot in her short life, who has something to say and much to learn. After class I told her I was proud of how powerfully she'd spoken.

RETREAT FROM POWER

Some emotional states make us feel big and powerful; others make us feel small. When we feel depressed, many feel like retreating from the world. Sleep becomes more of a refuge than a need. We close the curtains, seek less impact, mute rather than wield our power. So, too, when we are ashamed, we may look down and away. Our knees and spines bend to shrink our stature. We hide our faces. In shame, we reduce ourselves, shrink, lessen what people can see of us.

These are unhappy ways to be. We prefer happier states of being that help us feel bigger and more powerful and alive. Except for the very late stages of maturity, when the task for body and mind is to make peace with lying down and death, it feels right to be up and having an impact on the world rather than retreating from it. We outwardly seek happiness, belonging, and love through our gestures and in how they are returned.

Short of love, happiness, and belonging, most of us would rather feel anger or outrage than feel depression or shame. Though we may not feel happy in the moment, at least in outward anger we are more likely to be heard and feel powerful.

Our world is troubled and unfair, which makes anger understandable. Rage and violence become alluring and available pathways to feel our agency and impact. Indeed, outrage is more than just a likely pathway, it is among the pathways actively offered us. The ruling elite, who shape the inequities that makes us feel angry, actively fan the flames of our anger to divide us so they may continue to rule. News and social media companies, which thrive when our emotions make us hungry for content, will also fan those flames to keep us anxious, angry, and engaged.

Every day that we wake, what pathways to power are open to our children and to each of us? What opportunities to feel power and be happy are available to our neighbors, friends, family, and strangers?

Like Vanessa, we may feel anxious and angry because of the injustices we see or the losses we have known. What opportunities do we have to express these feelings and understand them in the company of others? We can certainly feel powerful casting insults in the hallways, making enemies of others in our outrage. Or instead we can feel powerful in conversation with our peers across the table, mining our experience, understanding theirs, in conversation about how to make the world a better place.

POLARIZATION LIMITS OUR OPTIONS

This book invites school leaders to consider how to exercise our influence in ways that honor and channel the power of people in democratic directions, toward mutual understanding and nonviolent belonging, away from ridicule and shame, the silencing of others, and the dehumanization of difference.

An acute challenge that school leaders will face in the present era, and perhaps for generations to come, is that a polarized society limits the range of options available for exercising our power and having an impact. The space for democratic practice and restorative justice will shrink as the society continues to polarize and people become less and less willing to engage in dialogue. The pathways for feeling power in peaceful ways, in collaboration across difference, become less visible and may feel less viable and more dangerous.

A progressive educator on the political left, someone I respect, once wrote to me on Twitter, questioning my impulse to dialogue. I had suggested that people involved in a public confrontation on social media be encouraged to meet face-to-face. He wrote:

> I wonder, is there a line that gets crossed where dialogue becomes counter productive, where the very act of hearing both sides solidifies the false equivalence, where hate and exclusion are given too much space to exist? In my experience, calling in doesn't always work.

My response was to validate the question, but also to say: "In my experience, one-on-one conversation with parents or other stakeholders almost always helps. Having dialogue [with] someone doesn't mean I validate a delusion. And it can help keep a delusion from doing further damage in the school."

It may not always work, but my impulse is to engage a dangerous idea and the person who believes it. I'm hoping to weaken the harmful notion, perhaps through persuasion but minimally through some discovery of common ground, rather than leave it alone and let the poisonous delusion potentially grow stronger.

But dialogue across difference is perceived as less viable in a polarized society. Trends today are toward deepening division, with schools as a site where much of the conflict plays out. What this means is that the reforms described in this book will be even harder embrace tomorrow than they were yesterday, when this book was written.

"IT TAKES SOCIAL LEADERS"

Democratic societies like ours, which are troubled by inequality and violence, can avoid the descent into more savage and widespread violence when leaders step into the public sphere to mobilize people in nonviolent directions. Even politicians corrupted by the influence of the wealthy few are still dependent on the middle and working classes for the votes that keep them in office. Rachel Kleinfeld, an expert in what makes some societies more violent than others, names the necessity of creative and courageous leadership in a polarized society:

> It takes social leaders to organize the middle class into movements that are focused on effective goals, strong enough to overcome entrenched interests, and broad and nonpartisan enough to achieve success in highly polarized countries.[1]

A school leader can be such a leader. Schools are small societies situated within larger societies. Schools are subject to the polarizing forces that disable dialogue and drive people apart, but schools are likewise positioned to center goals in which all can believe. A goal nearly all families and neighbors can share is that the community's children grow up healthy and happy. School leaders can articulate such goals, cultivate collective commitment to them, and shape the conditions of our small societies to achieve them. We can make and hold democratic spaces for dialogue, mutual understanding, and the repair and prevention of harm. We can engage children and adults in collaboration across difference to see and work toward solving the problems large and small that face us.

School leaders in this country will be instrumental in holding our communities together in nonviolent collaboration in years to come. If our nation is at risk of greater violence, our schools can be places where the courage of nonviolent collaboration lives.

"The United States now stands on a precipice," wrote Kleinfeld in 2018. "Do we continue to polarize politically and culturally or can we find a way to rebuild trust and a sense of shared nationhood across our differences?"[2] The school reforms described in this book, and the actions school leaders can take to achieve them, are small but important steps toward achieving trust and shared nationhood in an era when common cause can be hard to find.

Understanding schools and school leadership as a social endeavor with the highest of stakes can help us see the simplest of goals more clearly. The goal is the wellness of each individual child and the wider community in which they live. We will achieve the goal through collaborative solutions to the problems we share, empathic listening no matter how loud the cry, and the occasional quiet needed to hear the truth of other people's stories and our own.

Notes

PREFACE

1. "A Notorious Affair of Honor—William H. G. Butler," National Memorial to Fallen Educators, accessed 11.1.21, https://nthfmemorial.org/a-notorious-affair-of-honor-william-h-g-butler/.

2. "Bath School Disaster," National Memorial to Fallen Educators, accessed 11.1.21, https://nthfmemorial.org/bath-school-disaster/.

3. Trip Gabriel and Dana Goldstein, "Disputing Racism's Reach, Republicans Rattle American Schools," *New York Times*, 6.1.21, https://www.nytimes.com/2021/06/01/us/politics/critical-race-theory.html?smid=tw-share.

4. "Want to Know America's Most Armed Counties? Check This Map with Data from 2016," Wideopenspaces, March 12, 2021, accessed October 19, 2021, Want to Know America's Most Armed Counties? Check This Map With Data From 2016 (wideopenspaces.com).

5. Emma Garcia and Elaine Weiss, "US schools struggle to hire and retain teachers," *Economic Policy Institute*, 4.16.19, https://www.epi.org/publication/u-s-schools-struggle-to-hire-and-retain-teachers-the-second-report-in-the-perfect-storm-in-the-teacher-labor-market-series/.

INTRODUCTION

1. "High School Completion Rate Is Highest in US History," United States Census Bureau, 12.14.17, https://www.census.gov/newsroom/press-releases/2017/educational-attainment-2017.html.

2. "2 Cited In Confrontation Outside Courthouse After Hearing For Alleged Martinez BLM Mural," CBS 5 KPIX, 10.13.20, https://sanfrancisco.cbslocal.com/2020/10/13/2-cited-confrontation-protest-courthouse-hearing-alleged-martinez-blm-mural-vandals/.

3. "Curriculum Guide 2020–2021," Community High School District 117, accessed 11.1.21, https://core-docs.s3.amazonaws.com/documents/asset/uploaded_file/747668/2020-2021-Curriculum-Guide.pdf.

4. Nahlia Webber, "If You Really Want to Make a Difference in Black Lives, Change How You Teach White Kids," *Education Post*, 6.29.20, https://educationpost.org/if-you-really-want-to-make-a-difference-in-black-lives-change-how-you-teach-white-kids/.

CHAPTER 1

1. Jamila Lyiscott, *Black Appetite. White Food. Issues of Race, Voice, and Justice Within and Beyond the Classroom* (New York: Routledge, 2019), 90.

2. Stokely Carmichael, speech, accessed October 19, 2021, https://www.goodreads.com/quotes/7802915-if-a-white-man-wants-to-lynch-me-that-s-his.

3. Ibid.

4. W. E. B. DuBois, *Darkwater: voices from within the veil (*New York: Harcourt, Brace, 1921), accessed October 19, 2021, W. E. B. Du Bois—Darkwater (Chap. 2) | Genius.

5. Ijeoma Oluo, "White People: I Don't Want You To Understand Me Better, I Want You To Understand Yourselves," accessed October 19, 2021, https://medium.com/the-establishment/white-people-i-dont-want-you-to-understand-me-better-i-want-you-to-understand-yourselves-a6fbedd42ddf.

6. Myriam Gurba, *Mean* (Brooklyn: Coffee House Press, 2017), 6.

7. James Baldwin, *The Fire Next Time* (New York: Dell Publishing, 1964), 28.

8. "I Sexually Identify as an Attack Helicopter," Know Your Meme, accessed October 19, 2021, I Sexually Identify as an Attack Helicopter | Know Your Meme.

9. Sean Couglan, "2018 worst year for US school shootings," BBC News, December 12, 2018, 2018 'worst year for US school shootings'—BBC News.

10. "Want to Know America's Most Armed Counties? Check This Map with Data from 2016," Wideopenspaces, March 12, 2021, accessed October 19, 2021, Want to Know America's Most Armed Counties? Check This Map With Data From 2016 (wideopenspaces.com).

11. John Kruzel, "Newsweek Stated on October 2, 2017 in an Article: 'White Men Have Committed More Mass Shootings Than any Other Group,'" *Politifact*, October 6, 2017, https://www.politifact.com/factchecks/2017/oct/06/newsweek/are-white-males-responsible-more-mass-shootings-an/.

12. Western States Center, *Confronting White Nationalism in Schools Toolkit, Second Edition (*Portland, OR: Western States Center, 2019), 7.

13. Josh Bersin, "Why Aren't Wages Keeping Up? It's Not the Economy, It's Management," *Forbes,* October 31, 2018, accessed October 19, 2021. https://www.forbes.com/sites/joshbersin/2018/10/31/why-arent-wages-keeping-up-its-not-the-economy-its-management/?sh=596bd878397e.

14. James Baldwin, *No Name in the Street* (New York: Vintage Press, 2000), 125.

15. Chris Hedges, "Hedges: The Evil Within Us," Scheerpost, March 22, 2021, Hedges: The Evil Within Us—scheerpost.com.

16. James Baldwin, *Dark Days* (New York: Penguin Press, 1985) 2.

17. Emma Redden, *Power Means Who the Police Believe: Talking with Young Children about Race and Racial Violence*, (published by the author, 2019), 147.

18. Ibid., 27.

19. National Memorial for Peace and Justice, accessed October 19, 2021, Memorial (eji.org).

20. Ralph Ellison, *Invisible Man* (New York: Vintage Books, 1947), 5.

21. Ibid.

22. Jamila Lyiscott, *Black Appetite. White Food: Issues of Race, Voice and Justice Within and Beyond the Classroom* (New York: Routledge, 2019), 13.

23. Ibid., 4.

24. Ibid., 5.

25. Ibid., 19.

26. Alice Walker, review of *Strange Fruit*, by Lillian Smith, accessed October 19, 2021, Lillian Smith—Lillian Smith: Breaking the Silence (lilliansmithdoc.com).

27. James Baldwin, review of the writings of Lillian Smith, accessed October 19, 2021, Lillian Smith—Lillian Smith: Breaking the Silence (lilliansmithdoc.com).

28. John Inscoe, "*Killers of the Dream*," New Georgia Encyclopedia, last modified March 20, 2021. https://www.georgiaencyclopedia.org/articles/arts-culture/killers-of-the-dream/.

29. Lillian Smith, *Killers of the Dream* (New York: Norton, 1994), 37.

30. Ibid., 38.

31. Ibid., 39.

32. Ibid.

33. Ibid., 168.

34. Ibid., 164.

35. Heather McGhee, *The Sum of Us: What Racism Costs Everyone and How We Can Prosper Together* (New York, One World, 2021), 25.

36. Ibid., 20.

37. Jean-Paul Sartre, *Existentialism Is a Humanism* (New Haven, Yale University Press, 2007), 41.

38. Ibid., 41.

39. Franz Fanon, *Black Skin, White Masks* (New York: Grove Press, 1967), 222.

40. Lyiscott, *Black Appetite. White Food*, 22.

41. Center for Public Education, "Teaching the Teachers: Effective Professional Development in an Era of High Stakes Accountability," accessed November 11, 2021, http://conference.ohioschoolboards.org/2017/wp-content/uploads/sites/17/2016/07/1pm111317A114Job-embedPD.pdf.

42. James Baldwin, "James Baldwin Discusses His Book 'Another Country' and His Travels through Africa," interview by Studs Terkel, *Studs Terkel Radio Archive*, September 29, 1962, audio, 47:08, https://studsterkel.wfmt.com/programs/james-baldwin-discusses-his-book-another-country-and-his-travels-through-africa?t=1806.6%2C1810.499&a=ItHasTo%2CWherEverBegi.

43. Fanon, *Black Skin, White Masks*, 232.

CHAPTER 2

1. Carolyn Boyes-Watson and Kay Pranis, *Circle Forward: Building a Restorative School Community* (St. Paul: Living Justice Press, 2015),18.

2. Nelda Cambron-McCabe, "Schooling as an Ethical Endeavor," in *Schools That Learn: A Fifth Discipline Fieldbook for Educators, Parents, and Everyone Who Cares about Education,* ed. Peter Senge (New York: Doubleday, 2000), 279–281, 317.

3. Ibid., 279.

4. Ibid., 281.

5. Ibid., 317.

6. Cornel West, *Democracy Matters: Winning the Fight against Imperialism* (New York: the Penguin Group, 2004), 68.

7. Deborah Meier, *In Schools We Trust*: *Creating Communities of Learning in an Era of Testing and Standardization* (Boston: Beacon Press, 2002), 177.

8. "Position Description: High School Principal," Northfield Public Schools, Northfield, Minnesota, accessed October 26, 2021, https://cse.google.com/cse?q=&sa.x=11&sa.y=11&cx=005796229432434085693%3Az2nbjlwhts4&ie=UTF-8#gsc.tab=0&gsc.q=High%20School%20Principal&gsc.sort=.

9. Ibid.

10. John Dewey, *Democracy and Education: An Introduction to the Philosophy of Education* (New York: Macmillan Company, 1916), Ch 7. "The Democratic Conception in Education," 94–116. https://books.google.com/books?id=jqROAAAAMAAJ&pg=PR3&source=kp_read_button&hl=en&newbks=1&newbks_redir=0&gboemv=1.

11. John Dewey, *Experience and Education* (New York: Simon and Schuster,1938), 54–56.

12. Chelsea Parsons, "Gun Violence Prevention Priorities for a New Congress and a New Administration," Center for American Progress, January 26, 2021, accessed October 26, 2021, https://www.americanprogress.org/issues/guns-crime/news/2021/01/26/495035/gun-violence-prevention-priorities-new-congress-new-administration/.

13. Ibid.

14. Katherine Schaefer, "Key Facts About Americans and Guns," Pew Research Center, September 13, 2021, accessed October 25, 2021, https://www.pewresearch.org/fact-tank/2021/09/13/key-facts-about-americans-and-guns/.

15. Bill Chapel, "The Pentagon Has Never Passed an Audit. Some Senators Want to Change That," National Public Radio, May 19, 2021, accessed October 26, 2021, https://www.npr.org/2021/05/19/997961646/the-pentagon-has-never-passed-an-audit-some-senators-want-to-change-that.

16. Chris Hedges, "Hedges: The Collective Suicide Machine and the Fall of Kabul," Scheerpost, July 26, 2021, accessed October 26, 2021, https://scheerpost.com/2021/07/26/hedges-the-collective-suicide-machine/.

17. Nahlia Webber, "If You Really Want to Make a Difference in Black Lives, Change How You Teach White Kids," *Education Post*, June 29, 2020, accessed October 26, 2021, https://educationpost.org/if-you-really-want-to-make-a-difference-in-black-lives-change-how-you-teach-white-kids/.

18. Ibid.

19. Ralph Ellison, *Invisible Man* (New York: Vintage Books, 1947), 574.

20. School Reform Initiative (SRI), "Towards a General Theory of SRI's Intentional Learning Communities," SRI, accessed October 26, 2021, https://www.schoolreforminitiative.org/research/general-theory-of-intentional-learning-communities/.

21. See Maria Hantzopoulos, *Restoring Dignity in Public Schools: Human Rights Education in Action* (New York: Teachers College Press, 2016).

22. Sascha Brodsky, "Is Discipline Reform Really Helping to Decrease School Violence?," *The Atlantic*, June 28, 2016, accessed October 26, 2021, https://www.theatlantic.com/education/archive/2016/06/school-violence-restorative-justice/488945/.

23. Nikhil Goyal, "These People Think Your Kids Need High Stakes Testing—but Not Theirs," *The Nation*, March 29, 2016, accessed October 26, 2021, https://www.thenation.com/article/archive/these-politicians-think-your-kids-need-high-stakes-testing-but-not-theirs/.

24. InsideSchools.org, 2017, "James Baldwin School: A School for Expeditionary Learning," https://insideschools.org/school/02M313.

25. NYC (New York City) Department of Education, 2017, "School Quality Reports School Year 2015–2016," http://schools.nyc.gov/OA/SchoolReports/2015-16/School_Quality_Snapshot_2016_HST_M313.pdf.

26. See Mara Benitez, Jill Davidson, and Laura Flaxman, *Small Schools, Big Ideas: The Essential Guide to Successful School Transformation* (New Jersey, Hoboken: John Wiley & Sons, Inc., 2009).

27. Münire Erden and H. Eylem Korkmaz, "A Delphi Study: The Characteristics of Democratic Schools," *The Journal of Educational Research* 107, no.5 (March 2014): 365–73.

28. Michael W. Apple and James A. Beane, "The Case for Democratic Schools," in *Democratic Schools: Lessons in Powerful Education*, 2nd ed., ed. Michael W. Apple and James A. Beane (Portsmouth, NH: Heinemann 2007), 9.

29. See Ronald J. Newell and Irving H. Buchen, *Democratic Learning and Leading: Creating Collaborative School Governance* (Lanham, MD: Rowman and Littlefield, 2004).

30. Erden and Korkmaz, "A Dephi Study," 372.

31. Deborah Meier and Paul Schwartz, "Central Park East Secondary School: The Hard Part of Making It Happen," in *Democratic Schools: Lessons in Powerful Education*, ed. Michael W. Apple and James A. Beane, "The Case for Democratic Schools," in *Democratic Schools: Lessons in Powerful Education*, Second ed., ed. Michael W. Apple and James A. Beane (Portsmouth, NH: Heinemann, 2007), 147.

32. Dewey, *Experience and Education*, 54–56.

33. See Maria Hantzopoulos, "Deepening Democracy: How One School's Fairness Committee Offers an Alternative to 'Discipline,'" *Rethinking Schools* 21, no.1 (Fall 2006), https://www.rethinkingschools.org/articles/deepening-democracy. Also see Christine Olson, "The Deep Roots of the Fairness Committee in Kohlberg's Moral Development Theory," *Schools* 8, no.1 (Spring 2011): 125–35, https://doi.org/10.1086/659442.

34. See Martha Foote, "Keeping Accountability Systems Accountable," *Phi Delta Kappan* 88, no. 5 (January 2007): 359–63, https://journals.sagepub.com/doi/10.1177/003172170708800506.

35. Carl D. Glickman, *Renewing America's Schools: A Guide for School-Based Action* (San Francisco: Jossey-Bass, 1993), 34.

36. Ibid., 42.

37. Perry Weiner as cited in T. Elijah Hawkes, 2011. The James Baldwin School Faculty Handbook (New York: James Baldwin School, 2011).

38. Glickman, *Renewing America's Schools*, 9.

39. John Tierney, "Why Do So Many Teachers Quit Their Jobs: Because They Hate Their Bosses?," *The Atlantic* (November 2012), https://www.theatlantic.com/national/archive/2012/11/why-do-so-many-teachers-quit-their-jobs-because-they-hate-their-bosses/265310/?utm_source=copy-link&utm_medium=social&utm_campaign=share.

40. Deborah Meier, "So What Does It Take to Build a School for Democracy?" *Phi Delta Kappan* 85, no. 1 (September 2003): 15–21, https://doi.org/10.1177/003172170308500106.

41. School Reform Initiative (SRI), "Towards a General Theory of SRI's Intentional Learning Communities," SRI, accessed October 26, 2021, https://www.schoolreforminitiative.org/research/general-theory-of-intentional-learning-communities/.

42. Douglas R. Knecht, "Schooling for and with Democracy," *Schools: Studies in Education* 15, no. 1 (Spring 2018): 21, https://doi.org/10.1086/697092.

43. Ibid., 24.

44. Ibid.

CHAPTER 3

1. James Baldwin, *Dark Days* (New York: Penguin Press, 1985), 30.

2. Maria Hantzopoulos, "Deepening Democracy: How One School's Fairness Committee Offers an Alternative to 'Discipline,'" *Rethinking Schools* 8, no.1 (Spring 2011), https://doi.org/10.1086/659440.

3. Liz Kleinrock, *Start Here, Start Now: A Guide to Antibias and Antiracist Work* (Portsmouth, NH: Heinemann, 2021), 57.

4. *Leaders of Their Own Learning*, "Chapter 5: Student-Led Conferences," *Expeditionary Learning*, accessed November 1, 2021, https://eleducation.org/resources/chapter-5-student-led-conferences.

5. Nancy Riestenberg, *Circle in the Square: Building Community and Repairing Harm in School* (St. Paul, Minnesota: Living Justice Press, 2012), 6.

6. Howard Zehr, *The Little Book of Restorative Justice* (Intercourse, PA: Good Books, 2002), 37.

7. Zehr, *The Little Book of Restorative Justice,* 23.

8. Ibid., 19–20.

CHAPTER 4

1. Ben Heintz, ed., "For Teachers, a Classroom Lesson: The BLM Flag in Our Schools," *VT Digger*, October 10, 2021, https://vtdigger.org/wp-content/uploads/2021/10/For-Teachers_-A-Lesson-for-the-BLM-Flag-in-VTs-Schools.pdf.

2. Susannah Hutcheson, "Read the Speech That Got a High School Valedictorian Pulled from the Stage," *USA Today*, June 21, 2017, https://www.usatoday.com/story/college/2017/06/21/read-the-speech-that-got-a-high-school-valedictorian-pulled-from-the-stage/37433371/.

3. Lulabel Seitz, "Valedictorian Mic Cut: Uncensored Speech," *YouTube*, June 3, 2018, https://www.youtube.com/watch?v=SWbFmi_lqdo.

4. "Know Your Rights: Student Walkouts and Protest at School," *ALCU of Maine*, 2021, https://www.aclumaine.org/en/know-your-rights/know-your-rights-student-walkouts-and-protest-school.

5. Hannah Beausang, "Petaluma High School Valedictorian 'Appalled' after Mic Cut Off during Her Graduation Speech," *The Press Democrat*, June 6, 2018, https://www.pressdemocrat.com/article/news/petaluma-high-school-valedictorian-appalled-after-mic-cut-off-during-her/?gallery=60F18449-9AA2-4617-9D1C-04065F2E4ABE&sba=AAS.

6. Alyssa Lukpat, "When a Valedictorian Spoke of His Queer Identity, the Principal Cut Off His Speech," *New York Times*, June 28, 2021, https://www.nytimes.com/2021/06/27/nyregion/new-jersey-valedictorian-lgbtq-speech.html.

7. Dylan Kelley, "Schools Closed Due to Threat: National Shootings Have Area Schools on Edge," *Our Herald*, May 24, 2018, https://www.ourherald.com/articles/schools-closed-due-to-threat/.

8. Chris Hedges, *America: The Farewell Tour* (New York: Simon and Schuster, 2018), 243.

9. James Baldwin, *The Fire Next Time* (New York: Dell,1963), 132.

10. Hedges, *America: The Farewell Tour*, 307.

11. Ibid., 29.

12. Saul D. Alinski, *Rules for Radicals: A Pragmatic Primer for Realistic Radicals* (New York: Vintage,1989), xx.

13. Chris Hedges, *America: The Farewell Tour,* 259.

14. Heather McGhee, *The Sum of Us: What Racism Costs Everyone and How We Can Prosper Together* (New York: One World, 2021), 103.

15. "The Trump Effect: The Impact of the Presidential Campaign on Our Nation's Schools," Southern Poverty Law Center, April 13, 2016, https://www.splcenter.org/20160413/trump-effect-impact-presidential-campaign-our-nations-schools.

16. "Raising the Black Lives Matter Flag at MHS," Vermont NEA, accessed November 2, 2021, http://www.racialequityvtnea.org/wp-content/uploads/2018/12/Raising-the-Black-Lives-Matter-Flag-at-MHS.pdf.

17. See "New Chapter of SPLC's 'Sounds Like Hate' Looks at a Vermont High School Grappling with Racism," Southern Poverty Law Center, September 14, 2020, https://www.splcenter.org/presscenter/new-chapter-splcs-sounds-hate-looks-vermont-high-school-grappling-racism.

18. Chris Hedges, *America: The Farewell Tour*, 251.

19. Ibid., 252.

20. "The College, Career, and Civic Life (C3) Framework for Social Studies State Standards: Guidance for Enhancing the Rigor of K–12 Civics, Economics, Geography, and History," National Council for the Social Studies, Silver Spring, MD, June 2017, accessed November 2, 2021, https://www.socialstudies.org/sites/default/files/2017/Jun/c3-framework-for-social-studies-rev0617.pdf.

21. David Madland and Malkie Wall, "The Middle Class Continues to Struggle as Union Density Remains Low," Center for American Progress, September 10, 2019, https://www.americanprogressaction.org/issues/economy/news/2019/09/10/175024/middle-class-continues-struggle-union-density-remains-low/.

22. Derek Sivers, "First Follower: Leadership Lessons from a Dancing Guy," February 11, 2010, https://sive.rs/ff.

23. *30 Rock*, "The Ones," Northeast Ohio on Screen, May 12, 2009, http://neoscreen.blogspot.com/2009/05/30-rock-ones.html.

24. Richard M. Perloff, "Four Students Were Killed in Ohio: America Was Never the Same," *New York Times*, May 4, 2020, https://www.nytimes.com/2020/05/04/opinion/kent-state-shooting-protest.html.

25. Ibid.

26. Ibid.

CHAPTER 5

1. Eric K. Ward, "Winning the Peace: What If We've Already Won the War?," 8.19.2020, https://westernstatescenter.medium.com/winning-the-peace-what-if-weve-already-won-the-war-b0ab6cdc8738.

2. "Episode 104: Thank You for Not Smoking," Bad Faith Podcast, 9.6.21, https://www.patreon.com/posts/episode-104-you-55818244.

3. Ibid.

4. Ibid.

5. Kenneth Hardy and Dr. Tracy Laszloffy, *Teens Who Hurt: Clinical Interventions to Break the Cycle of Adolescent Violence* (New York: Guildford, 2005), 151.

6. Ibid.

7. Cynthia Miller-Idriss, *The Extreme Gone Mainstream: Commercialization and Far-Right Youth Culture in Germany* (Princeton: Princeton University Press. 2018), xv.

8. Cynthia Miller-Idriss, *Hate in the Homeland: The New Global Far Right* (Princeton: Princeton University Press, 2018), 1–2.

9. "Fatal Force," *Washington Post*, accessed 11.1.21, https://www.washingtonpost.com/graphics/investigations/police-shootings-database/.

10. Western States Center, *Confronting White Nationalism in Schools Toolkit, Second Edition* (Portland, OR: Western States Center, 2019), 5.

11. Ibid., 8.

12. Erik Erikson, *Identity, Youth and Crisis* (New York: W.W. Norton & Company, Inc., 1968), 190.

13. Ibid.

14. Miller-Idriss, *Hate in the Homeland*, 4.

15. "Building Resilience and Confronting Risk: A Parents and Caregivers Guide to Online Radicalization," Polarization and Extremism Research Innovation Lab and Southern Poverty Law Center, 2021, 5.

16. Ibid., 8.

17. Western States Center, "Confronting White Nationalism in Schools," 13.

18. Ibid., 14.

19. Ibid., 20.

20. Ibid., 27.

21. Ibid.

22. Polarization and Extremism Research Innovation Lab and Southern Poverty Law Center, "Building Resilience and Confronting Risk," 4.

23. Martin Luther King Jr., "The Other America" speech, The Other America, accessed 11.1.21, https://the-other-america.com/speech.

24. Audre Lorde, "Poetry Is Not a Luxury," 1985, https://makinglearning.files.wordpress.com/2014/01/poetry-is-not-a-luxury-audre-lorde.pdf, 1.

CONCLUSION

1. Rachel Kleinfeld, *A Savage Order: How the World's Deadliest Countries Can Forge a Path to Security* (New York: Vintage, 2018), 16.

2. Ibid., 259.

Works Cited

ALCU of Maine. "Know Your Rights: Student Walkouts and Protest at School." Accessed November 10, 2021. https://www.aclumaine.org/en/know-your-rights/know-your-rights-student-walkouts-and-protest-school.

Alinski, Saul D. *Rules for Radicals: A Pragmatic Primer for Realistic Radicals.* New York: Vintage,1989.

American Civil Liberties Union. https://www.aclu.org/.

Apple, Michael W., and James A. Beane. "The Case for Democratic Schools." In *Democratic Schools: Lessons in Powerful Education*, 2nd ed., edited by Michael W. Apple and James A. Beane, 9. Portsmouth, NH: Heinemann, 2007.

Au, Wayne, and Jesse Hagopian. "How One Elementary School Sparked a Citywide Movement to Make Black Student's Lives Matter." In *Teaching for Black Lives*, edited by Dyan Watson, Jesse Hagopian, and Wayne Au, 23–29. Milwaukee: Rethinking Schools, 2018. https://rethinkingschools.org/books/teaching-for-black-lives/.

Baldwin, James. *Dark Days.* New York: Penguin Press, 1985.

———. *No Name in the Street.* New York: Vintage Press, 2000.

———. "Review of the Writings of Lillian Smith." Accessed October 19, 2021. Lillian Smith—Lillian Smith: Breaking the Silence (lilliansmithdoc.com).

———. "James Baldwin Discusses His Book 'Another Country' and His Travels through Africa." Interview by Studs Terkel, *Studs Terkel Radio Archive*, September 29, 1962. https://studsterkel.wfmt.com/programs/james-baldwin-discusses-his-book-another-country-and-his-travels-through-africa?t=1806.6%2C1810.499&a=ItHasTo%2CWherEverBegi.

———. *The Fire Next Time.* New York: Dell, 1963.

Beausang, Hannah, "Petaluma High School Valedictorian 'Appalled' after Mic Cut Off during Her Graduation Speech." *The Press Democrat*, June 6, 2018. https://www.pressdemocrat.com/article/news/petaluma-high-school-valedictorian-appalled-after-mic-cut-off-during-her/?gallery=60F18449-9AA2-4617-9D1C-04065F2E4ABE&sba=AAS.

Benitez, Mara, Jill Davidson, and Laura Flaxman. *Small Schools, Big Ideas: The Essential Guide to Successful School Transformation.* New Jersey, Hoboken: John Wiley & Sons, Inc., 2009.

Bersin, Josh. "Why Aren't Wages Keeping Up? It's Not the Economy, It's Management." *Forbes,* October 31, 2018. https://www.forbes.com/sites/joshbersin/2018/10/31/why-arent-wages-keeping-up-its-not-the-economy-its-management/?sh=284f0fec397e.

Boyes-Watson, Carolyn, and Kay Pranis. *Circle Forward: Building a Restorative School Community.* St. Paul: Living Justice Press, 2015.

Brodsky, Sarah. "Is Discipline Reform Really Helping to Decrease School Violence?" *The Atlantic,* June 28, 2016. https://www.theatlantic.com/education/archive/2016/06/school-violence-restorative-justice/488945/.

Cambron-McCabe, Nelda. "Schooling as an Ethical Endeavor." In *Schools That Learn: A Fifth Discipline Fieldbook for Educators, Parents, and Everyone Who Cares about Education,* edited by Peter Senge, 317. New York: Doubleday, 2000.

Carmichael, Stokely. Speech. Accessed October 19, 2021. https://www.goodreads.com/quotes/7802915-if-a-white-man-wants-to-lynch-me-that-s-his.

Chapel, Bill. "The Pentagon Has Never Passed an Audit. Some Senators Want to Change That." National Public Radio, May 19, 2021. https://www.npr.org/2021/05/19/997961646/the-pentagon-has-never-passed-an-audit-some-senators-want-to-change-that.

Community High School District 117. *Curriculum Guide 2020–2021.* https://core-docs.s3.amazonaws.com/documents/asset/uploaded_file/747668/2020-2021-Curriculum-Guide.pdf.

Couglan, Sean. "2018 Worst Year for US School Shootings." *BBC News,* December 12, 2018. 2018 "worst year for US school shootings"—BBC News.

Delpit, Lisa, ed. *Teaching When the World Is on Fire: Authentic Classroom Advice, From Climate Justice to Black Lives Matter.* New York: The New Press, 2021.

Dewey, John. "The Democratic Conception in Education." In *Democracy and Education: An Introduction to the Philosophy of Education,* edited by John Dewey, 94–116. New York: Macmillan Company, 1916. https://books.google.com/books?id=jqROAAAAMAAJ&pg=PR3&source=kp_read_button&hl=en&newbks=1&newbks_redir=0&gboemv=1.

———. *Experience and Education.* New York: Simon and Schuster, 1938.

"Disputing Racism's Reach: Republicans Rattle American Schools." *New York Times,* June 1, 2021. https://www.nytimes.com/2021/06/01/us/politics/critical-race-theory.html?smid=tw-share.

Du Bois, W. E. B. *Darkwater: Voices from within the Veil.* New York: Harcourt Brace, 1921. https://genius.com/Web-du-bois-darkwater-chap-2-annotated.

Dufour, Richard, and Robert Eaker. *Personal Learning Communities at Work.* Bloomington, IN: Solution Tree, 2005.

Educating for American Democracy. https://www.educatingforamericandemocracy.org/.

Ellison, Ralph. *Invisible Man.* New York: Vintage Books, 1947.

Erden, Münire, and H. Eylem Korkmaz. "A Delphi Study: The Characteristics of Democratic Schools." *The Journal of Educational Research* 107, no. 5 (March 2014): 365–73.

Erikson, Erik. *Identity, Youth and Crisis.* New York: W.W. Norton & Company, Inc., 1968.
Expeditionary Learning. *Leaders of Their Own Learning.* "Chapter 5: Student-Led Conferences." Accessed November 1, 2021. https://eleducation.org/resources/chapter-5-student-led-conferences.
Extinction Rebellion. https://rebellion.global/.
Facing History and Ourselves. https://www.facinghistory.org/.
Fanon, Franz. *Black Skin, White Masks.* New York: Grove Press, 1967.
Flanagan, Nora, Jessica Acee, and Lindsay Schubiner. *Confronting White Nationalism in Schools: A Toolkit.* Second Edition. Portland, OR: Western States Center, 2019.
Foote, Martha. "Keeping Accountability Systems Accountable." *Phi Delta Kappan* 88, no. 5 (January 2007): 359–63. https://journals.sagepub.com/doi/10.1177/003172170708800506.
Fries, Kenny. "The Nazis' First Victims Were Disabled." *New York Times*, September 12, 2017. https://www.nytimes.com/2017/09/13/opinion/nazis-holocaust-disabled.html.
Fullan, Michael. *The Moral Imperative of School Leadership.* Corwin Press, 2003.
Garcia, Emma, and Elaine Weiss. "U.S. Schools Struggle to Hire and Retain Teachers." *Economic Policy Institute.* April 16, 2019. https://www.epi.org/publication/u-s-schools-struggle-to-hire-and-retain-teachers-the-second-report-in-the-perfect-storm-in-the-teacher-labor-market-series/.
Goyal, Nikhil. "These People Think Your Kids Need High Stakes Testing—but Not Theirs." *The Nation*, March 29, 2016. https://www.thenation.com/article/archive/these-politicians-think-your-kids-need-high-stakes-testing-but-not-theirs/.
Glickman, Carl D. *Renewing America's Schools: A Guide for School-Based Action.* San Francisco: Jossey-Bass, 1993.
Gulamhussein, Allison. "Teaching the Teachers: Effective Professional Development in an Era of High Stakes Accountability." Center for Public Education. September 2013. Accessed November 11, 2021, http://conference.ohioschoolboards.org/2017/wp-content/uploads/sites/17/2016/07/1pm111317A114Job-embedPD.pdf.
Gurba, Myriam. *Mean.* Brooklyn: Coffee House Press, 2017.
Hantzopoulos, Maria. "Deepening Democracy: How One School's Fairness Committee Offers an Alternative to 'Discipline.'" *Rethinking Schools* 21, no. 1 (Fall 2006): https://www.rethinkingschools.org/articles/deepening-democracy.
Hantzopoulos, Maria. *Restoring Dignity in Public Schools: Human Rights Education in Action.* New York: Teachers College Press, 2016.
Hardy Kenneth, and Tracy Laszloffy. *Teens Who Hurt: Clinical Interventions to Break the Cycle of Adolescent Violence.* New York: Guilford Press, 2005.
Hawkes, T. Elijah. 2011. The James Baldwin School Faculty Handbook. New York: James Baldwin School.
Hedges, Chris. "Hedges: The Collective Suicide Machine and the Fall of Kabul." *Scheerpost*, July 26, 2021. https://scheerpost.com/2021/07/26/hedges-the-collective-suicide-machine/.
———. "Hedges: The Evil Within Us." *Scheerpost*, March 22, 2021. Hedges: The Evil Within Us—scheerpost.com.

Hedges, Chris. *America: The Farewell Tour.* New York: Simon and Schuster, 2018.

Heintz, Ben, ed. "For Teachers, a Classroom Lesson: The BLM Flag in Our Schools." *VT Digger*, October 10, 2021. https://vtdigger.org/wp-content/uploads/2021/10/For-Teachers_-A-Lesson-for-the-BLM-Flag-in-VTs-Schools.pdf.

Hutcheson, Susannah. "Read the Speech That Got a High School Valedictorian Pulled from the Stage." *USA Today*, June 21, 2017. https://www.usatoday.com/story/college/2017/06/21/read-the-speech-that-got-a-high-school-valedictorian-pulled-from-the-stage/37433371/.

Inscoe, John. "Killers of the Dream." *New Georgia Encyclopedia*, last modified March 20, 2021. https://www.georgiaencyclopedia.org/articles/arts-culture/killers-of-the-dream/.

InsideSchools. https://insideschools.org/.

"I Sexually Identify as an Attack Helicopter." Know Your Meme. Accessed October 19, 2021. I Sexually Identify as an Attack Helicopter | Know Your Meme.

Kelley, Dylan. "Schools Closed Due to Threat: National Shootings Have Area Schools on Edge." *Our Herald*, May 24, 2018. https://www.ourherald.com/articles/schools-closed-due-to-threat/.

Kleinrock, Liz. *Start Here, Start Now: A Guide to Antibias and Antiracist Work in Your School Community.* Portsmouth, NH: Heineman, 2021.

Knecht, Douglas R. "Schooling for and with Democracy." *Schools: Studies in Education* 15, no. 1 (Spring 2018): 21–24. https://doi.org/10.1086/697092.

Kruzel, John. "Newsweek Stated on October 2, 2017 in an Article: 'White Men Have Committed More Mass Shootings than any Other Group.'" Politifact, October 6, 2017. https://www.politifact.com/factchecks/2017/oct/06/newsweek/are-white-males-responsible-more-mass-shootings-an/.

Lorde, Audre. "Poetry Is Not a Luxury." 1985. https://makinglearning.files.wordpress.com/2014/01/poetry-is-not-a-luxury-audre-lorde.pdf.

Learning for Justice. https://www.learningforjustice.org/.

———. "The Social Justice Standards." November 21, 2018. Accessed October 29, 2021. https://www.learningforjustice.org/the-moment/november-21-2018-the-social-justice-standards.

Lyiscott, Jamila. *Black Appetite. White Food. Issues of Race, Voice, and Justice Within and Beyond the Classroom.* New York: Routledge, 2019.

Madland, David, and Malkie Wall. "The Middle Class Continues to Struggle as Union Density Remains Low." Center for American Progress, September 10, 2019. https://www.americanprogressaction.org/issues/economy/news/2019/09/10/175024/middle-class-continues-struggle-union-density-remains-low/.

Meier, Deborah. *In Schools We Trust: Creating Communities of Learning in an Era of Testing and Standardization.* Boston: Beacon Press, 2002.

———. "So What Does It Take to Build a School for Democracy?" *Phi Delta Kappan* 85, no. 1 (September 2003):15–21. https://doi.org/10.1177/003172170308500106.

Meier, Deborah, and Paul Schwartz. "Central Park East Secondary School: The Hard Part Is Making It Happen." In *Democratic Schools: Lessons in Powerful Education*, edited by Michael W. Apple and James A. Beane, 147. Portsmouth, NH: Heineman, 2007.

McGhee, Heather. *The Sum of Us: What Racism Costs Everyone and How We Can Prosper Together*. New York: One World, 2021.

Miller-Idriss, Cynthia. *Hate in the Homeland: The New Global Far Right*. Princeton: Princeton University Press, 2018.

———. *The Extreme Gone Mainstream: Commercialization and Far-Right Youth Culture in Germany*. Princeton: Princeton University Press, 2018.

National Association for the Advancement of Colored People. https://naacp.org/.

National Council for the Social Studies. "The College, Career, and Civic Life (C3) Framework for Social Studies State Standards: Guidance for Enhancing the Rigor of K–12 Civics, Economics, Geography, and History." June 2017. https://www.socialstudies.org/sites/default/files/2017/Jun/c3-framework-for-social-studies-rev0617.pdf.

National Memorial for Peace and Justice. "Memorial." Accessed October 19, 2021. eji.org.

National Memorial to Fallen Educators. "Bath School Disaster." Accessed November 10, 2021. https://nthfmemorial.org/bath-school-disaster/.

———. "A Notorious Affair of Honor—William H. G. Butler." Accessed November 10, 2021. https://nthfmemorial.org/a-notorious-affair-of-honor-william-h-g-butler/.

Newell, Ronald J., and Irving H. Buchen. *Democratic Learning and Leading: Creating Collaborative School Governance*. Lanham, MD: Rowman & Littlefield, 2004.

News Literacy Project. https://newslit.org/.

NYC (New York City) Department of Education. 2017. "School Quality Reports School Year 2015–2016." http://schools.nyc.gov/OA/SchoolReports/2015-16/School_Quality_Snapshot_2016_HST_M313.pdf.

Northeast Ohio Onscreen. *30 Rock*: "The Ones." May 12, 2009. http://neoscreen.blogspot.com/2009/05/30-rock-ones.html.

Northfield Public Schools, Northfield, Minnesota. "Position Description: High School Principal." Accessed October 26, 2021. https://cse.google.com/cse?q=&sa.x=11&sa.y=11&cx=005796229432434085693%3Az2nbjlwhts4&ie=UTF-8#gsc.tab=0&gsc.q=High%20School%20Principal&gsc.sort=.

Olson, Christine. "The Deep Roots of the Fairness Committee in Kohlberg's Moral Development Theory." *Schools* 8, no. 1 (Spring 2011): 125–35. https://doi.org/10.1086/659442.

Oluo, Ijeoma. "White People: I Don't Want You to Understand Me Better, I Want You to Understand Yourselves." Accessed October 19, 2021. https://medium.com/the-establishment/white-people-i-dont-want-you-to-understand-me-better-i-want-you-to-understand-yourselves-a6fbedd42ddf.

Parsons, Chelsea. "Gun Violence Prevention Priorities for a New Congress and a New Administration." Center for American Progress. January 26, 2021. https://www.americanprogress.org/issues/guns-crime/news/2021/01/26/495035/gun-violence-prevention-priorities-new-congress-new-administration/.

Perloff, Richard M. "Four Students Were Killed in Ohio: America Was Never the Same." *New York Times*, May 4, 2020. https://www.nytimes.com/2020/05/04/opinion/kent-state-shooting-protest.html.

Raschka, Lydie. "James Baldwin School: A School for Expeditionary Learning." InsideSchools. May 2018, updated August 2020. https://insideschools.org/school/02M313.

Redden, Emma. *Power Means Who the Police Believe: Talking with Young Children about Race and Racial Violence.* Emma Redden (www.emmaredden.com) publisher, 2019.

Reeves, Douglas B. *Leading Change in Your School.* Association for Supervision and Curriculum Development, April 2007.

Rethinking Schools. https://rethinkingschools.org/.

Riestenberg, Nancy. *Circle in the Square: Building Community and Repairing Harm in School.* St. Paul, Minnesota: Living Justice Press, 2012.

Sartre, John Paul. *Existentialism Is a Humanism.* New Haven: Yale University Press, 2007.

Schaefer, Katherine. "Key Facts about Americans and Guns." Pew Research Center, September 13, 2021. https://www.pewresearch.org/fact-tank/2021/09/13/key-facts-about-americans-and-guns/.

School Reform Initiative (SRI). 2015, 1. https://www.schoolreforminitiative.org/.

———. "Towards a General Theory of SRI's Intentional Learning Communities." Accessed October 26, 2021. https://www.schoolreforminitiative.org/research/general-theory-of-intentional-learning-communities/.

Seitz, Lulabel. "Valedictorian Mic Cut: Uncensored Speech." YouTube, June 3, 2018. https://www.youtube.com/watch?v=SWbFmi_lqdo.

Senge, Peter. *The Fifth Discipline.* New York: Doubleday, 1990.

Sivers, Derek. "First Follower: Leadership Lessons from a Dancing Guy." February 11, 2010. https://sive.rs/ff.

Smith, Lillian. *Killers of the Dream.* New York: Norton, 1994.

Southern Poverty Law Center. https://www.splcenter.org/.

———. "Building Resilience and Confronting Risk: A Parents and Caregivers Guide to Online Radicalization." June 2021. file:///C:/Users/Kristin/AppData/Local/Temp/splc_peril_parents_and_caregivers_guide_june_2021_final.pdf.

———. "New Chapter of SPLC's 'Sounds Like Hate' Looks at a Vermont High School Grappling with Racism." September 14, 2020. https://www.splcenter.org/presscenter/new-chapter-splcs-sounds-hate-looks-vermont-high-school-grappling-racism.

———. "The Trump Effect: The Impact of the Presidential Campaign on Our Nation's Schools." April 13, 2016. https://www.splcenter.org/20160413/trump-effect-impact-presidential-campaign-our-nations-schools.

Tierney, John. "Why Do So Many Teachers Quit Their Jobs: Because They Hate Their Bosses." *The Atlantic,* November, 2012. https://www.theatlantic.com/national/archive/2012/11/why-do-so-many-teachers-quit-their-jobs-because-they-hate-their-bosses/265310/?utm_source=copy-link&utm_medium=social&utm_campaign=share.

Tonatiuh, Duncan. *Separate Is Never Equal: Sylvia Mendez and Her Family's Fight for Desegregation.* New York: Abrams Books for Young Readers, 2014.

United States Census Bureau. "High School Completion Rate Is Highest in U.S. History." December 14, 2017. https://www.census.gov/newsroom/press-releases/2017/educational-attainment-2017.html.

Vermont NEA. "Raising the Black Lives Matter Flag at MHS." Accessed November 2, 2021. http://www.racialequityvtnea.org/wp-content/uploads/2018/12/Raising-the-Black-Lives-Matter-Flag-at-MHS.pdf.

Walker, Alice. *Review of "Strange Fruit,"* by Lillian Smith. Accessed October 19, 2021. Lillian Smith—Lillian Smith: Breaking The Silence (lilliansmithdoc.com).

"Want to Know America's Most Armed Counties? Check This Map with Data from 2016." Wideopenspaces. March 12, 2021. Want to Know America's Most Armed Counties? Check This Map With Data From 2016 (wideopenspaces.com).

Ward, Erik. K. "Winning the Peace: What If We've Already Won the War?" Western States Center. August 19, 2020. https://westernstatescenter.medium.com/winning-the-peace-what-if-weve-already-won-the-war-b0ab6cdc8738.

Washington Post. "930 People Have Been Shot and Killed by Police in the Past Year." Updated November 10, 2021. https://www.washingtonpost.com/graphics/investigations/police-shootings-database/.

Webber, Nahlia. "If You Really Want to Make a Difference in Black Lives, Change How You Teach White Kids." *Education Post*, June 29, 2020. https://educationpost.org/if-you-really-want-to-make-a-difference-in-black-lives-change-how-you-teach-white-kids/.

West, Cornel. "Cornel West: The Difference Between Being 'Woke' & Fortified ft. Richard Wolff," *The Michael Brooks Show. YouTube,* December 28, 2019. https://www.youtube.com/watch?v=rZoRTIdYamA.

———. *Democracy Matters: Winning the Fight Against Imperialism*. New York: The Penguin Group, 2004.

Western States Center. https://www.westernstatescenter.org/.

———. *Confronting White Nationalism in Schools Toolkit*, Second Edition. Portland, OR: Western States Center, 2019.

"When a Valedictorian Spoke of His Queer Identify, the Principal Cut Off His Speech." *New York Times,* June 27, 2021. https://www.nytimes.com/2021/06/27/nyregion/new-jersey-valedictorian-lgbtq-speech.html.

Whitman, Walt. "An Old Man's Thought of School." In Walt Whitman, *Leaves of Grass and Selected Prose*. New York: Rinehart, 1959.

Wide Open Spaces. "Want to Know America's Most Armed Counties? Check This Map with Data from 2016." March 12, 2021. https://www.wideopenspaces.com/map-of-most-armed-counties/.

Zehr, Howard. *The Little Book of Restorative Justice.* Intercourse, PA: Good Books, 2002.

Zinn Education Project. https://www.zinnedproject.org/.

About the Author

T. Elijah Hawkes has been an educator for more than two decades in rural and urban school communities, including ten years as principal of Randolph Union in Central Vermont, and six years as principal of the James Baldwin School in New York City, where he was founding principal. He is the director of School Leadership Programs at the Upper Valley Educators Institute, serving school communities in Vermont and New Hampshire. He is an education advisor to the Polarization and Extremism Research and Innovation Lab at American University, a member of the Schools Committee at the American Psychoanalytic Association, and a contributing editor at the journal *Schools: Studies in Education*. His writings about adolescence, public schools, and democracy have appeared in various journals, magazines, and books, including *The New Teacher Book* and *Rethinking Sexism, Gender and Sexuality*, and *Teaching When the World Is on Fire*, edited by Lisa Delpit. He is the author of the book *School for the Age of Upheaval: Classrooms That Get Personal, Get Political, and Get to Work* (Rowman & Littlefield, 2020).

www.ingramcontent.com/pod-product-compliance
Lightning Source LLC
Chambersburg PA
CBHW020122240426
43673CB00038B/566